DUMBARTON OAKS STUDIES 51

SACRALIZING VIOLENCE IN BYZANTIUM

DUMBARTON OAKS STUDIES 51

SACRALIZING VIOLENCE IN BYZANTIUM

Hymns, Empire, and the Narrowing of Christian Identity

GEORGE E. DEMACOPOULOS

DUMBARTON OAKS RESEARCH LIBRARY AND COLLECTION
WASHINGTON, DC

Copyright © 2025 by Dumbarton Oaks Research Library and Collection
Trustees for Harvard University, Washington, DC
All rights reserved
Manufactured in the United States of America by
Sheridan Books, Inc., 613 East Industrial Drive, Chelsea, MI 48118 | (734) 475-9145

ISBN 978-0-88402-523-8

LIBRARY OF CONGRESS CATALOGING-IN-PUBLICATION DATA

Names: Demacopoulos, George E., author.
TITLE: Sacralizing violence in Byzantium : hymns, empire, and the narrowing of Christian identity / George E. Demacopoulos.
OTHER TITLES: Dumbarton Oaks studies ; 51.
DESCRIPTION: Washington, D.C. : Dumbarton Oaks Research Library and Collection, 2025. | Series: Dumbarton Oaks Studies ; 51 | Includes bibliographical references. | SUMMARY: "Christians had always been concerned, since the faith's inception, about the relationship between violence and belief. In Byzantium, this tension was explored not only in abstract theological texts but in the songs people sung: hymns, a multivalent, fluid form of devotion that served as the meeting place between theological conviction and lived religious experience. *Sacralizing Violence in Byzantium* is the first book to examine the complex and shifting perceptions of premodern Christians toward violence and war through the lens of hymnography. This book argues that the liturgical reflection on violence in Byzantium underwent a profound transformation—a sacralization of violence—at approximately the same time that Persian and then Arab armies conquered Jerusalem in the early seventh century, a turn that persisted into the tenth century. By focusing on hymnography, this book provides both correction and nuance to historical assessments of Eastern Christian attitudes toward war and violence and reveals how Byzantine culture dramatized, authorized, and even celebrated violence"—Provided by publisher.
IDENTIFIERS: LCCN 2024042606 | ISBN 9780884025238 (hardcover)
SUBJECTS: LCSH: Violence—Religious aspects—Christianity—History—Sources. | War—Religious aspects—Christianity—History—Sources. | Hymns—Byzantine Empire—Themes, motives—History—Sources. | Hymns—Byzantine Empire—History and criticism. | Violence—Byzantine Empire—History. | Violence in music.
CLASSIFICATION: LCC BT736.15 .D45 2025 | DDC 261.8/7309495—dc23/eng/20250313
LC record available at https://lccn.loc.gov/2024042606

COVER: Plate with the Battle of David and Goliath, Byzantine, 629–630. The Metropolitan Museum of Art, New York, Gift of J. Pierpont Morgan, 1917.

www.doaks.org/publications

EU GPSR Authorised Representative
LOGOS EUROPE, 9 rue Nicolas Poussin, 17000, La Rochelle, France
E-mail: Contact@logoseurope.eu

CONTENTS

ACKNOWLEDGMENTS   vii

INTRODUCTION   1

CHAPTER 1
   The *Jerusalem Georgian Chantbook*   27

CHAPTER 2
   Crucifixion and "the Jews":
   The Idiomela Hymns of Good Friday   49

CHAPTER 3
   Romanos the Melodist   67

CHAPTER 4
   Feast of the Exaltation of the Holy Cross   89

CHAPTER 5
   Herakleios, Exaltation of the Holy Cross,
   and the Violence of Empire   107

CHAPTER 6
   Tenth-Century Liturgical Rites before Battle and after Death   133

CONCLUSION   153

APPENDIX 1   165

APPENDIX 2   199

APPENDIX 3   207

BIBLIOGRAPHY   215

GENERAL INDEX   227

ACKNOWLEDGMENTS

The seeds for this project were planted many years ago when I participated in a multiyear (roughly 2009 to 2012), interdisciplinary seminar in Boston that examined various dimensions of Orthodox Christian attitudes toward war and violence. Those gatherings, generously funded by the Lelon family, did as much for my development as a scholar as any working group in which I have participated. I am deeply grateful to Thomas and Charles Lelon and to all of my fellow participants. Appendix 2 to this volume is a translation by John Klentos that he developed as part of the working group.

I did not know very much about the scholarly study of liturgy before I began this project. I read a lot, for sure, but I also leaned on the insights of many generous friends. In this regard, this volume would not have been possible without Stephen Shoemaker. His expertise runs throughout this work. Many others contributed in their own way. I would especially like to thank Stephanos Alexopoulos, Thomas Arentzen, Daniel Galadza, Susan Harvey, Derek Krueger, Alexander Lingas, Bissera Pencheva, Christopher Sweeney, and Gregory Tucker. Any blind spots and errors that remain are, of course, my own.

Along the way I have had the opportunity to present several aspects of this project while it was still a work in progress. For offering me kind invitations, critical feedback, and hospitality, I would like to thank colleagues at the Holy Cross Greek Orthodox School of Theology, Brookline, Massachusetts; the University of Missouri, Columbia; the University of New Hampshire, Durham; and the Volos Theological Academy, Greece. The majority of the research for this book was made possible by a Faculty Fellowship from Fordham University during the fall of 2021. I completed the project during a short visit to Dumbarton Oaks in 2023. I am grateful to both institutions.

I would like to offer a special note of appreciation to the publications team at Dumbarton Oaks, especially managing editor Colin Whiting. I have never worked with a more insightful or thorough partner. I would also like to thank Nikos Kontogiannis, director of Byzantine Studies at Dumbarton Oaks, who first encouraged me to submit the manuscript to the press, and Abigail Anderson, who carefully shepherded the project to completion.

When I published my first monograph and dutifully dedicated it to my wife and children several years ago, our youngest child, Grace, was not yet born. I would like to dedicate this work to her as she begins to pursue her own intellectual and artistic interests.

INTRODUCTION

On 14 June 2020, Patriarch Kirill of Moscow consecrated an imposing new cathedral honoring the Russian military.[1] Dedicated to the Resurrection of Christ and located in Kubinka, some 40 miles outside Moscow, the church is said to have cost around $100 million. The iconography adorning the temple boldly affirms military service as an act of religious devotion and military victory as granted by God, at least in Russia. The central dome intentionally resembles a nuclear missile silo. Orthodox Christian theologians and art historians alike have critiqued the iconographic scheme, which matter-of-factly presents Christ, the Virgin Mary, and the saints alongside the instruments of modern warfare.[2]

In a broad sense, there is nothing new about the Christian sacralization of the armed forces or violence deployed by the righteous. The valorization of the Christian soldier in art and literature dates back more than a thousand years, and in the Middle Ages represented a key element of the culture. The Kubinka cathedral is, however, noteworthy in at least two respects. First, it suggests a potent synthesis between the Christian faith and nationalism at a time when most advanced nations with historical ties to Christianity are unwinding those connections.[3] Second, and the more relevant issue for the present study, the cathedral—like

---

1 The consecration had initially been planned for 9 May, the seventy-fifth anniversary of the end of World War II, but was delayed due to the COVID-19 pandemic.

2 See, for example, the critique of the images of the Virgin Mary in M. Milliner, "Woman of Peace, Temple of War," *Public Orthodoxy*, 25 March 2022, https://publicorthodoxy.org/2022/03/25/woman-of-peace-temple-of-war/.

3 To be sure, in many nations the distancing of Western secular governments from the country's Christian roots has caused a backlash. Populist leaders, such as Hungarian prime minister Viktor Orban and Italian prime minister Georgia Meloni, have been successful by in large part championing the Christian roots of their constituents.

Patriarch Kirill's unambiguous defense of the Russian invasion of Ukraine in 2022—challenges the conventional wisdom that Eastern Christianity has generally resisted the sacralization of violence found in other religious traditions.[4]

For nearly the last one hundred years, historians, theologians, and ethicists have generally held that the people today called the Byzantines—that is, the Eastern Romans of the Middle Ages—were more ambivalent about violence than either their Western Christian or Islamic counterparts. Although scholars have looked at this issue from multiple disciplinary perspectives and examined a wide variety of sources, no extant scholarly work seeks to understand Byzantine Christian attitudes toward war and violence from the perspective of its hymnography. This is surprising given that hymnography, more than any other source, provides insight into the religious thought world of ordinary Christians, clerics, and soldiers alike. Few Byzantine Christians owned a Bible, and if they did, likely could not read it; even fewer had access to the theological treatises or exegetic works of famous theologians. That aside, all Christians had access to the daily, weekly, and annual cycles of hymns that communicated the scriptures, basic theological teachings, and moral injunctions of their faith. *Sacralizing Violence in Byzantium* fills the scholarly lacuna on hymnography and provides a plausible historical explanation for the profound shift that begins to occur in hymnographic presentations of violence during the sixth and seventh centuries.

Christianity and Violence

Violence can take many forms, including specific acts of physical harm, such as beating, mutilation, dismemberment, rape, and murder. The perpetrators of intentional acts of violence can be family members, neighbors, strangers, public officials (executioners, police, soldiers), or foreign armies. Nonhuman factors (disease, environmental disaster, animal attack, and so on) can also result in physical violence.

---

4 After a series of military losses in Ukraine, the Russian government ordered a mass mobilization of the male population. Patriarch Kirill's enthusiastic endorsement of the move included the declaration that any Russian soldier who died fighting in Ukraine would have his sins forgiven. See G. Demacopoulos, "Patriarch Kirill's Crusade," *Public Orthodoxy*, 30 September 2022, https://publicorthodoxy.org/2022/09/30/patriarch-kirills-crusade/.

Humans can, of course, inflict violence on nonhumans as well. For example, most religious traditions of the ancient world practiced animal sacrifice. The Hebrew scriptures offer graphic instructions not only for the slaughter of animals, but also for spreading their blood on the temple altar as an expiation for human sin. Beyond religious observance, humans have also practiced deliberate violence against animals (hunting, husbandry, and so on) as well as less intentional acts, such as through environmental degradation. In addition, one can say that humans today are conducting a whole-scale act of violence against the ecosystem.

Some nonphysical acts also constitute a kind of violence. These include certain types of speech (intimidation, threats, or ridicule, and so on) that anticipate or recall previous acts of physical violence. One can describe the emotional trauma of physical harm as a form of violence. Such emotional violence might occur in association with personal experience or on behalf of relatives, neighbors, or a broader real or imagined community. Then there is the memory of violence—a person's own account of something that has happened to them and also memories produced among members of a community through acts of memorialization. As Brent Shaw demonstrated in his study of sectarian violence between Christians in late ancient North Africa, the careful crafting of the memory of violence was just as potent as the actual threats, beatings, and killings associated with the violence.[5] Shaw also noted the ability of communal singing to not only reinforce these collective memories, but to also spur further violence.

One of the unique and paradoxical features of Christianity is that its god, Jesus Christ, willingly suffered violence and death in the very act of enabling eternal life for others. For the earliest Christian hymnographers, the events surrounding Jesus's death and Resurrection were both a source of celebration and of mourning; they were a spur for hope, but also the impetus for self-censure and for critiques of others. As Christianity grew, the subject matter adopted for hymnographic reflection expanded. This expansion initially took in other biblical characters and themes, and by the early Middle Ages, hymnographers were celebrating the lives of postbiblical saints and sought to address the real-time challenges of the day, such as heresy, famine, earthquakes, and war. By the sixth

---

5 B. D. Shaw, *Sacred Violence: African Christians and Sectarian Hatred in the Age of Augustine* (Cambridge, 2011), 1, 3–4.

century in the Christian East, hymnography also came to reflect the reality of the church's association with the Byzantine Empire, as evidenced by the composition of hymns celebrating the emperor and deriding his enemies.

The presence of violence is one of the most ubiquitous elements found among the thousands of hymns produced between the fourth and tenth centuries, and this study examines the way that violence, in its many forms, was described, decried, and celebrated in the ritualized songs of the Christian liturgy. There has been no shortage of scholars seeking to understand the connection between Christianity and violence. Nearly every field of Christian studies—biblical, historical, ethical, theological—has experienced periods of intense scholarly production and debate on the topic. One might explain the ongoing attention in part as a consequence of its continued relevance—Patriarch Kirill's view of the war in Ukraine as a moral necessity offering only the most recent example—but surely part of scholars' ongoing interest relates to the wide diversity of opinions since the establishment of Christianity on what Christian teaching is or what it should be. Even in New Testament studies, for which there is a very limited set of texts applicable to questions of violence, scholars have produced wildly different interpretations, with some suggesting that Jesus was a pacifist and others seeing Jesus and his followers as an armed resistance movement seeking to expel the Romans from Palestine.[6]

Things only become more complex if one follows the Christian story beyond its New Testament origins. Whether in late antiquity, the Middle Ages, or the modern era, Christians have lived in a variety of contexts and experienced varied relationships to political and military power. They have been a persecuted minority, during the early Roman Empire; an ascendant religious force, in late antiquity; followers of the official state religion, in Byzantium; and a religious minority, in Islamic caliphates. Naturally, proximity to power and the responsibility, or lack thereof, of providing security impacted the way in which individual Christian leaders thought about the moral responsibility born of the Christian faith vis-à-vis the reality of war and violence. Perhaps even more so, the diversity of experience conditioned the way ordinary lay Christians in the premodern

---

6 Contrast, for example, J. H. Yoder, *The Politics of Jesus: Vicit Agnus Noster*, 2nd ed. (Grand Rapids, MI, 1994), and D. Martin, "Jesus in Jerusalem: Armed and Not Dangerous," *Journal for the Study of the New Testament* 37.1 (2014): 3–24.

period understood the connection between their belief in a crucified god—one who died violently at the hands of the state—and the harsh realities of violence endemic to the cycle of life.

Byzantine Violence

As in other medieval societies, war and violence were an inherent part of the Byzantine world. As one example of this, Warren Treadgold estimated that nearly three-quarters of the overall imperial budget went to the armed forces from 842 through 1025.[7] Given the outsized role of the military in Byzantine society and the ample textual sources, military history has been a popular field of Byzantine studies.[8] A long-standing consensus, only occasionally challenged, is that the Byzantines understood the necessity of maintaining an elite fighting force, but they did not glorify war or military victories the way that some of their neighbors did.[9] Most scholars interpret this as a strategic choice; it was more cost-effective to pursue political alliances through marriage or to purchase peace through tribute than to prosecute wars. For some Orthodox Christian commentators, the restrained bloodlust in Byzantine imperial policy, and the society as a whole, can be directly linked to Orthodox Christian teachings.[10] Among Byzantine military historians, Walter Kaegi has devoted the most attention to the role of religion and religious difference in the army.[11] Given the extent to which every Byzantine

---

7 W. Treadgold, *History of the Byzantine State and Society* (Stanford, 1997), 576, table 13.

8 See, for example, the collective work of Warren Kaegi, the translations and commentaries of Byzantine military manuals by George Dennis, as well as Treadgold, *Byzantium and Its Army*, and J. Haldon, ed., *Byzantine Warfare* (Aldershot, 2007).

9 The position is well articulated in W. Kaegi, "Patterns of Political Activity of the Armies of the Byzantine Empire," in *On Military Intervention*, ed. M. Janowitz and J. van Doorn (Rotterdam, 1971), 4–35, at 6–7, and other of his works.

10 See, for example, A. Kyrou and E. Prodromou, "Debates on Just War, Holy War, and Peace: Orthodox Christian Thought and Byzantine Imperial Attitudes toward War," in *Orthodox Christian Perspectives on War*, ed. P. T. Hamalis and V. A. Karras (Notre Dame, IN, 2018), 215–48.

11 See, for example, W. Kaegi, "Arianism and the Byzantine Army in Africa 533–46," *Traditio* 21 (1965): 23–53; W. Kaegi, "The Byzantine Armies and Iconoclasm," *BSl* 27.1 (1966): 48–70; and Kaegi, "Patterns of Political Activity." Several European scholars in the late

military manual invokes religion, and given the extent to which some Christian hymns sacralize violence, it is surprising that the religious facet of military life has not received greater attention.[12]

When scholars of the Byzantine era have examined the intersection of Christianity and violence, they have often focused on the extent to which Byzantine attitudes matched those of their Islamic or Western counterparts, in particular with respect to notions of holy war, just war theory, and the crusading ideal.[13] In this respect, Thomas Sizgorich offers perhaps the most provocative challenge to the conventional scholarly wisdom, arguing that early Christianity and early Islam had far more in common with respect to their sacralization of violence than Western scholars have been willing to acknowledge.[14] According to Sizgorich, the defining features of both religious groups emerged through the fashioning of exaggerated, and even imagined, histories of persecution and triumph that were at their core violent. In Christianity, ascetics reinforced these histories by enacting multiple forms of violence against themselves, against pagans, against Jews, and others. Their actions symbolized a militant piety celebrated throughout the Christian world. One important insight by Sizgorich is

---

nineteenth and early twentieth centuries researched these issues as well. See, for example, H. Delehaye, *Les legends grecques des saints militaires* (Paris, 1909), for a study of the memorialization of military saints; C. Diehl, *L'Afrique byzantine: Histoire de la domination byzantine en Afrique* (Paris, 1896), on the question of Arianism in the African campaigns; and A. Lombard, *Études d'histoire byzantine: Constantin V, empereur des Romains* (Paris, 1902), esp. 25–26, 131–32, and 166, on the question of the faith of the army vis-à-vis iconoclasm.

12 W. Kaegi, *Army, Society, and Religion in Byzantium* (London, 1982). The military manual of Leo VI might be the best example of the convergence of a particular kind of Christian thinking and military service. For a recent analysis of Leo's theological understanding of war, see M. Riedel, *Leo VI and the Transformation of Byzantine Christian Identity: Writings of an Unexpected Emperor* (Cambridge, 2018).

13 See, for example, A. Noth, *Heiliger Krieg und heiliger Kampf in Islam und Christentum* (Bonn, 1966); T. Kolbaba, "Fighting for Christianity: Holy War in the Byzantine Empire," *Byzantion* 68 (1998): 194–221; G. Dennis, "Defenders of the Christian People: Holy War in Byzantium," in *The Crusades from the Perspective of Byzantium and the Muslim World*, ed. A. Laiou and R. P. Mottahedeh (Washington, DC, 2001), 31–39; and A. Laiou, "On Just War in Byzantium," in *To Hellenikon: Studies in Honor of Speros Vryonis, Jr.,* ed. J. S. Allen, C. Ioannides, J. Langdon, and S. Reinert (New Rochelle, NY, 1993), 153–74.

14 T. Sizgorich, *Violence and Belief in Late Antiquity: Militant Devotion in Christianity and Islam* (Philadelphia, 2009).

that ordinary people, Christian and Muslim, were more willing to live peacefully in multireligious contexts than were political elites, who used religious difference to authorize violence against minority communities.[15]

In a 2012 essay, Ioannis Stouraitis offered the most balanced and persuasive assessment to date of whether the Byzantines' approach to war fits within the current scholarly categories of "just war" and "holy war."[16] For Stouraitis, a just war might incorporate some elements of religious thought or religious determination, in large part because the premodern world was inherently religious, but a holy war should be understood to be war that is exclusively motivated by religious difference and not by other factors. While there is ample evidence that the Byzantines applied the language and concepts of just war repeatedly, there are no sources that evince that the Byzantines fought wars primarily on the basis of religious difference; the extant sources always offer additional justifications, even when religious difference is cited. For this reason, Stouraitis sees no reason to apply the category of holy war to the Byzantine experience, even if the Byzantine rhetoric of war routinely included language that suggests a kind of "sacralization" of war.[17]

"The sacralization of warfare was always present against any enemy of the imperial state, Christian or non-Christian," Stouraitis wrote.[18] The adoption of a sacralizing rhetoric by chroniclers, panegyrists, and military manuals was rooted in what he calls a "natural law" approach to just war that nevertheless included religious language based on the presumption that God would assist those who fought in just wars.[19] While Stouraitis never considers hymnography as a documentary source, his distinction between holy war and the rhetoric of sacralization provides helpful nuance to distinguish categories that scholars often

---

15 Sizgorich, *Violence and Belief*, 231–71.
16 I. Stouraitis, "'Just War' and 'Holy War' in the Middle Ages: Rethinking Theory through the Byzantine Case-Study," *JÖB* 62 (2012): 227–64.
17 See Stouraitis, "'Just War' and 'Holy War' in the Middle Ages," esp. 231–33, 243–46, and I. Stouraitis, "State War Ethic and Popular Views on Warfare," in *A Companion to the Byzantine Culture of War, ca. 300–1204*, ed. I. Stouraitis (Leiden, 2018), 59–91.
18 Stouraitis, "'Just War' and 'Holy War' in the Middle Ages," 231.
19 Stouraitis, "'Just War' and 'Holy War' in the Middle Ages," commenting on the *Taktika* of Leo VI, 238–42 (G. Dennis, trans., *The Taktika of Leo VI* [Washington, DC, 2010]).

conflate. For the purposes here, the interest is not so much in the precise categories of just war or holy war, as the ways in which hymnographers increasingly sacralized the imperial office and the violence it deployed. This they did by describing the emperor as God-appointed and by declaring that his armies fought on God's behalf or on behalf of faithful Christians. At least some hymnographers believed that the soldier who died protecting the Christian community should be granted the remission of sins on the basis of that service. With a nod to Stouraitis, it is argued here that these hymnographers sacralize violence without advancing holy war per se.

It is at the intersection of Orthodox Christian studies and Byzantine studies where one finds the most consistent attempt to explain the connection between Christian teachings and the Byzantines' actual approach to violence. Stanley Harakas and Alexander Webster, two ethicists working in the Orthodox Christian tradition, consistently looked to Byzantine patristic texts in their effort to articulate the Orthodox view of war and violence.[20] While historians of Byzantium might lament their persistent anachronism, generalization, and failure to acknowledge the wide diversity of Byzantine ideas and practices, Harakas and Webster helpfully identify some of the most influential Byzantine theologians to engage the topic of violence, and their work has spurred subsequent engagements with more nuanced and persuasive analyses of individual texts and authors.[21]

---

20 See S. Harakas, "The Teaching on Peace in the Fathers," in *Wholeness of Faith and Life: Orthodox Christians Ethic*, pt. 1, *Patristic Ethics* (Brookline, MA, 1999), 137–61, also available at *In Communion*, https://incommunion.org/2004/10/18/peace-in-the-fathers/; and S. Harakas, "No Just War in the Fathers," *In Communion*, rev. 15 August 2003, https://incommunion.org/2005/08/02/no-just-war-in-the-fathers/. For strikingly different positions, see A. Webster, *The Pacifist Option: The Moral Argument against War in Eastern Orthodox Theology* (San Francisco, 1998), and A. Webster and D. Cole, *The Virtue of War: Reclaiming the Classic Christian Traditions East and West* (Salisbury, MA, 2004).

21 Webster and Cole, *The Virtue of War*, has especially been critiqued for providing a one-sided account of the issue. See, for example, the scathing review by A. F. C. Louth, *In Communion* 33 (Spring 2004), https://incommunion.org/2011/07/22/review-of-the-virtue-of-war/. For a critique of Harakas, see G. E. Demacopoulos, "Constantine, Ambrose, and the Morality of War: How Ambrose of Milan Challenged the Imperial Discourse on War and Violence," in Hamalis and Karras, *Orthodox Christian Perspectives on War*, 159–94.

The most noted of the early Byzantine authors to offer a moral analysis of warfare, albeit surprisingly brief, was Basil of Caesarea (d. 379), who famously instructed a correspondent that a soldier who takes the life of another in the context of war should abstain from the Eucharist for a period of three years, as opposed to the much longer prescription for murder.[22] Basil's application of *oikonomia*—the lessening of a prescribed reprimand in order to achieve a pastoral good[23]—is often identified as emblematic of an Orthodox or Byzantine teaching that, on the one hand, recognizes the reality of violence in the world and, on the other, takes the theological view that the enactment of violence does damage to the soul.[24] Basil's recommendation was codified in canon law during the middle Byzantine period, and although it is unlikely that ordinary Christians or soldiers had any knowledge of it, Patriarch Polyeuktos and his synod in the tenth century apparently cited it as the reason that he could not consent to a request from Emperor Nikephoros II Phokas (r. 963–969) to declare martyrdom for soldiers who died fighting Muslims.[25]

---

22 Basil's "canon" originated as an answer (*Epistle* 188) to Amphilochius, who had asked for a series of recommendations regarding the pastoral application of the church's moral teachings. This particular teaching became known as Basil's Canon 13. In the centuries that followed, Basil's fame and the common sense of his recommendations developed in such a way that some canonical handbooks incorporated a number of his instructions.

23 For an analysis of the way that oikonomia functioned in early Christian pastoral works, see G. E. Demacopoulos, *Five Models of Spiritual Direction in the Early Church* (Notre Dame, IN, 2007).

24 For insightful analysis of Basil's canon and the way in which it came to dominate later Byzantine canonical teaching, see J. A. McGuckin, "A Conflicted Heritage: The Byzantine Religious Establishment of a War Ethic," *DOP* 65/66 (2011/2012): 29–44, at 32–33. Regarding violence and spiritual trauma in Orthodox Christian teachings, see A. Papanikolaou, "The Ascetics of War: The Undoing and Redoing of Virtue," in Hamalis and Karras, *Orthodox Christian Perspectives on War*, 13–35.

25 See P. Stephenson, "About the Emperor Nikephoros and How He Leaves His Bones in Bulgaria: A Context for the Controversial Chronicle of 811," *DOP* 60 (2006): 87–109. Some scholars have suggested that this tenth-century ruling by the Synod of Constantinople was not only a new intervention without precedent on the issue of Christian participation in the Byzantine army—the argument being that Basil's canon was largely unknown—but that it also directly contradicted what soldiers were being told in the field. See the commentary in G. Dagron and H. Mihaescu, eds., *Le traité sur la guérilla (De velitatione) de l'empereur Nicéphore Phocas (963–969)* (Paris, 1986), 284–86. Whatever its possible novelty, the synodal verdict was acknowledged and repeated by several Byzantine canonists in subsequent

Of course, Basil was not the only theological authority in the Byzantine period to comment on the pastoral needs of soldiers or the reality that the imperial government sought to maintain effective armies. Anecdotes to this effect can be found in the works of Athanasius, Gregory Nazianzen, Gregory of Nyssa, and John Chrysostom, to name some of the most influential theologians. These same authors and others also occasionally drew direct comparisons between the wars referenced in the Hebrew scriptures and the wars of their own day, but such statements tend to be remarkably brief, never rising to anything resembling a fully developed theological reflection on war or violence or a theory of just war as would be developed by Latin authors in the Middle Ages. It is for this reason that Basil's canon has drawn the greatest scholarly attention. It is also why the majority of scholars, theologians and ethicists included, have often turned to non-theological texts, such as Byzantine military manuals, to try to understand what made Byzantium different.

More than anyone else, John McGuckin has situated the complexity and nuance of the Byzantines' Orthodox theological tradition within its proper historical context.[26] Rather than seeing the Byzantine attitude toward war and violence as ambivalent or contradictory, McGuckin has proposed that there were multiple strands and contexts operating simultaneously within the Byzantine ecclesiastical world, which included monastic communities, court-appointed theologians, and other ecclesiastical authors whose distinctive relationships to state power conferred different understandings regarding the suitability of Christians enacting violence. For McGuckin, the Byzantine theological interpretation of violence runs along a series of partially overlapping tracks: an exegetical tradition, which typically interpreted the violence of scripture apocalyptically; a canonical tradition that continuously recycled Basil's canon; and the more organic traditions of saints' cults and liturgy, which developed over time and with considerable

---

centuries. See Stephenson, "About the Emperor Nikephoros and How He Leaves His Bones in Bulgaria"; McGuckin, "A Conflicted Heritage," 43; and P. Viscuso, "Christian Participation in Warfare: A Byzantine View," in *Peace and War in Byzantium: Essays in Honor of George Dennis*, ed. T. S. Miller and J. Nesbitt (Washington, DC, 1995), 33–40, at 37–39. Riedel has recently challenged the probability that Nikephoros II Phokas ever made this request. See M. Riedel, "Nikephoros II Phocas and Orthodox Military Martyrs," *Journal of Medieval Religious Cultures* 41 (2015): 121–47; also see chapter 6, in this volume, for further discussion.

26 McGuckin, "A Conflicted Heritage."

diversity. McGuckin devotes less than two pages to what is the most interesting and underdeveloped aspect of the entire issue here—but he identifies the way that hymnography indicates not only the multitude of Christian responses to violence but also the ways in which imperial patronage could shift the entire trajectory of a specific religious feast and, in doing so, present a theological vision that reinforced the needs of the state.[27]

Hymns as Evidence of Byzantine Attitudes toward Violence

Susan Ashbrook Harvey has done more than perhaps anyone to draw attention to the unparalleled access to lived religion made possible by the close study of hymnography.[28] As Harvey notes, hymnography provided biblical literacy to the early Christian community, by summarizing, interpreting, allegorizing, and typologizing well-known and other stories from the scriptures. The earliest sources indicate that the vast majority of these hymns focused on the Passion, Crucifixion, and Resurrection of Jesus Christ. Through hymnography, Christian poets could tell and retell the significance of those events in accessible language that everyone could understand. Unlike formal biblical exegesis—produced by elite bishops and theologians who routinely deployed archaicizing rhetorical flourishes—hymnography was composed for public consumption and devotion.[29] For some authors, such as Ephraim the Syrian or Jacob of Sarug, "hymnography as exegesis" provided a powerful mechanism for stimulating moral and ethical formation.[30] Public singing also provided a fertile space for female participation and even leadership.[31]

---

27 McGuckin rightly points to the role of the emperor Herakleios in the development of the Feast of the Exaltation of the Holy Cross and the ways in which that feast represents a kind of liturgical sacralization of violence.

28 See, for example, S. A. Harvey, *Song and Memory: Biblical Women in Syriac Tradition* (Milwaukee, 2010), and S. A. Harvey, "Bearing Witness: New Testament Women in Early Byzantine Hymnography," in *The New Testament in Byzantium*, ed. D. Krueger and R. Nelson (Washington, DC, 2016), 205–20.

29 Harvey, "Bearing Witness," 205.

30 Harvey, "Liturgy and Ethics in Ancient Syriac Christianity: Two Paradigms," *Studies in Christian Ethics* 26 (2013): 300–316.

31 Harvey, "Revisiting the Daughters of the Covenant: Women's Choirs and Sacred Song in Ancient Syriac Christianity," *Hugoye: Journal of Syriac Studies* 8 (2009): 125–49.

Hymnography was the one thing that all Christians heard and knew, thus making it an important resource for scholars seeking to understand the religious imagination of premodern peoples. As noted, whereas most Christians did not have access to famous theological texts, they did have access to the various cycles of hymns that communicated the scriptures and basic theological teachings of the Christian faith. Early Christians were unlikely to ever actually read the account of Jesus's death and Resurrection in one of the Gospels, but over the course of an eight-week Sunday cycle, they would have heard, and probably sung, nearly a thousand short hymns telling these events and celebrating their soteriological significance. That cycle would repeat itself, Sunday after Sunday, throughout Christians' lives. As Derek Krueger documents so compellingly, hymnography produced "liturgical subjects,"[32] and it did so across hierarchical, cultural, and gendered divides.

Another important feature of hymnography in particular, and liturgy more generally, is its organic, evolving nature. Throughout the Byzantine period, local churches possessed their own typika—guidebooks recording the cycle of liturgical festivals and assigned hymns—even though the basic structures of the liturgy were largely formed by the Christian communities of Jerusalem and Constantinople. Major monastic centers and cathedral churches experimented not only with new hymns, but also with entirely new genres of hymnography. Such experimentation was not haphazard but a direct response to the social, political, and religious conditions of the local community. As Harvey put it, "[Liturgy's] presentation, content, and enactment responded to the time and place it was performed, and to the social expectations and cultural needs of its context. Hence, liturgical texts—sermons, hymns, and prayers—can sometimes provide windows into what scholars refer to as 'lived religion': that reality of religious practice that people enact in their daily lives, which may or may not align easily with doctrine or institutional mandates."[33] Put more succinctly, hymnography offers an otherwise invisible window into the discrepancy between the thought world of ordinary Christians and the theological positions imparted

---

32 D. Krueger, *Liturgical Subjects: Christian Ritual, Biblical Narrative and the Formation of the Self in Byzantium* (Philadelphia, 2014).

33 S. A. Harvey, review of M. Doerfler, *Jephthah's Daughter, Sarah's Son: The Death of Children in Late Antiquity*, IOTA Forum: Reviews, 28 June 2021, https://iota-web.org/2021/06/28/doerfler-jephthahs-daughter-sarahs-son/.

from on high. For purposes here, hymnography has the potential to reveal popular understandings of the relationship between faith and violence, insights otherwise inaccessible through elite, theological sources or military handbooks.

Hymnography's multivalence also makes it a powerful, if slippery, source of data. Not only are these texts poetic in nature, potentially triggering a myriad of meanings, but as a focal point of lived religion, a fluidity exists between what a hymnographer might have had in mind at the time of composition, what a priest, cantor or choir might have thought when they sung the hymn, and what a lay participant in the service might have absorbed when hearing it sung. Of course, a priest or layperson's hermeneutical engagement with a hymn might be different from one century to the next, from one region to the next, as local power structures and the experience or threat of violence shifted.

While a few scholars have looked at the ways in which specific hymns offer evidence of violence and competition between religious groups, it is noteworthy that no single study explores hymnography as the source base for understanding Byzantine attitudes toward violence and war.[34] Violence is endemic in Byzantine hymnography, to a large extent because the majority of hymns produced from the fourth to the fourteenth century continued to reflect on the Passion and Resurrection of Christ, and the Passion–Resurrection cycle provided hymnographers an ongoing reason to reflect on the violence that Christ suffered. That being said, historical events, such as the Persian and Arab conquests of Jerusalem in the seventh century, and the development of new religious festivals, like the Exaltation of the Cross, coincided with profound shifts in the way that hymnographers reflected on violence.

Objective, Method, and Thesis

The purpose of this study is to assess the ways in which a close reading of select hymns alters, confirms, or refines current knowledge of Byzantine Christian attitudes toward violence and whether those attitudes changed over time.

---

34 See, for example, Shaw, *Sacred Violence*, esp. ch. 10, "Sing a New Song," 441–89. See also O. Münz-Manor and T. Arentzen, "Soundscapes of Salvation: Resounding Refrains in Jewish and Christian Liturgical Poems," *Studies in Late Antiquity* 3.1 (2019): 36–55; and J. Koder, "Imperial Propaganda in the Kontakia of Romanos the Melode," *DOP* 62 (2008): 275–91.

Hymnography offers a record of ideas that both originated among and was directed at ordinary Christians, and this study seeks to explore an otherwise ignored repository of evidence concerning the ways that Byzantine Christians imagined violence when they prayed. The language of liturgical violence changed considerably. In part, this was organic—related to the gradual expansion of the Christian festal cycle—and, in part, it appears to have been imposed by the imperial court.

Methodologically, *Sacralizing Violence in Byzantium* offers a close reading of clusters of hymns produced between the fourth and tenth centuries with two chapters relying on double translations, which render such close readings somewhat provisional.[35] In addition to a literary and theological analysis of specific hymns, this study routinely employs a historical-critical methodology to situate the composition and adoption of the hymns in their historical context. Shifting historical conditions coincided with profound changes in the hymnographic presentation of violence. Given the challenges of authorship and dating involved in the study of hymnography, I do not claim a direct correlation between historical events and the shifting patterns in hymnography, but do identify imperial policies or setbacks that changed conditions for Christians or the relationship between Christian communities and other religious groups—for example, relations between Christians and Jews in Palestine during the reign of Justinian (r. 527–565)—whenever a hymnographic innovation can be shown to have emerged at roughly the same time and in the same place.

This project can best be described as a genealogy rather than a narrative history. The concept of genealogy is employed in a general sense, for the most part. This means that important historical evolutions in Byzantine hymnography are identified and analyzed, but without the unbroken summary of events or exact causal precision—that is, x happened on this date for y reason—often typical of narrative history. Moreover, no effort is made to assess the entire body of Byzantine hymnography. In large part, this approach has been determined by the nature of the sources. Of the thousands of Byzantine hymns that survive, many do not deal with violence at all and, more importantly, it is not possible to identify the authorship, date, and (often) the provenance of most hymns. Given that

---

35 Chapters 1 and 4 deal with texts composed in Greek but today survive only in Old Georgian. In both cases, I have relied on English translations of the Georgian.

a general date and provenance can be established for only a select set of hymns, genealogy offers the best path for this analysis.

Acknowledgment must be made of a certain indebtedness to the more specific application of genealogy first introduced by Nietzsche and then popularized by Foucault, although it is not the primary focus of this study.[36] For both Nietzsche and Foucault, genealogy was more a method of critique than a form of historical analysis. Whether the target was Christian morality (as for Nietzsche) or the surveillance state (as for Foucault), genealogy provided a historical-philosophical means of undermining a popular contemporary idea or practice by illustrating the unethical origins and progressions that led to its formation.[37] The current project includes an element of critique, most notably in the conclusion, but its principal purpose is to document changes in the way Christians conceptualized violence over time and, where possible, to point to the historical factors that may have spurred those changes. What is more, the critique offered in the conclusion incorporates theological reasoning, which obviously marks a clear break from the methodology of Nietzsche and Foucault.

The thesis of this study is rather straightforward: Byzantine hymnography underwent a profound transformation in the way that it engaged violence at roughly the same time that Christian and Roman identity became fully intertwined and as Roman armies suffered unprecedented setbacks in the early seventh century. The Feast of the Exaltation of the Holy Cross appears to have provided the first occasion for this transformation, but it was under Emperor Herakleios (r. 610–641)—and specifically, the importation of the feast to Constantinople in 628—that one finds the most profound reconceptualization of violence in Byzantine hymnography. The subsequent development of liturgical services explicitly for imperial soldiers before battle and after death in the late ninth or tenth century evinces a further expansion of this imperialization of violence.

---

36 See F. Nietzsche, *On the Genealogy of Morals and Ecce Homo*, trans. W. Kaufmann and R. J. Hollingdale (New York, 1967), and M. Foucault, *The Archaeology of Knowledge*, trans. A. M. Sheridan Smith (New York, 1972).

37 For both Foucault and Nietzsche, albeit in different ways and extents, the purpose of genealogy was to show the shameful and contingent origins of generally popular contemporary ideas and practices. For analysis of Foucault's notion of genealogy and how it departs from Kant and Nietzsche, see C. Koopman, *Genealogy as Critique: Foucault and the Problems of Modernity* (Bloomington, IN, 2013).

Generally speaking, the earliest Christian hymns engaged violence by reflecting on the violence that Christ suffered historically or by exploring the theological ramifications of that suffering. In some instances, such as the hymns of Romanos the Melodist, this approach extended to reflections on the suffering of saints, who were often positioned as a typology for Christ's suffering. Two important aspects of these early hymns differentiate them from those that began to emerge in Jerusalem in the middle of the sixth century. First, no hymn of Christian composition prior to Justinian's reign asks God to inflict violence on others, and second, none of those early hymns presumed Christian and Roman identity to be one and the same. But both of those facets of early Byzantine hymnography begin to change with the introduction of hymns composed in Jerusalem for the Feast of the Exaltation, which likely occurred during the reign of Justinian.

At roughly the same time that Emperor Herakleios imported the Feast of the Exaltation to Constantinople and issued a directive, in 628, that it be commemorated throughout the empire, new hymns transformed the ways in which Byzantine liturgy conceptualized and sang about violence. Not only did hymnographers begin to sacralize violence in the sense that they incorporated prayers for the destruction of others, but they also intimately tied this sacralization to the notion that the basileus—the Eastern Roman emperor—was God's chosen political and military instrument on earth; God was on the side of the Roman basileus. The soldiers of the basileus were God's soldiers, and the basileus's enemies were God's enemies. This new conceptualization of violence did not supplant the previous one that focused on Christ's Passion and Crucifixion. Indeed, the older model remained the more common expression in Byzantine hymns, but the sacralization of imperial violence continued and expanded within contexts closely associated with imperial interests and identity, such as the Feast of the Exaltation, and with new prayer services designed for imperial armies.

Parameters of This Study and Echoes of Ancient Israel

Sometimes the parameters of a book are best defined by what it is not. *Sacralizing Violence in Byzantium* is not a study of Byzantine music. Rather, the focus lies on the content—the words—of the hymns, not their meter, melody, tone, arrangement, or choirs. This is not a study of the way in which the act of singing or the hearing of music functions within the brain or shapes the conscious or subconscious. All of these aspects of liturgy are relevant to our understanding of lived religion in Byzantium, but do not feature here.[38]

Moreover, it is hoped that this book will spur subsequent scholarship that reappraises extant interpretations of the Byzantine canonical and exegetical tradition, but this study itself does not do so. The analysis of each chapter concerns the content of the hymns themselves, rather than comparisons between hymns and the writings of Byzantine theologians or works of exegesis. There are, however, two minor exceptions to this guiding parameter. The first is a short survey, in the paragraphs that follow, of the way early Christian theologians typologized the violence of the psalms. The second is in chapter 4, which examines Eusebius of Caesarea's presentation of Constantine as a divine instrument as well as an analysis of Eusebius's efforts to link Constantine and the cross; these motifs are addressed because they were deliberately appropriated in subsequent hymnography developed for the Feast of the Exaltation.

In addition, this book only explores hymns written by Christians. Thus, it does not examine the presentation of violence in the psalms, even though the psalms were the first hymns that the followers of Jesus sang in their eucharistic gatherings,[39] and even though the Byzantines steadily came to envision their empire as New Israel. This decision was made for several reasons, the principal ones being a desire to focus the analysis on hymns composed by Byzantine Christians and to show that changing historical conditions coincided with the production of hymns that conceptualized violence in new ways. Because the ancient Hebrews produced most of the psalms more than a millennium before the oldest surviving Byzantine hymns, the central objective of the study precluded their study. To be sure, the continued use of the psalms by Byzantine Christians demonstrates the extent to which they found the content relevant to

---

38 For a recent examination of the ways in which music and ritual movement shaped identity and faith commitments in early (Latin) Christian communities, see the excellent examination of the hymns of Ambrose in B. Dunkle, *Enchantment and Creed in the Hymns of Ambrose of Milan* (Oxford, 2016).

39 For a concise summary of the function of the psalms in early Christian liturgy and the ways in which they inspired but also limited subsequent hymns, see Dunkle, *Enchantment and Creed*, 14–24.

their liturgical and personal needs.[40] Which psalms were sung in parish churches and when remains largely unknown, however, with the exception of elaborate choral singing at Hagia Sophia and the singing of an entire psalter in the course of a week in certain monastic circles.[41]

Another reason for excluding the psalms from detailed analysis is the way early Christian theologians typologized their meaning, often elaborately. Any attempt to trace whether the Byzantine exegetical traditions were communicated or absorbed by lay communities over the centuries would simply take this project too far afield. This would be especially true for the so-called imprecatory psalms—that is, Psalms 57/58, 68/69, 108/109, and 136/137—which on the surface appear to celebrate expressions of anger and grief and then build on these emotions to request divine vengeance against human enemies.

While many Christians in the modern world might recoil at the content of the imprecatory psalms, it is important to note that early Christian theologians did not. Gregory of Nyssa, for example, understood the imprecatory psalms as key to the entirety of the Psalter, not because he celebrated their violence, but because of the way his typological analysis so transformed their meaning that they became, in his hands, prayers for noetic stillness.[42] For Nyssa, the psalmist,

---

40 For an overview of the ways in which the Byzantines developed multiple regimens for reciting the psalms, see Krueger, *Liturgical Subjects*, 17–23.

41 It is known that in the fourth and fifth centuries, some influential theologians, among them Athanasius and Gregory of Nyssa, encouraged ascetic correspondents to read the psalms frequently and that aristocratic families in the middle and later Byzantine periods commissioned and used psalters for personal devotion. Neither of these situations, however, reveals much about lay community rituals. See G. R. Parpulov, "Psalters and Personal Piety in Byzantium," in *The Old Testament in Byzantium*, ed. P. Magdalino and R. Nelson (Washington, DC, 2010), 77–105.

42 As Gary Anderson notes, Nyssa's interpretation is preconditioned on two important elements: (1) he accepts Davidic authorship for the whole of the Psalter, and (2) he carefully reads the Psalter alongside 1 Samuel, which chronicles David's struggles with Saul. According to Anderson, when these psalms are read against the history recorded in 1 Samuel, one begins to see the anger and desire for revenge in a different light in alignment with David's patient willingness to endure the torturous efforts of Saul against David. G. Anderson, "King David and the Psalms of Imprecation," *Pro Ecclesia: A Journal of Catholic and Evangelical Theology* 15 (2006): 267–80, esp. 278. See, also, H. Boersma, "The Church Fathers' Spiritual Interpretation of the Psalms," in *Living Waters from Ancient Springs: Essays in Honor of Cornelis Van Dam*, ed. J. Van Vliet (Eugene, OR, 2011), 41–56.

that is, David, prefigured Christ; the former's patient endurance of Saul's attacks anticipated Christ's endurance of his rejection by Jewish leaders. More importantly, Nyssa claims that David overcame his animosity toward Saul through the act of articulating it in prayer. He argues that this is known because 1 Samuel makes clear that David never acted on the animosity against Saul articulated in the psalms.[43] Thus, Gregory counsels readers that Christians should read these psalms to overcome their own anger or grief.

John Chrysostom took a different tact but equally deflected from calls for violence. Rather than read the psalms as typology, he interpreted them as prophecy, although not so much as prophecy for the ancient Jews as for his own audience.[44] In his hands, David did not "want" bad things to happen to his enemies; instead, he "predicted" that bad things would happen. In other words, Chrysostom suggests that the psalms were composed in this way so that contemporary readers might fear what might happen to themselves so that they could reform their lives accordingly.[45] As Elizabeth Sunshine Koroma has observed, when the text does not lend itself to reading in this way, Chrysostom typically redirected his audience to see the imprecatory passages as calls to repentance, modeled on David's own life.[46] When all else failed, Chrysostom instructed his audience to follow the example of the psalmist, rather than the psalms.[47]

Another dimension of potential violence in the psalms is the way God, Yahweh, is occasionally presented as a kind of divine warrior. Arguably, the most explicit expression of the divine warrior motif occurs in Psalms 67/68, where Yahweh is presented as a combination of king and conqueror. For most Christian commentators of this psalm in the fourth and fifth centuries, the psalmist is not describing Yahweh's activity in ancient Israel, but prophetically

---

43 For Gregory's interpretation of the psalm, see R. Heine, trans., *Gregory of Nyssa's Treatise on the Inscriptions of the Psalms* (Oxford, 1995), 200–201.

44 In other words, as elsewhere in John's exegesis, he is principally concerned with the moral formation of his audience, and he develops his exegetical strategies accordingly. On John's exegetical strategy, see M. Mitchell, *The Heavenly Trumpet: John Chrysostom and the Art of Pauline Interpretation* (Tübingen, 2000). For John's interpretation of the imprecatory psalms, see E. S. Koroma, "Imprecatory Psalms as Prophecy: How John Chrysostom's Commentary on the Psalms Address the Moral Problem of Anger," *JEChrSt* 31 (2023): 33–56.

45 See Koroma, "Imprecatory Psalms as Prophecy," 47.

46 See Koroma, "Imprecatory Psalms as Prophecy," 44 and 51.

47 See Koroma, "Imprecatory Psalms as Prophecy," 47.

anticipating Christ, whose triumph occurs through the Resurrection.[48] This type of typological reading was especially prevalent among the Alexandrian School, which tried to find Christ in every psalm, but some Antiochian interpreters pursued it as well, including Theodoret of Cyrrhus. As James Wellington observes, for Theodoret, Psalms 67/68 are a victory song of the risen and glorified Christ. The opening statement, "Let God arise," is interpreted not only as an invocation for God to address the suffering of his people, but also in anticipation of the Resurrection itself. According to Theodoret, this is not a rising for war in a material or physical sense—it is a rising for war in a spiritual sense, through resurrection.[49] Thus, the enemies of Psalms 67/68 are not the human enemies of Israel, or their Christian successors, but the "demons warring against human beings."[50]

In short, whether concerning the expressions of anger or grief voiced by the psalmist, requests for divine vengeance, or portrayals of God as a kind of divine warrior, early Christian commentators typically typologized or spiritualized the violence in the imprecatory psalms in ways aimed at leading their audience toward self-reform and inner peace. They did not derive from these texts any sort of authorization for the reader to inflict violence against others in the present or in the future. The earliest hymns of Christian composition that engage themes of violence approach their subject in much the same way as these theological expositions of the psalms: the violence speaks to a spiritual realm dominated by the victory of Christ over death. By the tenth century, however, hymnographers began to compose special services for imperial soldiers that included requests for divine vengeance against human enemies. How and to what extent those hymns were inspired directly by a more literal reading of the imprecatory psalms is impossible to gauge.

---

48 See J. Wellington, "Let God Arise: The Divine Warrior Motif in Theodoret of Cyrrhus' Commentary on Ps. 67," *StP* 96 (2017): 265–71.

49 Thus, the soldiers in the psalm are not actual soldiers but those who proclaim the gospel, and their fight is not physical but spiritual. Similarly, the spoils of victory described in the psalm are allegorized to represent humans' liberation from sin, formerly belonging to Satan, now belonging to Christ.

50 Theodoret of Cyrrhus, PG 80:1376D; R. C. Hill, trans., *Theodoret of Cyrus: Commentary on the Psalms,* 2 vols. (Washington, DC, 2000–2001), 1:381. Also see Wellington, "Let God Arise," 268.

The connection between the psalms' supposed author, King David, and the Byzantine vision of their empire as New Israel requires careful reflection. In 627, shortly after Constantinople escaped pillaging by the Avars and just as the decades-long conflict with the Persians was turning in the Byzantines' favor, the orator Theodore Synkellos delivered a panegyric on behalf of Herakleios that draws a direct link between the emperor and King David.[51] As Claudia Rapp has observed, to Synkellos, Herakleios was not just a "new" David; he was "the David" who lived in biblical times and had been transported to the present.[52] With the exception of Eusebius, an outlier in many respects, this was the first official court panegyric to link a Byzantine emperor to David.[53] Although it would take centuries before court panegyric and Byzantine chronicles would consistently combine Byzantine political rhetoric with the notion of New Israel, the reign of Herakleios stands out as a key moment in that integration.[54]

Perhaps the best-known artistic connection between David and the Byzantine throne, between ancient Israel and New Israel, is also linked to Herakleios: a set of nine silver dinner plates, known as the David Plates, which were created in

---

51 Theodore Synkellos, *On the Avar Siege of Constantinople* 38, ed. L. Sternbach, *Analecta Avarica* (Krakow, 1900), 17 [313], lines 35–39, with the specific link noted at line 37; repr. in F. Makk, ed. and trans., *Traduction et commentaire de l'homélie écrite probablement par Théodore le Syncelle sur le siege de Constantinople en 626*, Opuscula Byzantina 3, Acta Universitatis de Attila József Nominatae: Acta Antiqua et Archaeologica 19 (Szeged, 1975), 73–118, at 89, lines 35–39.

52 C. Rapp, "Old Testament Models for Emperors in Early Byzantium," in Magdalino and Nelson, *The Old Testament in Byzantium*, 175–98, at 194–95.

53 For the importance of the Byzantines' successful delivery from the Avar siege and the imagining of Herakleios as the new David, see G. Dagron, "L'Église et la chrétienté byzantines entre les invasions et l'iconoclasme (VIIe–début VIIIe siècle)," in *Évêques, moines et empereurs (610–1054)*, ed. G. Dagron, P. Riché, and A. Vauchez, Histoire du christianisme 4 (Paris, 1993), 9–91, at 20.

54 Indeed, in the twentieth century, it was commonplace to associate Herakleios's reign with the introduction of political self-identification as New Israel. In addition to Dagron, see, for example, O. Treitinger, *Die oströmische Kaiser- und Reichsidee nach ihrer Gestaltung im höfischen Zeremoniell* (Jena, 1938), and P. Alexander, "The Strength of Empire as Seen through Byzantine Eyes," *Speculum* 37.3 (1962): 339–57, both of whom pointed to physical symbols or relics of ancient Israel brought to Constantinople as evidence of this link. It has also been observed that there are very few examples of this motif in Byzantine chronicles before the twelfth century. On this, see E. Jeffreys, "Old Testament 'History' and the Byzantine Chronicle," in Magdalino and Nelson, *The Old Testament in Byzantium*, 155–74.

Constantinople between 614 and 630 CE.⁵⁵ Each of the plates depicts a different scene from the life of David with artistic gestures linking him to Roman imperial traditions. The high quality of the plates has led most of the art historical world to believe that they were crafted in Herakleios's palace workshops, possibly at the successful conclusion of the Persian war to celebrate Herakleios as the new David. Despite their majestic quality and the clear conceptual connection between the plates and the panegyric of Synkellos, it remains noteworthy that there is no other surviving artistic link between the imperial throne and David until the ninth century, when new images appeared under Basil I (r. 867–886), at which point the motif became standard in Byzantine ideology and court ceremony.⁵⁶

In a brilliant, albeit brief, study Rapp examined four distinctive genres within early Byzantine literature—chronicles, panegyrics, conciliar acts, and correspondence—to understand the ways in which the Byzantines employed Old Testament models in their discussions of imperial figures.⁵⁷ Noting that Byzantine authors used both the Roman tradition of exempla and the Christian exegetical tradition of typology, Rapp observed that it was conciliar acts and episcopal correspondence to the emperor in the wake of conciliar gatherings, in particular the Council of Chalcedon in 451, that were the first to consistently employ the Old Testament kingly motifs for Byzantine emperors. To be sure, these authors' positive associations between their addressee and King David, or Solomon, were meant to flatter the emperor through acclamation, in the hope that he might be persuaded to adopt a particular theological position. Early ecclesiastical historians, such as Socrates and Sozomen, rarely employed the motif, and when they did, they typically did so negatively—that is, comparing a bad ruler to one of the Old Testament villains, such as Pharoah or Ahab.⁵⁸ Apart from Eusebius, the motif does not appear in official court panegyrics until Herakleios, in the Synkellos example noted above, which Rapp interprets as the first true embrace of the motif in that genre. The imperial chroniclers were the

---

55 See M. M. Mango, "Imperial Art in the Seventh Century," in *New Constantines: The Rhythm of Imperial Renewal in Byzantium, 4th–13th Centuries*, ed. P. Magdalino (Aldershot, 1994), 109–38.

56 See I. Kalavrezou, N. Trahoulia, and S. Sabar, "Critique of the Emperor in the Vatican Psalter gr. 752," *DOP* 47 (1993): 195–219, at 199.

57 Rapp, "Old Testament Models for Emperors."

58 Rapp, "Old Testament Models for Emperors," 187.

last group to adopt the Old Testament models in their writing, but some of them had begun to introduce Old Testament events in their world histories during the mid-sixth century.[59]

For Stephen Shoemaker, the connection between the Old Testament and the Byzantine imperial imagination was not so much to be found in the way that chroniclers and panegyrists incorporated the histories of the ancient Jews into the Byzantine political and religious realms so much as it was to be found in the Jewish apocalypses, especially in the book of Daniel's pronouncements that the world would experience only four global kingdoms before the end-time.[60] Several influential Christian writers in the fourth and fifth centuries—including Cyril of Alexandria, Ephraim, Eusebius, and John Chrysostom—believed the Roman/Byzantine Empire constituted the last historical stage of the people of God and that it had been specifically selected to pave the way for the eternal kingdom of God.[61] By the seventh century, this understanding gave rise to the last emperor conceit, an expectation that a mythical emperor would pacify the world, that is, vanquish the Arabs, and institute a new Pax Romana until the end-time.[62] This motif of the last emperor, which blended Old Testament and Roman imperial themes, would come to dominate middle and later Byzantine apocalyptic thinking.[63] By the tenth century, the hymns composed for the benefit of imperial soldiers carefully wove together the threads of the emperor as a new David,

---

59 Rapp, "Old Testament Models for Emperors," 187, notes that the seventh-century *Chronicon Paschale* (Herakleios's reign) does not contain comparisons between Old Testament figures and ruling emperors. John Malalas, writing in the 560s, was the first Byzantine chronicler to include events from the Old Testament in his chronicle. He was also the first to have a broader, even monastic, audience in mind as he composed his text. See Jeffreys, "Old Testament 'History' and the Byzantine Chronicle," 163 and 167.

60 S. Shoemaker, *Apocalypse of Empire: Imperial Eschatology in Late Antiquity and Early Islam* (Philadelphia, 2018), esp. ch. 3, 65–84.

61 Shoemaker, *Apocalypse of Empire*, 41.

62 See, also, A. Kraft, "The Last Roman Emperor 'Topos' in the Byzantine Apocalyptic Tradition," *Byzantion* 82 (2012): 213–57, and D. Olster, "Byzantine Apocalypses," in *The Encyclopedia of Apocalypticism*, ed. J. J. Collins, B. McGinn, and S. J. Stein (New York, 1998), 2:48–73.

63 For Shoemaker, *Apocalypse of Empire*, 146–79, it is not just that Byzantine religious thinking in the age of Islam became increasingly apocalyptic, but that the Roman people were considered the directly hand-chosen people of God, selected to further the legacy of ancient Israel in preparing the way for the eternal kingdom of God.

confidence in the Romans being the lone people of God, and invocations by soldiers to call upon God to destroy their enemies.

Overview of the Chapters

Sacralizing Violence in Byzantium consists of six chapters and proceeds in general chronological order. Given the nature of the sources, the individual chapters contain discrete analyses of a manuscript collection of hymns organized around a liturgical cycle (such as the cycle of Sunday hymns), an annual liturgical event (Good Friday and the Feast of the Exaltation), or a single liturgical service; one chapter features a collection of hymns known to have been penned by a single author, Romanos the Melodist. All of the hymns examined were composed in Greek, but in two cases, in chapters 1 and 4, the original Greek hymns have been lost and survive only in an ancient Georgian translation. In both cases, I have relied on English translations of the Georgian by Stephen Shoemaker.

Chapter 1 examines the oldest surviving collection of Christian hymns, which is found in the *Jerusalem Georgian Chantbook*, a sixth-century translation of older Greek hymns. The book includes approximately one thousand short hymns, organized into an eight-week cycle for the vesper, matin, and Sunday liturgy services performed at the church of the Anastasis (Holy Sepulcher) in Jerusalem. The vast majority of these hymns narrate or reflect on the Passion, death, and Resurrection of Jesus Christ, which was the focus of the ancient Sunday liturgical cycle. Many of these hymns reflect on the violence Christ endured through his Crucifixion, some of them graphically. For the purposes here, the most noteworthy aspect of the collection is that the engagement with violence is exclusively focused on the violence that Christ suffered or on the soteriological consequences of that violence.[64]

A much smaller collection of hymns, the Good Friday Idiomela, is examined in chapter 2. Its contents are likely the oldest surviving hymns composed exclusively for Good Friday and originated in Palestine. The engagement with violence in these mid-sixth-century hymns is similar to that of the Sunday liturgical cycle

---

64 On a few occasions, the hymns look back to various heroes of the Hebrew scriptures, especially the three Chaldean children of Babylon, and portray the violence that they suffered as a kind of prefiguration for Christ's suffering.

in focusing on violence suffered by Christ and the soteriological benefit of that suffering for humanity. What most differentiates these hymns from those of the Sunday services is the extent to which some of them identify "the Jews" as being responsible for the death of Christ. In the hymns of the chantbook, the explicit or implicit assumption is that all humans are responsible for Christ's death because all humans needed him to die. The chapter not only connects this hymnographic shift to on-the-ground events pitting Jews against Christians in Palestine at the time of composition, but it also offers a brief theological analysis of the consequences of this change.

Chapter 3 examines three kontakia by the Constantinopolitan hymnographer Romanos the Melodist, who was active in the early and middle part of the sixth century. Romanos's hymns differ from those of the chantbook and idiomela collections in several ways. As kontakia, these hymns deploy dramatic, extrabiblical conversations between biblical characters in a way that allows Romanos to mine the thoughts and motivations of famous biblical heroes, such as the Virgin Mary, and villains, including Herod and Satan. As a result, the presentation of violence is more expansive than the others, even if it continues to follow existing parameters. For example, Romanos extended reflection on violence beyond that suffered by Christ to include that suffered by the saints—both the physical violence experienced by the "holy innocents" slain by Herod and the emotional violence endured by Mary as she watched her son die.

Chapters 4 and 5 present a two-part analysis of the development and expansion of the Feast of the Exaltation, commemorated 14 September in the Byzantine Church. More than any other liturgical commemoration, this feast provided the impetus for two things that transformed liturgical engagement with violence in the Byzantine Church. Analyzing the oldest surviving hymns for the Jerusalem feast, chapter 4 shows that the festival emerged in such a way that it celebrated the Christianization of the Roman Empire by explicitly connecting commemoration of the cross to the figure of Constantine. Stephen Shoemaker completed a translation of these hymns, which survive only in Old Georgian, and this translation is included as appendix 1. Chapter 5 discusses not only how the emperor Herakleios expanded the imperial dimensions of the feast, but also the way in which new hymns composed during his reign were the first to ask God to destroy the enemies of the basileus. As the centuries passed, the imperial and militant dimensions of this feast remained key elements of each successive wave of hymnographic composition. These chapters also demonstrate that proximity to imperial power became the determinant factor in the degree to which new compositions leaned into those themes.

An altogether different type of hymnography is explored in chapter 6, which features analysis of two special occasion prayer services—one for soldiers on the evening before battle and the other as a memorial for the soldiers who died in battle or in captivity. Agostino Pertusi edited the first service, known simply as Akolouthia before Battle, in 1948. The liturgical scholar John Klentos has provided an English translation of Pertusi's Greek text, which is included in this volume as appendix 2. Akolouthia before Battle suggests a hymnographic sacralization of both the basileus and his soldiers. It repeatedly positions the army of the basileus as God's army, the enemies of the basileus as God's enemies. The text invokes the saints, angels, and Christ not only to protect the baslieus and his army in battle, but also, and in graphic detail, to bring death and destruction to his enemies. The second service, Akolouthia for Fallen Soldiers, was likely introduced in Constantinople during the tenth century for Saturday of the Souls, the annual commemoration on the last Saturday before Lent. The text is not concerned with the sacralization of the basileus, but it repeatedly presents the sacrifice of fallen soldiers as a religious act that should merit the forgiveness of sins. Thus, both texts represent a high point in the Byzantines' sacralization of violence through liturgy. An English translation of this service based on the Greek text edited and published by Theocharis Détorakis and Justin Mossay is included as appendix 3.[65]

---

65 T. Détorakis and J. Mossay, "Un office byzantine inédit pour ceux qui sont morts à la guerre, dans le Cod. Sin. Gr. 734–735," *Le Muséon* 101.1 (1988): 183–211.

CHAPTER 1

THE *JERUSALEM GEORGIAN CHANTBOOK*

The *Jerusalem Georgian Chantbook* is the oldest surviving collection of Christian hymns.[1] As its name suggests, the chantbook originated in Jerusalem and was written in Old Georgian. By the fourth century, Jerusalem had become a major pilgrimage site for Christians of diverse ethnic backgrounds, and the production of this text in Georgian a century or two later reflects the need at that time to translate the Greek-language hymns being used in Jerusalem into Georgian to accommodate resident Georgian speakers and visiting Georgian pilgrims. One of the more remarkable features of this manuscript collection is its age: it is so old that more than 80 percent of its hymns do not exist in any surviving Greek manuscripts. Thus, the assembled ancient hymns had already been replaced by subsequent compositions by the time the oldest surviving Greek manuscripts came into existence.[2] In short, the chantbook is a one-of-a-kind document preserving the most ancient testimony to the content of early Christian worship

---

1 As I do not read Georgian, this chapter relies heavily on the published work (and personal consultation) of S. Shoemaker, *The First Christian Hymnal: The Songs of the Ancient Jerusalem Church; Parallel Georgian-English Texts,* Middle Eastern Texts Initiative 10 (Provo, UT, 2018).

2 There are, in fact, two major recensions of the chantbook in the Georgian manuscript. Interestingly, one of them mirrors surviving Greek hymnbook collections dating to the start of the seventh century, indicating that the other recension is the older one, reflecting practices in the Greek tradition that no longer survive. See Shoemaker, *The First Christian Hymnal,* xiv–xv.

as communicated and practiced by believers in the region that gave birth to Christianity.[3]

The *Jerusalem Georgian Chantbook* consists of three major sections, all of which developed over time.[4] The oldest section, examined in this chapter, contains the hymns used for the vesper, matins, and Eucharist sequence of services for "regular" Sundays throughout the year.[5] This means that it does not include those for Lent, Holy Week Sundays, or various annual feasts; the hymns for those appear in other sections of the chantbook.[6] The weekly Sunday liturgy was the oldest liturgical cycle for the Christian community, having been designed to commemorate and celebrate the Resurrection on a weekly basis. Over the course of a lifetime, the hymns of the Sunday liturgy would have been sung so many times that early Christians likely memorized them. Perhaps more than any other written source, these hymns would have shaped a layperson's understanding of Christian teaching, not only with respect to the historical events of the Passion, which they memorialized, but also with respect to what could or should be asked of a God who become human and died to grant them eternal life.

In the chantbook, the Sunday hymns are organized according to a cycle of eight musical modes, or tones, known as the Octoechos.[7] These eight tones are

---

3 For a comprehensive synopsis of the Georgian witness to Jerusalem worship and the likelihood that the Georgian texts reflect the Greek original, see S. S. R. Frøyshov, "The Georgian Witness to the Jerusalem Liturgy: New Sources and Studies," in *Inquiries into Eastern Christian Worship: Selected Papers of the Second International Congress of the Society of Oriental Liturgies, Rome, 17–21 September 2008*, ed. B. Groen, S. Hawkes-Teeples, and S. Alexopoulos (Leuven, 2012), 227–68.

4 For a critical edition of the chantbook, see E. Metreveli, C. Čankievi, and L. Xevsuriani, *Uzvelesi iadgari* [The oldest chantbook], Żveli k'art'uli mcerlobis żeglebi 2 (Tbilisi, 1980). The final section contains the Octoechos, on pages 367–512.

5 Early Christianity, like ancient Judaism, marked the beginning of the day with sunset. In the Eastern Christian liturgy, the vesper service typically began at sundown, the matins (or orthros) service took place at sunrise, and the Eucharist (Divine Liturgy) typically followed the matins service.

6 See Shoemaker, *The First Christian Hymnal*, xiv. Eastern Christians would eventually also develop a separate liturgical plan for festal days that might fall on a Sunday and disrupt certain portions of the Octoechos cycle, but that does not appear to have happened at this stage.

7 See S. S. R. Frøyshov, "The Early Development of the Liturgical Eight-Mode System in Jerusalem," *SVThQ* 51 (2007): 139–78. Among other insights, Frøyshov proposes that

provided in the chantbook in the following sequence: first, second, third, fourth, first plagal, second plagal, third plagal, and fourth plagal. Each week of this eight-week cycle had its own complete set of hymns for the vesper, matins, and liturgy services, and each of those sets of hymns would have been sung according to a distinctive tonal melody now lost.[8] It is important to note that the hymns in the chantbook would not have constituted the entirety of the liturgical ritual for the vesper, matins, and liturgy cycle. Some elements of these services never changed—such as the recitation of certain psalms, a stock set of petitions, and the Lord's Prayer—and they are not included in the chantbook. Other elements, such as lectionary readings, changed according to another schedule, and those were also excluded from the collection.[9] The chantbook does, however, contain most of the hymns for the vesper, matins, and liturgy services that repeated in the eight-week cycle of the Octoechos, and these would have constituted the majority of the hymnographic regimen for those services.[10] The current scholarly consensus dates the composition of the original Greek hymns of the Octoechos to sometime between the late fourth century, or possibly even earlier, and the early sixth century.[11] Scholars are confident of the terminus date; internal evidence in

---

the cycle of eight modes derives from the Christian commitment to the idea of Sunday as the "eighth" day (extending the Jewish cycle of seven), which was then adopted to the Jewish pentecontad of seven weeks by adding an eighth (esp. 149–53).

8 While it is true that the present-day Orthodox Churches, both Chalcedonian and some non-Chalcedonian, use an eight-part tonal register, scholars acknowledge that they are unable to determine the precise ancient tonal registry. Moreover, as Frøyshov notes, the eight-week liturgical cycle of the Octoechos is a separate, if overlapping, element from the eight-part tonal system. Frøyshov, "The Early Development of the Liturgical Eight-Mode System in Jerusalem," 140.

9 The oldest surviving lectionary from Jerusalem is the Armenian Lectionary, which Athanase Renoux dates to the fifth century. See A. Renoux, ed., *Le Codex arménien Jérusalem 121*, 2 vols., *PO* 35, fasc. 1, no. 163; *PO* 36, fasc. 2, no. 167 (Turnhout, 1969–1971).

10 The surviving manuscript is missing pages, so the collection is incomplete. Shoemaker, *The First Christian Hymnal*, xx (following Renoux, *Le Codex arménien Jérusalem 121*), privileges Sinai manuscript 40 over 41 for his reconstruction of the text. The latter manuscript is missing folios for the third plagal and fourth plagal modes.

11 See Shoemaker, *The First Christian Hymnal*, xvii, but especially C. Renoux, trans., *Les hymnes de la Résurrection* vol. 1, *Hymnographie liturgique géorgienne: Textes du Sinaï 18*, Sources liturgiques 3 (Paris, 2000), 30–64. Renoux dates the hymns to the fourth century on the basis of the content of the Christological statements in them and a comparison of that content to notable fourth-century Jerusalem-based theologians (44–45).

the text affirms that the Georgian translation of this section of the Greek text was complete by the year 600.[12]

The chantbook provides a Georgian translation of the Greek hymns sung in the church of the Anastasis (Holy Sepulcher), the major Christian shrine in the vicinity of Jerusalem. The Roman emperor Constantine commissioned the Anastasis in the early fourth century, and it was built just outside of the city, at the presumed site of Christ's tomb. It is important to note that the church of the Anastasis followed a liturgical structure open to all lay Christians and clergy, which distinguished it from the more closed monastic rites developing in Palestine and elsewhere to accommodate the different liturgical needs of the various monastic communities. Indeed, the very notion of a liturgical Octoechos originated within the context of a public "cathedral" setting rather than a monastic environment.[13] Given the dominant influence of Jerusalem in the development of liturgy elsewhere, it is likely that the hymns in the chantbook also point to patterns of Christian devotion being practiced by lay Christians beyond Palestine.[14]

One final note by way of introduction is the intriguing possibility, summarized by Shoemaker in the introduction to his translation of the hymns, that lay Christians—as opposed to ordained clergy or monks—composed at least some of these hymns in the earliest years of the Christian community in Jerusalem. As Shoemaker notes, officials in the Jerusalem bishop's office would ultimately have been responsible for the codification of hymns in a now lost Greek text replicated as the chantbook, but that does not necessarily mean that all of the hymns in the chantbook were composed by clerics in the bishop's office.[15] This possibility is

---

12 See Shoemaker, *The First Christian Hymnal*, xiv–xv.

13 See Frøyshov, "The Early Development of the Liturgical Eight-Mode System in Jerusalem," 145. It is customary for scholars of Byzantine liturgy to differentiate between a cathedral rite and a monastic rite. Typically, when scholars use the term *cathedral rite*, they are referring to the church of Hagia Sophia in Constantinople or possibly to the church of St. Demetrius in Thessalonica. Here the term is used in reference to the church of the Anastasis in the general sense to showcase the difference between an open public liturgical space and a closed, monastic one.

14 This possibility is, of course, speculative as there is no surviving evidence of liturgical rites elsewhere that are as old as the *Chantbook*.

15 Shoemaker, *The First Christian Hymnal*, xvii–xviii.

The Jerusalem Georgian Chantbook

noted here simply to reinforce the point that unlike any other source available to scholars, early Christian hymnography provides a window into the thought-world and faith of ordinary Christians. This is especially important in seeking to understand early Christian understandings of violence.

The Violence of Christ's Passion

Even after accounting for the challenge of double translation—from Greek to Old Georgian and from Old Georgian to English—it is quite clear that the Octoechos hymns regularly reference violence. More often than not, the hymns employ the language of violence to describe, commiserate, or celebrate the violence that Jesus suffered during his Crucifixion. Typically, the remembrance of Christ's suffering is tied to its salvific effect—that Christ's death and Resurrection open eternity to all those otherwise destined for death and oblivion. The sheer number of instances of this violence in the chantbook precludes analyzing each one individually, so a few representative examples must suffice: to start, a short refrain from the matins service in the third tone. Here, the ninth hymn following the gospel reading proclaims,

> You were nailed to the cross,
> And by the shedding of your blood,
> You delivered the world from corruption,
> Have mercy on us.[16]

In this single short hymn, the hymnographer describes the historical, macabre details of Christ's death, asserts the central theological claim of Christians about that death—that it delivers the world from death—and implores the same God, who suffered death, to have mercy on those who affirm these Christian truths through prayer or song.

In another representative example, from the matins service in the second plagal tone, the congregation sings,

---

16 *Jerusalem Georgian Chantbook*, third tone, matins (Shoemaker, *The First Christian Hymnal*, 105).

> You who endured, Savior, for the salvation of the world,
> Spreading out your hands on the cross,
> And by the opening of your side,
> You purified us from sin.
> We all bless the true God with glory.[17]

Here, the description of Christ's Crucifixion is more graphic, more drawn out. Christ endures the slow, painful agony of crucifixion. He spreads his hands on the cross; his side is opened by a spear. As in the previous short hymn, the hymnographer ties these graphic remembrances to the theological promise of Christianity—that Christ's death enables the salvation of the world, that it purifies the singers of their sin. For this suffering, for this act of salvation, the congregation praises the true God.

In another, more extended example that strings together a series of short hymns for the vesper service in the third plagal tone, the text further emphasizes the connection between Christ's suffering via crucifixion and death and the soteriological benefit of that suffering for the Christian community:

> You willingly suffered, O Christ God,
> For the salvation of humankind.
> When you went up on the cross,
> You tramped down the sting of death,
> And those who were in darkness
> You brought into the light
> And clothed with light.
> You presented them to the Father, as you promised.
>
> We offer you the prayer of evening, O Lord.
> You were intentionally nailed to the cross;
> You took hell captive
> Glory to your Resurrection, O Christ our God.

---

17 *Jerusalem Georgian Chantbook*, second plagal tone, matins (Shoemaker, *The First Christian Hymnal*, 209).

> For us you were placed in the tomb as a human being,
> And you arose on the third day.
> You brought forth Adam from the bonds of death.
> Glory to your Resurrection, O Christ our God.[18]

In this sequence of hymns, as elsewhere, the text connects Christ's suffering to its soteriological end—the salvation of the people of God. Although this connection is a mainstay of Christian identity and reflection, the centrality of this connection for the Christian is so essential, so commonplace, that one might simply take it for granted and thereby lose sight of the frequency with which these hymns incorporate the language and themes of violence.

It is worth recalling that hymnographers had a variety of possible ways to memorialize the Resurrection of Jesus. Nothing required them to register the nails, spear, blood, or suffering of Christ's Passion; rather, they chose to do so. By way of comparison, early Christian iconographers, unlike hymnographers, typically did not draw attention to the violence of Christ's death.[19] It is a commonplace among art historians of the period to note that there are far more images of Christ's Resurrection than his Crucifixion. Perhaps even more to the point, the few images of the Crucifixion that do survive from the early period consistently illustrate a Christ unfazed by violence, seemingly immune to any suffering that crucifixion might inflict, even if the various instruments of violence are included in the image. In contrast to later Western depictions of the Crucifixion, which emphasize Christ's suffering and blood, early Eastern Christian depictions typically do not draw attention the actual violence of crucifixion. So, too, the earliest surviving theological reflection on the Crucifixion consistently deflects from meditation or reflection on the violence Christ suffered on the cross. As Christopher Sweeney has compellingly argued, church leaders focused their theological energies on the significance of a joyful hope in the Resurrection to

---

18 *Jerusalem Georgian Chantbook*, third plagal tone, vespers (Shoemaker, *The First Christian Hymnal*, 221).

19 See R. Jensen, "*Crux Abscondita*: The Late-Emerging Crucifix," in *The Cross: History, Art, and Controversy* (Cambridge, MA, 2017), 74–96.

counter any lingering fear of death among Christians.[20] Indeed, Christian leaders routinely sought to suppress lay efforts to mourn Christ's suffering.[21]

For the hymnographers of the *Jerusalem Georgian Chantbook* and its subsequent users, however, it was insufficient to pass over the details of Christ's death en route to a celebration of his Resurrection. They composed, and the Christian community sang, of Christ's violent, painful, and bloody death. Why the disconnect between hymnography and other forms of Christian reflection on the Crucifixion? Why did early Christians in Jerusalem emphasize this violence through song? Was the goal to chronicle the historical reality of the Crucifixion, much as the Gospels had? Was the goal to reinforce the theological claim of Christ's genuine humanity, to emphasize that he suffered as a human, that his death was not a passive experience? Was it to connect the lived experience of suffering Christians to that of their Lord? Is it possible that the survival of these hymns reflects a divergence between the theological concerns of a clerical elite, the authors of the surviving commentaries, and the lived concerns of the laity, who extended their ritualized mourning practices to the death of Christ?[22]

Although it is impossible to know why any single poet chose to detail the violence endured by Christ during the Passion, it would seem that the Jerusalem community in late antiquity believed not only that Christ had suffered, but also that his suffering was worthy of commemoration and veneration through liturgical singing. Perhaps the simplest approach to the above questions is to acknowledge the probability that hymnographers of the chantbook emphasized the violence of Christ's death for the very reason they articulated in their hymns: it was believed to be a constitutive element of their own salvation.

---

20 C. Sweeney, "Grief and the Cross: Popular Devotion and Passion Piety from Late Antiquity to the Early Middle Ages" (PhD diss., Fordham University, 2019).

21 Sweeney points to the evidence from Cyril of Jerusalem as well as the presbyter Hesychius, who corrected lay Christians for mourning on Good Friday. C. Sweeney, "'The Wailing of the People': The Lay Invention of Passion Piety in Late Antique Jerusalem," *Journal of Orthodox Christian Studies* 2.2 (2019): 129–48, esp. 130.

22 Sweeney, "The Wailing of the People," advances this last thesis.

The Rebounding of Violence

One of the more interesting methods by which the chantbook engages themes of violence concerns the way the violence inflicted upon Christ rebounds on the poetic personification of death and the "enemy," both of which are taken captive or destroyed. One version of this emphasizes the theological claim that Christ "took death captive" through his Passion and Resurrection. Often, but not always, this and similar expressions in the chantbook explain the granting of eternal life to Christians. Eternity is made possible for Christians by death's destruction or captivity. For example, a string of short hymns in the matins service in the first tone proclaims,

> We exalt you, God our Savior,
> Who arose from the dead,
> You trampled down death.
>
> The host of angels rejoices
> And we sing to the resurrected Christ.
>
> You took captive the power of death
> You who were crucified for us
> Glory to You, lover of mankind.[23]

The Resurrection is more than a historical event for the God-man Jesus Christ. It transforms the very existence of death. For purposes here, the use of violent imagery to speak of the death of death personified is even more noteworthy than the theological claim of eternal salvation. As a divinely ordered irony of sorts, the violence of the Crucifixion rebounds on death personified. Death is trampled, taken captive. It is defeated.[24] Angels and humans alike rejoice at death's violent end.

---

23 *Jerusalem Georgian Chantbook*, first tone, matins (Shoemaker, *The First Christian Hymnal*, 13).

24 Of course, here, one must note the limitations of a double translation to perceive the precise language of the Greek original.

The vesper service in the first plagal tone employs this motif of rebounding violence but expands it in interesting ways:

> You were nailed to the cross, as you intended,
> You were counted among the dead,
> You annihilated hell with great benevolence,
> You took death captive by your precious cross,
> You appeared as a Light for the world,
> Glory to you, glory to your power, O Lord.[25]

Here, the hymnographer portrays Christ as always in control. He suffers violence—from the nails of the cross and death—but this is his plan, his intention. More notable is the subtle, perhaps paradoxical, way in which Christ annihilates hell with benevolence. Goodness is achieved through the suffering of violence. The endurance of crucifixion is a victory.

Note also that Christ captures death with a "precious" cross. The text uses the language of violence to describe the rebounding of violence suffered by Christ on the forces of death, but it does so subtly, in ways that reinforce the theological claim that Christ was always in control, that everything proceeded according to a divine script.

The hymnographers of the chantbook expand these themes by deploying the metaphor of a military campaign to describe Christ's conquest of death. For example, just after the gospel reading for the matins service in the first tone, the text notes,

> By the cross Christ entered hell for our sake.
> He destroyed the enemy's power,
> And by his victory he led forth those in it to the light.[26]

---

[25] *Jerusalem Georgian Chantbook*, first plagal tone, vespers (Shoemaker, *The First Christian Hymnal*, 163).

[26] *Jerusalem Georgian Chantbook*, first tone, matins (Shoemaker, *The First Christian Hymnal*, 35).

Possibly drawing inspiration from 1 Peter 3:19—which early Christians interpreted to mean that Christ preached to the dead between his own death on Good Friday and his Resurrection on Easter Sunday—the hymn's text recalibrates the traditional account of Christ's preaching to the deceased to appear more like a clandestine military operation designed to liberate prisoners of war. Somewhat unusual about this particular example is its placement in a sequence of short hymns lacking any reference to violence. The opening two hymns of this section, just before the one in question, as well as the dozen or so that follow it all focus on the joy of the Resurrection, such as the myrrh-bearing women, the pronouncement to the apostles, the celebration of the angels. The short burst of violence in the hymn, however, recalls not only the violence Christ endured on the cross, but also the means by which that suffering destroyed the source of suffering. Equally noteworthy is the description of an enemy—ostensibly death, possibly Satan—whose power is utterly vanquished by means of crucifixion, the means of violent suffering.

The use of militarized language to describe the Resurrection features in another hymn drawn from the matins service in the fourth tone:

> You arose on the third day from the grave,
> You who put death to death and tramped down on the enemy's armament
> You saved those who believe in you by the Resurrection.[27]

The Resurrection destroys death; it tramples upon the enemy's armament, and it does so for the benefit of those who believe. Who, however, is the enemy?

A pair of sequential hymns in the matins service in the third plagal tone continue this militarized language, but in one case, the hymnographer identifies Satan as the enemy.

> He who stretched forth his hands on the cross
> And shattered the power of Satan
> And delivered the world from the violence of the enemy,
> You priests, sing to him, peoples, exalt him above all unto the ages.

---

27 *Jerusalem Georgian Chantbook*, fourth tone, matins (Shoemaker, *The First Christian Hymnal*, 119).

He who trampled down the strength of death
And rose from the grave on the third day,
And delivered the faithful by the Resurrection,
You priests sing to him, peoples, exalt him above all unto the ages.[28]

Having lost the Greek original, it is difficult to know if Satan, mentioned in the first line, is the same enemy referenced by the poet in the second. Either way, these hymns continue the theme employed elsewhere, whereby the poets draw on military motifs to describe Christ's victory by means of his violent suffering.

Throughout the chantbook, the Resurrection is narrated as a rebounding of the violence Christ endures unto death on the very source and power of that death—the "power of Satan" vis-à-vis death. By shattering the power of Satan, Christ delivers the world from the "violence of the enemy." Divine violence defeats Satan's violence; the divine conquering of death destroys death.

One final observation about the rebounding of violence in the hymns of the Octoechos is that the destruction of death, Satan, or the enemy is achieved through an overabundance of love rather than actual violence. Yes, the hymnographers took poetic license to present the destruction of death as a kind of retribution for the violence against Christ, but Christ's actual action—his suffering, his enduring the cross, the nails, the spear—is as an act of love. Death is defeated, destroyed, annihilated by love.

Stirrings of a Weaponized Cross

Even though it would be impossible to appreciate Christ's suffering apart from his death by crucifixion, there has been to this point no explicit mention of the cross as an instrument of violence. As noted in the introduction, the genealogy of the sacralization of violence in Greek hymnography developed, in large part, alongside the recalibration of the Feast of the Exaltation of the Holy Cross in the Greek liturgical tradition in the seventh century. What is important for now is the multiple ways in which the cross of Christ factors into the discourse of violence in the hymns on the Resurrection in the chantbook.

---

28 *Jerusalem Georgian Chantbook*, third plagal tone, matins (Shoemaker, *The First Christian Hymnal*, 241).

To be sure, the chantbook contains numerous references to the cross that do not draw explicit attention to the violence Christ suffered on it, but instead treat it as a sign of God's love and as a protection from evil.

> Grant peace, O God,
> To those who hope in your cross.
> Protect your people from every evil.[29]

In this example, the cross functions as a promise of God's love and his commitment to his creation, a commitment to protect his people and ensure life everlasting.

The hymns of the fourth tone, especially, provide a number of examples in which the hymnographers present the cross as a weapon of the faithful. For example, the final hymn of the vesper service declares,

> As a victorious weapon, Christ,
> You have given us the cross,
> And by it we will triumph,
> In battle against the enemy.[30]

The hymns for the vesper service prior to this one do not reference the cross at all; thus, there is no indication of how to interpret this one. Nevertheless, several things about this particular hymn are clear. For example, the hymn continues and expands the notion of rebounding violence against the forces of death through an instrumentalization of the cross. However, the principal means of Christ's suffering, the cross, is recalibrated in the text to make it not only a weapon in the hands of the faithful, but an object given directly to them by Christ himself. In other words, the instrument that killed Christ is then presented by Christ to the faithful for their benefit. With the cross in hand, the faithful will "triumph, in battle against the enemy."

---

29 *Jerusalem Georgian Chantbook*, first tone, matins (Shoemaker, *The First Christian Hymnal*, 17).

30 *Jerusalem Georgian Chantbook*, fourth tone, vespers (Shoemaker, *The First Christian Hymnal*, 113).

Other aspects of the connection between the cross and violence in this particular hymn are less clear. For instance, what is the battle, and who is the enemy? Once again, one might wish for the Greek original. Perhaps the hymn hearkens to the Pauline expectation that all Christians will engage in spiritual warfare against demonic forces, as stated in Ephesians 6.[31] In the Pauline passage, the enemy is plural—a variety of demonic forces—whereas the hymn appears to identify a singular, unnamed enemy. Perhaps, the battle should be understood as a contest between (eternal) life and death (as a result of sin). If so, the enemy would once again be the personification of death. Alternatively, perhaps, the enemy is Satan, as identified elsewhere. However one interprets the battle and the enemy, this hymn posits a different poetic use of violence, via the cross, than any of the previous hymns of the chantbook considered here, testifying to the multivalent conception of violence operative in the Octoechos cycle.

The chantbook includes several other hymns that refer to the cross as an instrument of violence against the enemies of God. For example, the matins hymns of the fourth tone, which would have been sung the morning after the hymn just examined, continue the same themes. Invoking similar language, the eighteenth hymn of the matins text reads,

> Take heed, O Lord, with mercy for your people,
> Protect us by your holy cross,
> Which you have given to us as a weapon against the enemy.[32]

---

31 Ephesians 6:10–17 (NIV): "Finally, be strong in the Lord and in his mighty power. Put on the full armor of God, so that you can take your stand against the devil's schemes. For our struggle is not against flesh and blood, but against the rulers, against the authorities, against the powers of this dark world and against the spiritual forces of evil in the heavenly realms. Therefore, put on the full armor of God, so that when the day of evil comes, you may be able to stand your ground, and after you have done everything, to stand. Stand firm then, with the belt of truth buckled around your waist, with the breastplate of righteousness in place, and with your feet fitted with the readiness that comes from the gospel of peace. In addition to all this, take up the shield of faith, with which you can extinguish all the flaming arrows of the evil one. Take the helmet of salvation and the sword of the Spirit, which is the word of God."

32 *Jerusalem Georgian Chantbook*, fourth tone, matins (Shoemaker, *The First Christian Hymnal*, 117).

In this short hymn, the singers beseech Christ's mercy, asking that he protect them with the cross, which he has given to them as "a weapon against the enemy." Here, again, the cross is simultaneously the instrument of Christ's suffering and death, but also a protection for Christians against the enemy, and, perhaps most notably, as previously, it has been provided to Christians by Christ. Once again, one might ask, who is the enemy? Is it death? Satan? Other humans?

If one presumes an authorial or editorial consistency throughout the Octoechos, then the likely enemy in this particular hymn would appear to be death incarnate or Satan rather than other humans. Such an assumption, however, would be easily misplaced. At any given moment, these hymns would have been heard and interpreted differently by priests, singers, and lay participants, including soldiers. When also considering that these hymns were produced over decades, if not centuries, and were sung for centuries longer, certainty becomes even more difficult. The possibility that someone might interpret the enemy to be a human is found in a hymn from the matins service in the third plagal tone. The hymn makes a brief biblical reference to human enemies who were defeated by the cross—the ancient Egyptians.

> Moses, by the sign of the cross,
> Put the enemies of the Lord to shame.
> Christ, who by being nailed to the cross, annihilated hell,
> And the creatures held captive from the ages
> He freed from darkness.[33]

According to Exodus 14, Moses parts the Red Sea by making the sign of a cross with his staff. This allows the Jews to escape their captors, the Egyptians, many of whom drown in the sea when Moses restores the water to its natural condition. During late antiquity and throughout the Byzantine period, the episode served as a popular scriptural referent for Christian exegetes and hymnographers looking to identify prefigurations of the cross in the Hebrew Bible. For the purposes here, most noteworthy about the reference to the Moses story is the explicit claim that the cross had been historically employed to defeat the human enemies of

---

33 *Jerusalem Georgian Chantbook*, third plagal tone, matins (Shoemaker, *The First Christian Hymnal*, 225).

the Lord. Specifically, the hymn uses the cross to connect the humiliation of the ancient Egyptians to the liberation of the dead from Hades. Implicit in this hymn is the elision between the "enemies of the Lord" and the enemies of the Lord's people. From the perspective of fifth-century Christians, the Lord's people would be the ancient Jews as well as themselves, the Christians singing the hymn.

The hymn does not say so explicitly, but one can assume that the Christian community of Jerusalem understood themselves to be in the direct line of divine privilege, along with the ancient Jews.[34] As such, the enemies of the Lord and the enemies of the ancient Jews were Christian enemies. Just as the Jews of Moses's day were the people of God, so too were the Christians of Jerusalem. Of course, the threat of the ancient Egyptians was not a genuine danger to the community of the chantbook. Thus, the enemy in this hymn is more a type of threat that can be defeated by Christ and his cross. What, however, does this say about the possibility of human threats to the Christian community during the period from the fourth to the seventh century?

No hymn in the *Jerusalem Georgian Chantbook* names or even insinuates a contemporary human threat to the people of God, apart from the people themselves through their sins. There is no contemporary version of the ancient Egyptians. There is no human enemy or source of anger like that found in the imprecatory psalms. Also the hymns of the Octoechos contain no recollection of the threats once posed to the community by the Romans. In fact, the Romans never appear at all, which is perhaps odd, given that the community at the time was, by definition, Roman. There is also no reference to the Persians, the most pressing foreign threat to the Christians of Palestine.

Just as no foreign threat to the singers of the chantbook is named, the hymns never suggest, not even metaphorically, that the cross could or should be used by the community as an instrument against a human enemy. To the extent that Christians should use the cross as a weapon, they are to do so within the confines of spiritual warfare. Yet, it is not too difficult to see how this language in the hymns could be appropriated, transformed, and deployed against human enemies, including not only those who impede the salvation of Christians, but those who stand in the way of the Christian community's progress.

---

34 As noted in the introduction, even the rhetoric of imperial panegyrists and historians came to adopt this point of view in subsequent centuries.

Chaldean Children

While the overwhelming majority of references to violence in the hymns of the chantbook refer to the suffering of Christ, the deliverance of one group of individuals from suffering is acknowledged and celebrated—the Chaldean children. In fact, apart from Christ and the Virgin Mary, the three Chaldean children receive more attention in the hymns than any other individuals. According to the book of Daniel, during the Babylonian captivity, three Jewish children who were acquaintances of the prophet were brought as slaves to King Nebuchadnezzar's court. When the children refused to pay homage to a golden image of the king, Nebuchadnezzar ordered them cast into a fiery furnace. Inside the furnace, one of the children prayed for the forgiveness of their sins as well as the sins of their fellow Jews. He then asked God to demonstrate his power by delivering them from the furnace. Immediately after the request, an angel of the Lord appeared inside the furnace, quenched the fire with a heavenly dew, and delivered the children from their captivity. Upon their miraculous exit from the furnace, Nebuchadnezzar ordered his people to worship the God of the Jews.

The three Chaldean children became a frequent subject of early Christian interpretation and hymnography not only because of the way their story functioned as a prefiguration of Christ's entombment and Resurrection, but also because of their "triune number," which comported as a symbol of the Trinity.[35] Given the focus of Christ's death and Resurrection in the *Jerusalem Georgian Chantbook*, it is unsurprising that the text incorporates the story of the children into its hymnographic scheme. The matins service in the third tone features a sequential pair of hymns highlighting the multiple ways in which the children prefigure key Christian claims:

> They were a foreshadowing type,
> The holy youths of Babylon,
> For they mocked the fire
> And would not worship the idol of gold.

---

35 For example, the matins service in the first tone declares, "He who appeared in the furnace in Babylon / Saved the youths numbered as the Trinity from fire / Sing and exalt the Lord above all, unto the ages." *Jerusalem Georgian Chantbook*, first tone, matins (Shoemaker, *The First Christian Hymnal*, 29).

> They tirelessly confessed you,
> God who is seated upon the cherubim, and said:
> Blessed are you, O God of our fathers.
>
> By their faith they trampled upon
> Babylon's wicked law of transgression.
> By their triune number they loved you, the Trinity,
> And did not worship the idol of gold,
> And they tirelessly confessed you,
> God who is seated upon the cherubim and said:
> Blessed are you, O God of our fathers.[36]

Four stanzas later,[37] the chantbook returns to the Chaldean children, but focuses more squarely on the violence that they avoided as a result of receiving God's protection.

> You who appeared in Babylon,
> In the midst of the furnace
> And delivered from the fire your servants,
> Who tirelessly were crying out:
> Blessed are you, O God of our fathers.
>
> The Chaldeans were burning around the furnace,
> But those who were singing
> Were preserved unharmed by the dew,
> Who were proclaiming:
> Blessed are you, O God of our fathers.[38]

---

36 *Jerusalem Georgian Chantbook*, third tone, matins (Shoemaker, *The First Christian Hymnal*, 92–93).

37 The intervening stanzas focus on the Trinity, the myrrh-bearing women, and the foundation of the church, respectively.

38 *Jerusalem Georgian Chantbook*, third tone, matins (Shoemaker, *The First Christian Hymnal*, 92–93).

Whereas most engagements of violence in the chantbook reflect on the violence that Christ suffers during his Passion, here the emphasis is on the violence that the faithful avoid as a consequence of their devotion to God. The children are saved from painful, fiery violence and certain death because they sang to the Lord in their time of need. This connection between the Chaldean children, singing, and escaping violence is referenced in the matins service in the second tone as well.

> The angel of the Lord descended from heaven to Babylon,
> In the middle of the furnace,
> And changed into dew the flame of the furnace,
> In which the three youths singing said:
> Blessed are you, O Lord God of our Fathers.[39]

The repeated affirmation of the children singing is an invocation for the community to sing as they did. The hymns invite the community to use the example of the faithful children to offer their own concerns and fears to God through song. The repeated meditation on the children being saved from a fiery death instills confidence in the singers that they, too, will be spared from violence. Perhaps this violence is not so much the lived reality of rampant violence in the late ancient world, but the metaphorical violence inflicted by any number of potential threats to the Christian—that is, the violence of idolatry, death, or Satan. The liberation of the children from violence offers a typological foreshadowing of the Christian community's liberation from death, all of which is made possible by Christ's suffering and Resurrection.

Whereas most of the examples of the Chaldean children in the chantbook appear as the inverse of Christ's experience of violence—the children are spared it, but Christ endures it for humanity's sake—their stories mirror one another in one important way—the rebounding of the violence intended for them instead impacts those meant to harm them. A hymn from the matins service in the second tone offers a clear example:

---

39 *Jerusalem Georgian Chantbook*, second tone, matins (Shoemaker, *The First Christian Hymnal*, 59).

> The three youths in the furnace
> Vanquished the ungodly king by the power of the Trinity
> And destroyed all the seduction of the idols and said:
> Blessed are you, O Lord God of our fathers.[40]

Just as Christ destroyed death or Satan or the enemy in some of the previous hymns analyzed, here the Chaldean children vanquish King Nebuchadnezzar. What is more, the children destroy "the seduction of the idols." The children's faith makes them active agents of violence, though metaphorically, in much the same way that Christ actively destroyed death or vanquished the enemy. The chantbook never explicitly invokes Christian singers to vanquish or destroy a human enemy, but it repeatedly invites them to draw inspiration from and to imitate the faith of the children who did.

Conclusion

The oldest surviving hymns in the Christian world—hymns devoted to the weekly commemoration of the Resurrection—consistently reference explicit violence. Most of the examples in the chantbook refer directly to the violence that Christ suffered during his Passion, most notably during the Crucifixion. The references are sometimes brief and matter-of-fact, a simple affirmation that Christ did, in fact, suffer in the flesh, that he did, in fact, die. Other instances are more detailed, drawing attention to the graphic details of the nails, the spear, and the outstretched arms, to hang from them, and the suffocation that accompanied this posture. Indeed, not a Sunday would pass in the eight-week cycle of the Octoechos during which the Christians of late ancient Jerusalem would not meditate, through song, on the suffering Christ.

In addition to the sheer frequency of the language of violence, it was employed in the chantbook hymns in several other noteworthy ways. One of the more interesting aspects is the poets' descriptions of the violence intended for Christ as rebounding against death itself. Death is conquered, vanquished, destroyed. In some instances, the hymns supplement this rebounding of violence

---

40 *Jerusalem Georgian Chantbook*, second tone, matins (Shoemaker, *The First Christian Hymnal*, 57).

by adding additional metaphors of military conquest or liberation. One of the more intriguing, if not surprising, metaphors they deployed is the transformation of the cross into a weapon against the forces of death; it is not only a weapon employed by Christ, but a weapon offered by Christ to the faithful for spiritual contests against the enemy. This transformation of the cross from a weapon against spiritual forces into a weapon that Christians could deploy against human enemies will become one of the most important steps in the gradual sacralization of violence in the Byzantine tradition.

The frequent references to the Chaldean children serve as an important predecessor to subsequent hymns celebrating Christian saints, especially the martyrs, whose suffering not only imitated Christ's but also contributed to their own salvation. The inclusion of the Chaldean children in the chantbook hymns also points to the way in which liturgical poets used historical events not only to celebrate divine interaction, but also to remind the Christian community of the potential threat of foreign enemies, who will ultimately be undone by the power of God.

CHAPTER 2

CRUCIFIXION AND "THE JEWS"

The Idiomela Hymns of Good Friday

In the *Jerusalem Georgian Chantbook*, the dozen hymns known as the Idiomela appear in the section dedicated to the major annual liturgical feasts, organized according to the calendar of late ancient Jerusalem and completed before the year 600.[1] This particular Idiomela consists of a set of hymns sung exclusively on Good Friday.[2] Like the hymns of the Sunday Resurrection cycle, these *idiomela* were also composed in Greek and translated into Georgian at some point prior to the composition of the chantbook, but they stem from a slightly later period than those of the Sunday cycle, likely the mid-sixth century. The first noteworthy aspect of these idiomela is that they did not originate at the church of the Anastasis (Holy Sepulcher). Rather, they were almost certainly composed by monks in the Palestinian desert.[3] While there is some debate as to whether the

---

1 For dating, see S. Shoemaker, *The First Christian Hymnal: The Songs of the Ancient Jerusalem Church; Parallel Georgian-English Texts*, Middle Eastern Texts Initiative 10 (Provo, UT, 2018), xv. The portion of the manuscript that contains the major annual feasts is the first and longest section of chantbook. The Octoechos, the oldest component of the manuscript, is the third and final section of the chantbook.

2 The hymns were most likely termed *idiomela* (meaning "idiomatic") because each one follows its own unique tune.

3 Until recently, scholars fixed the dating of these idiomela to the period of 450–560. See, for example, D. Galadza, *Liturgy and Byzantinization in Jerusalem* (Oxford, 2019), 239.

monks of the famous Chalcedonian lavra of Mar Saba crafted the hymns[4]—the alternative thesis being that Miaphysite monks in Gaza composed them and Mar Saba adopted them after 553—Mar Saba had definitely included these idiomela in its Good Friday services by the mid-sixth century.[5] The church of the Anastasis then, in turn, adopted the hymns for its own Good Friday services.[6] Thus, at some point prior to the translation of this section of the chantbook into Georgian, the Idiomela was incorporated into the Good Friday liturgical practices of lay Christians in Jerusalem and performed at the church of the Anastasis.[7]

Christopher Sweeney has compelling argued, however, that the dating of these idiomela could be narrowed to the time of the Theopaschite controversy because of lines in the hymns suggesting sympathy for the theological claim that God suffered on the cross. He states, "The most likely explanation for the composition of these hymns and their survival is that they were originally products of the Miaphysite network of Gazan monks. By or about the year 553 with the imperial endorsement of Theopaschitism, these texts were assimilated into the Jerusalemite liturgy. From there, they were adopted by the Sabaites [i.e., the monks of Mar Saba], where the texts survive in their earliest form in Ms. H2123." C. Sweeney, "Grief and the Cross: Popular Devotion and Passion Piety from Late Antiquity to the Early Middle Ages" (PhD diss., Fordham University, 2019), 183.

4 Scholars have spent considerable time debating the merits and variations of the cathedral versus monastic liturgy dichotomy. For a recent account of the state of the question, see R. Taft, "Cathedral vs Monastic Liturgy in the Christian East: Vindicating a Distinction," *Bollettino della Badia Greca di Grottaferrata*, 3rd ser., 2 (2005): 173–219. As Galadza notes, "The distinction between 'cathedral' and 'monastic' liturgy is useful, but must be handled carefully and with some nuance when analyzing the situation of the patriarchate of Jerusalem—a territory that included both urban and desert monastics, in constant interaction with the Holy City's cathedral." Galadza, *Liturgy and Byzantinization in Jerusalem*, 32.

5 Mar Saba is approximately 12.5 kilometers (7.8 miles) from the church of the Anastasis. From the seventh to the ninth century, it became one of the most influential monasteries for the composition and transmission of Greek-language Christian hymns. For the connection between the Idiomela and Mar Saba, see C. Renoux, "Hymnographie géorgienne ancienne et hymnaire de Saint-Sabas (V^e–VIIIe siècle)," *Irénikon* 80 (2007): 36–69, esp. 48.

6 In the Christian community in Palestine, there was considerable interaction between the patriarchal churches, like the Anastasis, and the various ascetic communities in the city and the nearby desert. This resulted in both the patriarchal and monastic communities influencing the development of the liturgy.

7 Given their sixth-century composition, these hymns did not exist at the time of Egeria's famous pilgrimage to Jerusalem.

Whereas most of the Octoechos hymns in the chantbook do not survive in Greek manuscripts, those of the Idiomela do. Not only are they the oldest surviving Greek hymns of the Good Friday liturgical commemorations, they also remain in use throughout the Orthodox Christian world today, sung during the service of the Royal Hours, typically performed on the morning of Good Friday.[8] The only substantial difference between the Georgian and Greek versions of the hymns is the sequence of presentation in the manuscripts.[9] In Greek manuscripts, the hymns of the Good Friday Idiomela are often designated as belonging to three different hymnographic types: troparia (τροπάρια), stichera idiomela (στιχηρὰ ἰδιόμελα), or troparia of the Passion (τροπάρια τῶν παθῶν).[10] The twelve idiomela for Good Friday are of different lengths, but they are, on average, about 50 percent longer than the hymns of the Sunday Resurrection cycle of the chantbook.

While the twelve hymns vary in precise content, they all focus on the Passion and Crucifixion and either implicitly or explicitly draw attention to the violence that Christ suffered. For example, one of the shorter idiomela reads, "You were led as a sheep to the slaughter, O Christ our king, and as an innocent lamb, you were nailed to the cross by wicked men for our sins, in your love for mankind."[11] Here in the figurative language of the violence that Christ suffers, "slaughtered as an innocent lamb," one hears an echo of the Sunday Resurrection hymns from

---

8 One of the hymns, "Today Was Hung upon the Cross," is performed three times during modern Holy Week services in the Orthodox Church—the Friday matins (typically on Thursday evenings), the Royal Hours (on Good Friday in the morning), and the Apokathelosis (on Good Friday in the afternoon).

9 Sweeney, "Grief and the Cross," includes an English-language translation of the Georgian version of the Idiomela as an appendix, but I have chosen to follow the sequencing and translation provided by Mother Mary and K. Ware, trans., *The Service Books of the Orthodox Church*, vol. 2, *The Lenten Triodion* (South Canaan, PA, 1994), 600–610, which is based on the Greek text.

10 S. Janeras, *Le Vendredi-saint dans la tradition liturgique byzantine: Structure et histoire de ses offices*, Analecta liturgica 13 (Rome, 1988), 235–36. In Byzantine hymnography, a troparion is the earliest form of strophic hymnographic composition. Eventually, the term *troparion* became synonymous with a stanza or distinctive hymn of which there were many different types, including the kontakion, kanon, and sticheron.

11 Second idiomelon (in the Greek sequencing); Mother Mary and Ware, *The Lenten Triodion*, 601. This translation is lightly edited and modernized throughout.

the chantbook. Also like the Sunday hymns, the violence is coupled with the theological claim that Christ's suffering enabled the remission of sins and was offered freely by Christ as an act of love.

Without question, the most famous of the idiomela is the last one (but positioned first in the Georgian version), which is performed in three different services in the modern Orthodox commemoration.[12] It reads as follows:

> Today he who hung the earth upon the waters is hung upon the cross.
> He who is king of the angels is arrayed in a crown of thorns.
> He who wraps the heaven in clouds is wrapped in the purple of mockery.
> He who in Jordan set Adam free receives blows upon his face.
> The bridegroom of the church is transfixed with nails.
> The son of the Virgin is pierced with a spear.
> We venerate your Passion, O Christ.
> Show us also your glorious Resurrection.[13]

Although the poetic force of this hymn lies in the lyrical juxtapositions of the God-man, who simultaneously suffers and sustains the world, one should not lose sight of the number of ways in which the hymn draws attention to specific forms of violence: Christ is "hung upon the cross," "arrayed in a crown of thorns"; he "receives blows upon his face"; he is "transfixed with nails" and "pierced with a spear." Grammatically, the context of each verbs is passive. Christ is the recipient of aggressive action. For all of its poetic beauty and soteriological consolation, the hymn is extraordinarily violent. The original Greek text, like the English translation, opens with the exhortation that all of this violence occurs "Today!" That declaration not only reinforces the timeliness of the commemoration, it also brings to life the violence Christ endured. These themes run throughout the other idiomela in the set.

---

12 Whereas the full set of twelve hymns is performed during the Royal Hours of Good Friday, this particular hymn is also sung at the Friday matins service (typically performed on Thursday evening) as well as the Apokathelosis (on Friday afternoon).

13 Twelfth idiomelon (in the Greek sequencing); Mother Mary and Ware, *The Lenten Triodion*, 609.

Emotional Violence

The idiomela in the chantbook differ from the Sunday hymns of the Octoechos. First, many of the idiomela employ speech-in-character, a literary device mostly absent from the Octoechos hymns.[14] This device allows the hymnographer to interject non-biblical, first-person speech in the voice of Christ (and, in one idiomelon, the apostle Peter). Not only can this dramatize a biblical scene by expanding its duration and amplifying its message, it also requires the singers to confront the emotional world of the biblical characters themselves. The singers vocalize as though they are Christ or St. Peter, rather than singing about them. In this way, they delved into the emotional depths of the characters at the time of the events they narrate—namely, the Crucifixion. Note in the following example the way the singers, in the persona of Christ, ask the Jews which of the miracles that he performed for their benefit led to the Crucifixion:

> When you were led to the Crucifixion, you cried, O Lord: "For what deed do you seek to crucify me, O you Jews? Is it because I made your paralyzed walk, because I raised the dead as though from sleep? I healed her who had an issue of blood, and I took pity on the woman of Canaan; for what deed do you seek to kill me, O you Jews." But O transgressors, you shall look upon Christ whom now you pierce.[15]

Whereas the biblical texts that describe the Crucifixion provide only meager insight into Christ's emotional or psychological state throughout the Passion—for example, his request to the Father that he might "let this cup pass"—this hymn adds considerable emotional weight to the scene. The hymnographer goes well beyond a description of the physical pain of Crucifixion to dramatize and thereby maximize the emotional distress that Christ suffers by having been betrayed by the very people he came to save.

---

14 Speech-in-character, or what the ancient Greeks called *ethopoiia*, served as a chosen vehicle for Greek drama and was also an important element in advanced education. Students would, in effect, be asked to compose invented speech in attempting to understand and analyze the figures being studied. For the Sunday hymns of the Octoechos, see chapter 1.

15 Sixth idiomelon (in the Greek sequencing); Mother Mary and Ware, *The Lenten Triodion*, 604.

The same pattern continues in the next idiomelon, which contains a fresh set of juxtapositions. It concludes with Christ's decision to extend the benefit of his sacrifice—a sacrifice initially meant for the Jews—to the Gentiles:

> Thus says the Lord to the Jews: "O my people, what have I done unto you? Or wherein have I wearied you? I gave light to the blind and cleansed your lepers, I raised up the man who lay upon his bed. O my people, what have I done unto you, and how have you repaid me? Instead of manna you have given me gall, instead of water vinegar; instead of loving me you have nailed me to the cross. I can endure no more. I shall call my Gentiles and they shall honor me with the Father and the Spirit and I shall bestow on them eternal life.[16]

One should not lose sight of the poetic and performative significance of presenting the emotional violence that Christ suffers from a first-person perspective. The Christian affirmation of Christ's divinity is on full display in the dialogue while he is on the cross. Christ declares that it is he, God, who offered manna, but he is repaid with gall. It is he who offers love but is repaid with the violence of the cross.

Because the community sings from the perspective of Christ, the emotional toll of rejection, a different form of violence, is not something the community observes from a distance. Rather, the suffering they enunciate, that they voice, becomes their own. Christ's pain is their pain; Christ's sense of betrayal becomes their own betrayal. Through the performance of the hymn, the Christian singers internalize the betrayal that Christ felt. The entirety of the Christian community annunciates the pain of his betrayal as if done to them.

Speech-in-character would become the most significant feature of the kontakion hymnographic style, greatly expanding the dramatic and exegetical possibilities available to hymnographers. Five of the twelve idiomela employ speech-in-character—although not in a manner as developed or expansive as that adopted by the contemporary Constantinopolitan liturgical poet Romanos the Melodist—and in doing so open new possibilities for interpreting the Passion

---

16 Seventh idiomelon (in the modern sequencing); Mother Mary and Ware, *The Lenten Triodion*, 606.

and the Crucifixion. What is most significant here is the expansion of Christ's suffering from physical violence to emotional violence through the act of betrayal.

Christians, Jews, and Violence

The second noteworthy feature of the Good Friday Idiomela is the extent to which "the Jews," as a people, are identified as the perpetrators of violence against Christ. Four of the twelve idiomela explicitly single out the Jews as being responsible for the Crucifixion.[17] A fifth idiomelon speaks indirectly of the Jews by juxtaposing the "transgressors" (παράνομοι) and the Gentiles.[18] Thus, nearly half of the Idiomela hymns develop their exegetical or theological points about the Crucifixion by blaming the Jews for Jesus's violent death. By way of comparison, of the approximate one thousand hymns in the Octoechos, only fourteen identify and disparage the Jews.[19]

Theologically implicit in this identification and condemnation of the Jews in the Idiomela is a rhetorical positioning in which "they" (the Jews), rather "we" (all mortals), are responsible for the violence that Christ suffered during the Passion and Crucifixion. This is a noteworthy shift from the rhetorical and theological structure of most of the hymns of the Octoechos that speak about the Crucifixion. Those hymns typically emphasize the culpability of all humans in the death of Christ. To be sure, they do not explicitly name Christians as the ones responsible for his death, but neither do they single out the Romans or Jews as the historical agents of it. Thus, the Octeochos hymns indirectly implicate Christians in the death of Christ because it is they who are singing them.

---

17 The fourth, sixth, seventh, and eighth idiomela directly reference the Jews. Several others within the set of hymns more generically refer to the "transgressors" (παράνομοι) or "lawless priests" (ἱερεῦσι ἀνόμοις).

18 In the eleventh idiomela, Christ welcomes the Gentiles because he knows that they will glorify God as the Father, Son, and Holy Spirit.

19 For example, the third tone contains two references to the "ungodly Jews." *Jerusalem Georgian Chantbook*, third tone, matins; Shoemaker, *The First Christian Hymnal*, 97, 99. See, also, S. Shoemaker, "Passion Piety and Anti-Judaism in Late Ancient Jerusalem: Hymns for Holy Week from the *Jerusalem Georgian Chantbook*," in *The Byzantine Liturgy and the Jews*, ed. H. Buchinger and A. Ioniță (Münster, forthcoming).

Of particular note, none of the idiomela call for divine retribution against the Jews. Rather, the hymns suggest a shift in the way Palestinian Christians had begun to conceptualize Jewish and Christian differences in their prayers between the creation of the Octoechos (circa the fourth to sixth centuries) and the Idiomela (mid-sixth century). It would also appear that this shift extended beyond Palestinian Christians. Evidence from mid-sixth-century Constantinople suggests that historical remembrance of the events of the Passion had begun to change among the capital's Christians toward exclusively blaming the Jews for the violence that Christ suffered.[20] Good Friday provided an obvious occasion for such a focus.[21]

As noted, in the sixth idiomelon Christ rhetorically asks the Jews which of his many miracles caused his Crucifixion. The list of miracles not only serves to reinforce Christian belief in Jesus's divinity and love for humanity, it also calls attention to the failure of the Jews to acknowledge Christ's efforts on their behalf. The speech-in-character dynamic of the hymn dramatizes this failure and further isolates the Jews from the Christian community. More importantly, the explicit naming of the Jews suggests that culpability for Christ's suffering belongs exclusively to them. The implicit "we" of the Octoechos hymns has been replaced by the not-so-subtle accusation that it is the Jews alone who have put Christ to death. As such, there is a distinct shift from speaking of the Crucifixion as an ontological event that alters the relationship between God and humanity to speaking of the Crucifixion as a historical event in which Christ is murdered by a specific group of people who remain culpable for his death.

In the seventh idiomelon, which also employs speech-in-character, Christ rhetorically asks the Jews which of his miracles, presenting a different set of examples, has led them to want to crucify him. This time, however, the hymn ends with Christ declaring that he will call together the Gentiles and that they

---

20 For an overview of the transformation of early Byzantine attitudes toward Jews, see D. Olster, *Roman Defeat, Christian Response and the Literary Construction of the Jew* (Philadelphia, 1994), and the review essay of that work, A. Cameron, "Byzantines and Jews: Some Recent Work on Early Byzantium," *BMGS* 20 (1996): 249–74.

21 See, for example, the Good Friday sermon of the presbyter Leontius, *Homily* 7.50–63, in C. Datema and P. Allen, eds., *Leontii Presbyteri Constantinopolitani Homiliae*, CCSG 17 (Turnhout, 1987). For a translation, see P. Allen and C. Datema, trans., *Leontius, Presbyter of Constantinople: Fourteen Homilies* (Brisbane, 1991).

will "glorify me with Father and Spirit." In return, Christ then promises that he "will grant them everlasting life."[22] This transferal of responsibility from the Jews to the Gentiles appears again in the eleventh idiomelon:

> When the transgressors nailed you, O Lord of glory, to the cross, you cried aloud to them: "How have I grieved you? Or where have I angered you? Before me, who delivered you from tribulation? And how do you now repay me? You have given me evil for good: In return for the pillar of fire, you have nailed me to the cross; in return for the cloud, you have dug a grave for me. Instead of manna, you have given me gall; instead of water, you have given me vinegar to drink. Henceforth I will call the Gentiles, and they will glorify me with the Father and Holy Spirit.[23]

Whereas the hymn does not name the Jews explicitly, the closing statement on inviting the Gentiles suggests a juxtaposition between the singers, who recognize God as Trinity, from others who do not sing. Because the Jews do not recognize Christ as God, they are in theological error, and more pointedly, are also guilty of his murder. It is for this reason that the hymn explicitly connects the violence perpetrated by the Jews against Christ as the reason for Christ's embrace of the Gentiles. The Jews nail Christ to the cross, dig Christ's grave, and give him gall and vinegar. As a consequence, Christ calls the Gentiles, for they will glorify him.

By speaking of the Jews and the Jews alone as the "transgressors" responsible for Christ's death, the authors of the Idiomela hymns ignore key historical aspects of the Gospels' account of Christ's Passion. This erasure reflects a profound transformation in late ancient Christian identity vis-à-vis imperial Rome. Indeed, it is noteworthy that the Idiomela, which so artfully revisits the final hours of Christ's life, makes no mention of the role of the Romans in the Crucifixion even though crucifixion was primarily a Roman form of punishment. The hymns also make no reference to Pilate, or his wife, or the Roman soldiers who performed the Crucifixion. Why? Because Christian identity among Palestinian Christians had evolved to such a degree that the authors of the Idiomela fully viewed themselves

---

22 Seventh idiomelon (in the Greek sequencing); Mother Mary and Ware, *The Lenten Triodion*, 606.

23 Mother Mary and Ware, *The Lenten Triodion*, 609.

as Romans to the point of deliberately ignoring Roman culpability in the violence that Christ suffered. Perhaps more importantly, why did the authors of the Idiomela speak of the Jews as though they were some foreign, external community when, in fact, Jesus, his disciples, and the vast majority of his early followers were not only Jews by birth but Jews by observance? In short, why did these hymns transfer the assignment of guilt for Christ's death from the "we" of the Octoechos to "they," the Jews? What changed theologically or contextually for Palestinian Christians between the composition of the Octoechos and the Good Friday Idiomela that might explain this profound transformation of the positional identity of the community of singers?

A few aspects of the interaction and competition between Christians and Jews in Palestine during late antiquity were relevant to the production of the Good Friday Idiomela.[24] One of the most important contextual dynamics is that Palestine was home to a sizable Jewish community even after the legalization of Christianity by the Roman emperor Constantine in 313.[25] Indeed, at the time of Constantine's accession, in 306, the Jewish community was both larger and stronger than the Christian community in Palestine. Like other parts of the empire, Palestine did not become majority Christian until the early part of the fifth century; even then, however, the number of Jews, and Samaritans, in Palestine remained significant.[26] The continued presence of so many Jews may have posed an existential threat to Christians in the region. As Stephen Shoemaker wrote, "If Jesus was truly the Jewish messiah, and Christianity was, as it claimed, the completion of Judaism, why then did Jews remain?"[27]

The larger presence of Jews in Palestine was not only an existential question for Christians, it also resulted in more tangible problems. For example, Jewish

24 See Cameron, "Byzantines and Jews."

25 G. Stroumsa, "Religious Contacts in Byzantine Palestine," *Numen* 38 (1989): 16–42, at 25–26. Emperor Constantine, though an obvious advocate of Christianity, and despite reissuing Hadrian's decree forbidding Jews from entering Jerusalem, did little to change the official approach of the empire toward the Jews. See M. Avi-Yonah, *The Jews under Roman and Byzantine Rule: A Political History of Palestine from the Bar Kokhba War to the Arab Conquest* (New York, 1976; repr., Jerusalem, 1984), 160–66.

26 See Avi-Yonah, *The Jews under Roman and Byzantine Rule*, 220–23.

27 S. Shoemaker, "'Let Us Go and Burn Her Body': The Image of the Jews in the Early Dormition Traditions," *ChHist* 68 (1999): 775–823, at 781.

communities in Palestine actively proselytized among Christians.[28] There was also the confusion posed by Judaizing Christians, who not only insisted upon the continuation of Jewish rituals within the Christian community but frequently attended Jewish ceremonies.[29] Both of these practices were perennially criticized by Christian leaders in the fourth and fifth centuries, which suggests how widespread they were. Given the close proximity of Christians and Jews in Palestine, the active competition between their communities for members, and the obvious connection or disagreement about their shared religious inheritance, the evidence of Jewish-Christian conflict in both Christian and Jewish literature from the fourth through the seventh century should not be surprising.[30]

An increase in the number of foreign Christians settling in the region was one way in which the legalization of Christianity transformed the lived experience of Jews and Christians in Palestine.[31] Wealthy imperial patrons, such as Constantine's mother, Helena, made Palestine a focal point of their public beneficence. Aristocratic interest in Jerusalem, in turn, further enticed would-be

---

28 While there is some debate about whether this occurred in an earlier period, there is near unanimity among scholars that Jews actively sought converts during late antiquity. See, for example, M. Simon, *Verus Israel: A Study of the Relations between Christians and Jews in the Roman Empire, AD 135–425*, trans. H. McKeating (Liverpool, 1996), 271–305; J. G. Gager, *The Origins of Anti-Semitism: Attitudes toward Judaism in Pagan and Christian Antiquity* (New York, 1983), 55–66; M. Goodman, *Mission and Conversion: Proselytizing in the Religious History of the Roman Empire* (Oxford, 1994), 129–53; W. Horbury, *Jews and Christians in Contact and Controversy* (Edinburgh, 1998), 98–102; and V. Déroche, "La polémique anti-judaïque au VIᵉ au VIIᵉ siècle," *TM* 11 (1991): 284–90.

29 For Stroumsa, the continued existence of this community posed something of an existential threat to both Jews and Christians because it called into question the very division between the two communities that had become so essential to identity making. Among other things, he cites a paschal letter of Cyril of Jerusalem, who complains about the continued embrace of the term *ioudaioi* even though they worship Christ. Stroumsa, "Religious Contacts in Byzantine Palestine," 28; also see Shoemaker, "Let Us Go and Burn Her Body," 779–82, and G. Dagron, "Judaïser," *TM* 11 (1991): 359–80.

30 There is some debate about whether this literature reflects actual, on-the-ground interactions between Christians and Jews or whether, perhaps, it was constructed for interreligious rhetorical purposes. For a summary and compelling case of a middle ground approach, see Shoemaker, "Let Us Go and Burn Her Body," 783–88.

31 Indeed, Constantine supported efforts to spread Christianity among the Jews by building churches in Jewish towns throughout the Galilee. See Avi-Yonah, *The Jews under Roman and Byzantine Rule*, 165.

settlers to relocate to the land of Christ's birth, death, and Resurrection. By the mid-fourth century, Palestine had become the leading destination for pilgrimage and settlement by a group of international Christians who were perhaps more determined than the local Christian population to spar with religious nonconformers, especially the Jews. Indeed, from the mid-fourth to the mid-fifth century, ample evidence documents monastic vigilantes—many of them of foreign origin—setting fire to Jewish buildings and terrorizing Jewish communities.[32]

The situation for the Jews also deteriorated legally and financially after Constantine's legalization of Christianity. The Romans had imposed certain restrictions on Jews since antiquity, but they had always exempted them from imperial requirements vis-à-vis religious conformity. Constantine maintained that status quo, but his successors enacted new laws that introduced strict boundaries between Christian and Jewish communities.[33] These new laws incorporated many anti-Jewish rhetorical slurs, such as referring to them as savage (*feralis*) and abominable (*nefaria*) and describing their religious gatherings as meetings of blasphemers (*sacrilege coetus*).[34] In response to their declining status, some Jews and Samaritans undertook periods of armed resistance against the Romans during the mid-fourth to mid-fifth century. Of particular note, the uprisings were followed by some seventy-five years of relative peace—from the Council of Chalcedon, in 451, to the accession of Justinian, in 527[35]—a period that coincides

---

32 See Avi-Yonah, *The Jews under Roman and Byzantine Rule*, 211–13, who attributes the end of this period of monastic vigilantism to the Council of Chalcedon, which required obedience of monks and monasteries to the local bishop.

33 For example, the Theodosian Code (16.8.1, 16.8.6, and 16.9.2) preserves a series of laws forbidding intermarriage between Christians and Jews, protecting Jewish converts to Christianity from Jewish mistreatment, and prohibiting Jews from owning Christian slaves, respectively. See Avi-Yonah, *The Jews under Roman and Byzantine Rule*, 174–75.

34 See Avi-Yonah, *The Jews under Roman and Byzantine Rule*, 176.

35 The same cannot be said of Palestinian Samaritans, who launched a major revolt against Roman authority in 484 and again at the beginning of Justinian's reign, in 529. Avi-Yonah offers two hypotheses to explain the relative calm: (1) the Council of Chalcedon had forcibly placed monks under the supervision of their local bishop, which in turn prevented monastic vigilantism against Jewish communities, and (2) many Palestinian desert monastics' rejection of the council led to such a high degree of inter-Christian factionalism that anti-Jewish fervor waned among Christians. Avi-Yonah, *The Jews under Roman and Byzantine Rule*, 236–37.

with the likely production of the Octoechos, which shows far fewer signs of anti-Jewish rhetoric or disposition than the later Idiomela.

The relative calm between Jews and Christians came to an end under Justinian (d. 565), who imposed vigorous anti-Jewish legislation that, among other things, revised the legal definition of heresy to include anyone who was not "Orthodox." This meant that the punishments for doctrinal nonconformity—fines, confiscation of property, forced exile, and so on—could now be leveled against non-Christians, whereas previously it had applied only to intra-Christian dissenters.[36] Justinian was the first emperor to prohibit Jews from serving as members of the curia, local town councils, which greatly diminished civic and financial opportunities for Jewish landowners.[37] He also expanded the penalties for Jews holding slaves and decreed a law requiring Jews to release any slave who sought baptism, whether genuine in motivation or not.[38] Whereas some laws financially burdened Jewish communities, Justinian's *Novella* 37 and 131, forbidding construction of new synagogues, imposed religious restrictions on them. In the Palestinian town of Borion, the effort to encumber or suppress Jewish worship went further still when Justinian ordered the transformation of a local synagogue into a church and likely forced many of the Jews to convert to Christianity.[39] As Michael Avi-Yonah notes, there was nothing revolutionary in the approach of these various laws, but, cumulatively, they greatly increased the pressure on Palestinian Jews.[40] One might arguably presume that Justinian's anti-Jewish legislation only emboldened individual Christians to harass Jewish interests in additional ways.

With the amplification of anti-Jewish measures, Justinian's reign fomented the largest outbreak of anti-Christian violence by Jews in the late ancient period. The most dramatic such uprising occurred in the early 550s in Palestine; the precise date varies in the sources and the event may have occurred in 552, 555,

---

36 *Corpus iuris civilis* 1.5.12.2.

37 Avi-Yonah, *The Jews under Roman and Byzantine Rule*, 247–48.

38 Avi-Yonah, *The Jews under Roman and Byzantine Rule*, 248.

39 Procopius, *De aedificis* 6.2. As Shoemaker notes, widespread forced conversion did not occur until the early seventh century, under Herakleios, but sporadic episodes like the one in Borion became increasingly common in the sixth century as well. Shoemaker, "Let Us Go and Burn Her Body," 782–83.

40 Avi-Yonah, *The Jews under Roman and Byzantine Rule*, 247.

or 556.[41] In this particular instance, a mob of Jews and Samaritans joined forces to assault the Christians of Caesarea, the coastal city and capital of the Roman province. In addition to killing a number of Christians, including the provincial governor, the mob plundered and burned a series of Christian churches.[42] Additional uprisings followed, consistently pitting Palestinian Christians and Jews against one another well into the seventh century. The acrimony between the communities was such that local Jews and Samaritans may have joined forces with the Persians when the latter invaded Palestine in 614.[43]

In redating the Good Friday Idiomela, Christopher Sweeney compellingly argued that the hymns were produced some time between Justinian's first edict on the Theopaschite controversy, in 533, and the transformation of the liturgical calendar in Jerusalem, which occurred in 560.[44] According to Sweeney, either Miaphysite monks in Gaza composed the hymns between 533 and 553, and the Chalcedonian monks of Mar Saba adopted them after Justinian's pro-Theopaschite edict, or the monks of Mar Saba produced the hymns in the narrow window of 553–560.[45] Either scenario lends itself to monastic composition at precisely the point when Jewish and Christian communities in Palestine were

---

41 Shoemaker, "Let Us Go and Burn Her Body," 783, n. 39. See also E. Stein, *Histoire du Bas-Empire*, vol. 2, *De la disparition de l'Empire d'occident à la mort de Justinien (476–565)* (Paris, 1949), 374, n. 2.

42 See, among others, A. Sharf, "Byzantine Jewry in the Seventh Century," *BZ* 48.1 (1955): 103–15; J. Starr, "Byzantine Jewry on the Eve of the Arab Conquest (565–638)," *JPOS* 15 (1935): 280–93; G. Dagron and V. Deroche, "Juifs et Chrétiens dans l'Orient du septième siècle," *TM* 11 (1991): 17–273, esp. 17–43, as well as Avi-Yonah, *The Jews under Roman and Byzantine Rule*, 251, and Shoemaker, "Let Us Go and Burn Her Body," 782–83.

43 The extent of Jewish collaboration with the Persians has been a matter of some scholarly debate. See E. Horowitz, "'The Vengeance of the Jews Was Stronger Than Their Avarice': Modern Historians and the Persian Conquest of Jerusalem in 614," *Jewish Social Studies* 4.2 (1988): 1–39. Also see "Byzantines and the Jews," esp. 253–57, for her revision of previous historical accounts that she believes did not sufficiently account for the rhetorical exaggeration and retrospection of the historical sources.

44 See Sweeney, "Grief and the Cross," 182–83.

45 Between 533 and 553, Chalcedonian monks, like those at the lavra of St. Sava, would have been opposed to the hymns' view that God suffered on the cross. The situation changed with the Second Council of Constantinople in 553, at which point it became possible for the monks of St. Sava to endorse Theopaschite-leaning hymns of the Idiomela or even required that they do so. See Sweeney, "Grief and the Cross," 182–83.

engaged in unprecedented levels of conflict. In addition, both scenarios reflect the precise moment in Byzantine history when imperial legislation and rhetoric took their harshest anti-Jewish turn. In other words, the amplification of anti-Jewish rhetoric in the Idiomela is entirely consistent with the realities of Jewish-Christian conflict on the ground at the time of their composition.

To be sure, the Idiomela is not the first Christian text to employ anti-Jewish rhetoric. One might argue that the Gospels themselves trade in ahistorical anti-Jewish invective in their accounts of the Passion and Crucifixion.[46] The second-century author Melito of Sardis clearly trades in a kind of supersessionism with frequent attacks against the Jews.[47] By the mid-fourth century, texts like Eusebius's *Life of Constantine* describe Jews as having killed their Lord and being blind in their soul.[48] Similar examples of anti-Jewish rhetoric abound in the writings of fourth- and fifth-century Christian writers, but when one looks exclusively at hymnography, the contents of the Idiomela are among the earliest-surviving Christian hymns that not only consistently and inherently isolate the Jews as a group, as the "other," but also present them as singularly responsible for the violence that Christ suffers. It would appear that the content of Christian hymnography trailed the excesses of Christian anti-Jewish polemic by at least one hundred years only to emerge precisely at the point in history when harsh rhetoric and unprecedented violence coincided.

The Implications of Anti-Jewish Invective

While historical context may help in understanding why Christian authors of the Idiomela chose to adopt explicit anti-Jewish rhetoric in their hymnographic accounts of the Crucifixion, the acknowledgment of this context does not, in and of itself, address the theological significance of this shift or register how the adoption of this anti-Jewish rhetoric suggests a new trend in imperial Christian

---

46 The unlikely storyline related to Pilate's release of the insurrectionist Barabbas is often identified as an example of the Gospels' authors exaggerating Jewish culpability in Jesus's death.
47 See A. S. Sykes, "Melito's Anti-Judaism," *JEChrSt* 5.2 (1997): 271–83.
48 Eusebius, *Life of Constantine*, chs. 18–19. Such accusations and others are put in Constantine's mouth.

hymnography that would open a space for the full-blown sacralization of violence against Christian enemies to become a topos in hymnographic literature.

To understand the theological significance of recalibrating who is responsible for the violence that Christ suffers, one can compare the idiomela that isolate the Jews for censure and those that do not. The second idiomelon in the chantbook affirms that Christ was "nailed to the cross by wicked men for our sins."[49] The third idiomelon states that Christ "suffered the transgressors to lay hold" of him.[50] Even if this language is derivative of prophetic critiques in the Hebrew scripture, the use of such terms as "wicked men" or "transgressors" to identify the culprits of Christ's Crucifixion, without any other indication of their identity, is both more historically accurate and more amenable to a constructive theological exegesis of the Crucifixion than those that simply transfer all of the guilt to a discrete group, such as the Jews. This is because early Christian theology taught, as the Octoechos affirms, that Christ suffered on behalf of all of humanity because all humans sinned and were in need of the saving act of Christ's death and Resurrection. From a Christian theological perspective, Christ suffers on the cross because Christians need him to do so; thus, it is they, the Christians, who are responsible for his death on the cross.[51] By shifting the focus of culpability for Christ's death from the collective group of singing sinners to an external community that is not singing, the Jews, the four relevant Good Friday idiomela ignore one of the most important theological dimensions of the Christian claim of Christ's death and Resurrection.

Looking exclusively at the category of violence, one notices that the anti-Jewish rhetorical turn in the Idiomela is significant but also quite limited by comparison to the sacralization of violence that emerged in Christian hymnography in subsequent centuries. Like the Octoechos, the Idiomela focuses all of its attention on the violence that Christ suffers.[52] There is no invocation or prophecy of

---

49 Second idiomelon (in the modern sequencing); Mother Mary and Ware, *The Lenten Triodion*, 601.

50 Third idiomelon (in the modern sequencing); Mother Mary and Ware, *The Lenten Triodion*, 602.

51 On this, see K. Anatolios, *Deification through the Cross: An Eastern Christian Theology of Salvation* (Grand Rapids, MI, 2020).

52 As noted in the previous chapter, the Octoechos extended its discussion of violence beyond Christ to include the three Chaldean children, who served an important typological role for Christ and salvation.

violence against others, no destruction of anyone. No explicit language designates a group an enemy of God. All these elements feature, however, in hymns produced in later centuries.

Where the Idiomela does mark an important interruption in the genealogy of the hymnographic sacralization of violence is in the assignment of blame for Christ's death outside the Christian community. In several of the hymns, the violence that Christ suffered is a violence perpetrated by the Jews alone. In those hymns, it is no longer a collective "we" that sings of their own guilt; rather, guilt resides elsewhere. The implicit consequence of Jewish collective guilt is that the Jews are abandoned by God; more importantly, they are replaced by the Gentiles—that is, the singers of the Idiomela, the Romans of Palestine, the Christians. The Idiomela may not ask that God inflict violence on the Jews, but the hymns mark the Jews as a people seemingly beyond Christ's salvific effort.

In the past twenty years or so, a number of scholars have examined the anti-Jewish character of the Holy Week hymns used in the modern Orthodox Church.[53] Universally, albeit in different ways, they have called for a revision of individual lines or the elimination of certain hymns for a variety of theological and historical reasons. While a few of the idiomela have been included in the scholarly discussions, none of the studies has identified the Idiomela as the oldest surviving set of Holy Week hymns or historicized this particular group of hymns in the precise context of Jewish-Christian interactions in Palestine at the time of their production; none has sought to compare the hymns to those that predate their composition to assess the escalation in anti-Jewish rhetoric. These historical insights only further the justification for liturgical correction to align more closely with the theological vision presented in the Gospels and in the Octoechos.

---

53 See, for example, M. Azar, "Prophetic Matrix and Theological Paradox: Jews and Judaism in the Holy Week and Pascha Observances of the Greek Orthodox Church," *Studies in Christian-Jewish Relations* 10.1 (2015): 1–27; B. G. Bucur, "Anti-Jewish Rhetoric in Byzantine Hymnography: Exegetical and Theological Contextualization," *SVThQ* 61.1 (2017): 39–60; A. Ioniță, "Byzantine Liturgical Hymnography: A Stumbling Stone for the Jewish–Orthodox Christian Dialogue?," *Review of Ecumenical Studies* 11.2 (2009): 253–67; and B. Groen, "Anti-Judaism in the Present-Day Byzantine Liturgy," *Journal of Eastern Christian Studies* 60 (2008): 369–87.

CHAPTER 3

ROMANOS THE MELODIST

There is likely no Byzantine hymnographer more familiar to Orthodox Christians and Roman Catholics than Romanos the Melodist, whose feast is commemorated by both their churches on 1 October. Romanos's popularity might be somewhat surprising given that little is known about his life and because his elaborate style of hymns, kontakia, fell out of use for the Byzantine Church's festal cycle more than eight hundred years ago.[1] Most of what scholars think they know about Romanos's life derives from hagiographies and hymnographic tributes composed several hundred years after his death.[2] It is generally agreed that Romanos was

---

1 The prooemion, or prelude, of a kontakia is sung in most matins service in the modern Orthodox Church, but the majority of the original compositions are no longer used. For the disappearance of kontakia from the Byzantine liturgical cycle, see A. Lingas, "The Liturgical Place of the *Kontakion* in Constantinople," in *Liturgy, Architecture and Art of the Byzantine World: Papers of the XVIII International Byzantine Congress (Moscow, 8–15 August, 1991) and Other Essays Dedicated to the Memory Fr. John Meyendorff*, ed. C. C. Akentiev (St. Petersburg, 1995), 50–57.

2 The *Typikon of the Great Church* is the oldest surviving text identifying his feast and includes a reference to the church in the Kyrou district of the city that he served as a deacon. For a critical edition of the typikon of Hagia Sophia, see J. Mateos, ed., *Le Typicon de la Grande Église*, 2 vols. (Rome, 1962–1963), 56–57. Several additional apocryphal details are included in the Menologion of Basil II, a remarkable, illustrated version of the Synaxarion of Constantinople, a list of feast days with short biographies of the saints, produced in Constantinople after 974.

born at the end of the fifth century in Emesa (modern-day Homs, Syria) and that he was ordained by the diaconate in Berytus (modern-day Beirut).[3] He moved to Constantinople under the emperor Anastasios I (r. 491–518) and served at a church dedicated to the Virgin Mary in the Kyrou district of the capital until his death, which must have occurred after 555.[4] It is generally assumed that Romanos came from a Jewish background and may have converted to Christianity as a young adult, based on an eighth-century encomiastic hymn assigned to his feast that claims he was "of the Hebrew race."[5] Whatever his religious ancestry, there is little doubt that Romanos's development of the kontakion hymnographic form owes a great deal to the religious matrix of late antique Syria, where Jewish and Christian communities lived in close proximity and where a great deal of cross-fertilization of exegetical and lyrical forms took place.[6] Indeed, as Thomas Arentzen notes, a variety of religious communities in the Eastern Mediterranean

---

3 B. Baldwin, "Romanos the Melode," *ODB* 3:1807–8. For a general overview of his career, including a detailed account of the biographical sources, see J. Grosdidier de Matons, *Romanos le Mélode et les origins de la poésie religieuse à Byzance* (Paris, 1977). For a more recent overview, see A. Mellas, "Romanos the Melodist," in *Liturgy and the Emotions in Byzantium: Compunction and Hymnody* (Cambridge, 2020), 71–112, esp. 71–74.

4 The district is likely named after Cyrus of Panapolis, a mid-fifth century aristocratic benefactor of the city and poet. According to the late Byzantine chronicler Kallistos Xanthopoulos, Cyrus was the benefactor of the church dedicated to the Virgin that Romanos served. Evidence in his corpus indicates that he was alive in 555.

5 See A. Prelipcean, "Γένος μέν ἐξ ἑβραίων or the Jewish Origin of Roman the Melodist: From *Overestimations* to *Underestimations* and Finding Bridges between the West and the East," *Review of Ecumenical Studies* 11.2 (2019): 199–208.

6 On the mutual assimilation of religious practices between Jews and Christians in late antique Syria, see L. Lieber, "Portraits of Righteousness: Noah in Early Christian and Jewish Hymnography," *Zeitschrift für Religions- und Geistesgeschichte* 61.4 (2009): 332–55; L. Lieber, "'You Have Skirted This Hill Long Enough': The Tension between Rhetoric and History in a Byzantine Piyyut," *Hebrew Union College Annual* 80 (2009): 63–114; L. Lieber, "The Rhetoric of Participation: Experiential Elements of Early Hebrew Liturgical Poetry," *JR* 90.2 (2010): 119–47; and L. Lieber, "Setting the Stage: The Theatricality of Jewish Aramaic Poetry from Late Antiquity," *JQR* 104.4 (2014): 537–72. See, also, S. Brock, "From Ephrem to Romanos," *StP* 20 (1989): 139–51.

during the fifth and sixth centuries all began to retell their sacred stories in longer, stanzaic and metrical hymns.[7]

The kontakion form of hymnography flourished in the early Byzantine period, especially from the late fifth century through the eighth century, and was unique to the so-called cathedral office of Constantinople.[8] Several notable features differentiate kontakia from other Greek-language hymns of early and medieval Christianity. Most notably, kontakia are typically quite long, often eighteen to twenty-four stanzas, and they function primarily as a sermon sung in verse form. Uffe Ericksen may have made the most useful assessment of a kontakion, when he described it as the blending of a sermon, a drama, and a hymn.[9] A kontakion typically consists of one or more preludes (prooemia) followed by metrically identical stanzas, or oikoi; a short refrain connects the stanzas. The first stanza, or heirmos, functions as a model in that it signals the melody and metrical pattern that the other stanzas will follow. The opening letter of each stanza typically forms an acrostic—for Romanos, it usually spells "the humble Romanos"—and all of the stanzas follow a complex metrical structure based on patterns of stressed syllables.[10]

Ordinarily, kontakia were sung during an evening service in anticipation of a major feast or in honor of a saint of scriptural origin.[11] It is generally assumed

---

7 T. Arentzen, *The Virgin in Song: Mary and the Poetry of Romanos the Melodist* (Philadelphia, 2017), 7.

8 For a brief overview, see E. Jeffries, "Kontakion," *ODB* 2:1148, and Arentzen, *The Virgin in Song*, 6–16.

9 U. H. Ericksen, "The Poet in the Pulpit: Drama and Rhetoric in the *Kontakion* 'On the Victory of the Cross' by Romanos the Melodist," *Transfiguration: Nordic Journal of the Arts* (2010/2011): 103–23, at 106.

10 The melody and metrical structure of the prooemion and the stanzas tend to differ. Also, Arentzen notes that the term *meter*, when applied to kontakia, requires some qualification: Byzantine liturgical poets maintained a complex pattern of stressed and unstressed syllables, but did not employ the pattern of pitched accents used in classical antiquity. Arentzen, *The Virgin in Song*, 10.

11 There is some debate as to whether these services were formal, structured services, such as vespers, or perhaps night vigil (*pannykis*). The original view, proposed by the French cardinal and theologian Jean-Baptiste-François Pitra, was that kontakia belonged to the matins service. José Grosdidier de Matons challenged this, arguing for an all-night vigil service, a view supported by others, including Alexander Lingas. For a summary, see Ericksen, "The Poet in the Pulpit," 106–7. See, also, Lingas, "The Liturgical Place of

that a single chanter or cleric sang the stanzas from the ambo, the raised pulpit in the center of the church, and a choir or the entire laity responded with the refrain.[12] As a sung sermon, a kontakion is exegetical, meaning that it interprets scripture.[13] Unlike typical biblical commentaries in the early church, however, kontakia unleashed new possibilities for biblical interpretation because they used dramatization, in particular speech-in-character, to expand the biblical scene to introduce events and speeches (monologues and dialogues) not included in the canonical text. By doing so, kontakia offered audiences additional layers of meaning. In much the same way that Athenian drama expanded on the "canonical" text of Homer by introducing new storylines and themes to the original, Romanos, through kontakia, introduced imagined encounters between biblical characters to drive home theological points on the proper way to interpret passages. With this technique, Romanos provided greater depth to well-known characters, such as the Virgin Mary and St. Peter, and gave voice to characters who had no, or very few, lines in the canonical text, such as the Magi and the sinful woman who washes Jesus's feet. Perhaps more than any other hymnographic form, the kontakia as conceived by Romanos enabled him to probe religious emotion and the supposed thinking of biblical heroes and villains.[14] The inclusion of a refrain between each stanza allowed the community to engage with the characters through their alleged state of mind, without requiring knowledge of ancient poetic forms or theological training.[15]

---

the *Kontakion* in Constantinople," and G. Frank, "Romanos and the Night Vigil in the Sixth Century," in *Byzantine Christianity: A People's History of Christianity*, ed. D. Krueger (Minneapolis, 2006), 59–78.

12 According to Lingas, "The Liturgical Place of the *Kontakion* in Constantinople," 56–57, Romanos's kontakia continued to be performed in Constantinople until the cessation of the cathedral rite, a consequence of the Fourth Crusade in 1204, when the Crusaders displaced local worship in both Hagia Sophia and monastic practice.

13 Arentzen challenges the scholarly consensus of treating kontakia as sermons. While they certainly employed exegesis of scriptural texts, he argues that their use in nocturnal services, rather than the Divine Liturgy, and their performance by lower clergy indicate a quality and standing different than a formal sermon, which would follow the gospel reading in the Divine Liturgy. Arentzen, *The Virgin in Song*, 11.

14 See, among others, A. Mellas, "Liturgical Emotions in Byzantine Hymns: Reimagining Romanos the Melodist's *On the Victory of the Cross*," *Phronema* 32 (2017): 49–75.

15 Arentzen, *The Virgin in Song*, 8.

Although Byzantine hagiographers have attributed more than one thousand hymns to Romanos, only some eighty-five survive in manuscripts under his name. Paul Maas and Constantine Trypanis argued that fifty-nine of these kontakia are authentic; the correct number remains a matter of scholarly debate, however.[16] As Arentzen observed, even Romanos's authentic kontakia underwent revision in subsequent generations, with later editors adding or replacing individual stanzas.[17] The most contested attribution is the famous Akathist Hymn—consisting of twenty-four stanzas and, uncharacteristically, an acrostic of the Greek alphabet—that details the encounter between the archangel Gabriel and the Virgin Mary at the time of the Annunciation. The hymn is the only kontakion still performed in its entirety in the Orthodox Christian liturgical cycle.[18] It likely originated in the early sixth century, but the current consensus holds that Romanos is not the author.

Unlike the hymns in the *Jerusalem Georgian Chantbook* that address the theme of violence surrounding Christ's Crucifixion, death, and Resurrection, Romanos's kontakia explore themes of violence unrelated to the Passion, such as Herod's massacre of the innocent children of Bethlehem. Two particular kontakia set at the time of the Crucifixion feature, respectively, an imagined conversation between Mary and Jesus and an "offstage" dialogue between Satan and Hell personified. In each of these hymns, Romanos transforms the scriptural record to advance new theological explanations for the suffering of the righteous. A close reading of these three kontakia show, however, that Romanos's theological conception of violence largely aligns with the hymns of the chantbook, even though the two sets of hymns treat the biblical text in demonstrably different ways: the chantbook hymns stick close to the biblical text, but Romanos's

---

16 See P. Maas and C. A. Trypanis, eds., *Cantica Genuina*, vol. 1 of *Sancti Romani Melodi Cantica* (Oxford, 1963); P. Maas and C. A. Trypanis, eds., *Cantica Dubia*, vol. 2, *Sancti Romani Melodi Cantica* (Berlin, 1970). See, also, the introduction to de Matons's edition of Romanos for Sources chrétiennes: J. Grosdidier de Matons, *Hymnes*, vol. 1, SC 99 (Paris, 1964), 13–56.

17 Arentzen made this observation during an informal conversation at a scholarly gathering in Volos, Greece, in 2023.

18 In the Hellenistic tradition, the Akathistos, or a part of it, is performed on each Friday evening during Lent. In the Slavic tradition, it is performed during the matins service of the fifth Saturday of Lent.

kontakia consistently present imagined dialogues and actions not included in the scriptures.

As in the chantbook, Romanos offers a largely unambiguous account of violence, which is perpetuated by the wicked against the good. In the case of Herod and the innocent children, the violence results from the emperor's disordered soul; in the case of Christ's Crucifixion, Romanos presents the violence endured by Christ as a necessary component of the enactment of salvation. While Romanos's theological conception of violence may be similar to that in the chantbook, the presentation is quite different. Not only are Romanos's descriptions of violence far more vivid, but the emotional toll of the violence is explored in greater depth.

On the Massacre of the Holy Innocents

No hymn among the fifty-nine authentic kontakia attributed to Romanos presents an account of violence as graphic as *On the Massacre of the Holy Innocents*.[19] Set as eighteen stanzas,[20] the hymn centers around the thoughts and actions of Herod just as he begins to fear being replaced by the newborn babe. Indeed, "That his power will soon be destroyed" is the hymn's refrain. As the poet walks the listener through ancient prophecy and reports of the Magi, Herod's anxiety builds. By the fourth stanza, Herod orders his army, "in full armor," to "assume a garb of mercilessness" and "slay all of the sons of Bethlehem."[21] The soldiers initially disobey the order (stanza 5), but eventually consent (stanza 7).[22] Stanzas 7–14 alternate between an alarmingly graphic account of the slaughter and a series of illusions to other biblical passages that help one interpret the massacre typologically and metaphorically. The remaining stanzas lead the listener

---

19 For the critical edition of the Greek text, see Mass and Trypanis, *Cantica Genuina*. For an English translation, see M. Carpenter, ed., *Kontakia of Romanos*, vol. 1, *On the Person of Christ* (Columbia, MO, 1969), 23–34.

20 An eighteenth strophe appears in the manuscript tradition, but it contains a different refrain and is typically assumed to have been a subsequent addition. In strophes 1–17, the refrain focuses on the destruction of Herod's power.

21 Romanos, *On the Massacre of the Holy Innocents*, stanza 4 (Carpenter, *Kontakia of Romanos*, 27–28).

22 Carpenter interprets the unexplained reversal by the soldiers as a compositional error, leading her to conclude that the hymn "is not one of the poet's most pleasing works." Carpenter, *Kontakia of Romanos*, 24.

through the holy family's flight to Egypt and the soteriological ramifications of Christ's escape.[23]

More than any other hymn evaluated in this book, *On the Massacre of the Holy Innocents* offers an extended and graphic account of acts of violence. At Herod's instruction, soldiers strip children from their mothers' arms. Some children drown in their own blood, others are cut in two.[24] Still others are beheaded, their bodies falling away with their lips still latched to their mother's breast.[25] Romanos describes earth soaked with blood and mountains echoing the thunderous screams of mothers.[26] In the eleventh stanza, some women are so distraught that they throw their sons to the ground and present themselves to the soldiers, pleading that they be killed rather than witness the slaughter of their children.[27]

From a theological perspective, there are several significant aspects to Romanos's presentation of violence in this kontakion. For starters, *On the Massacre of the Holy Innocents* leaves no doubt as to who perpetrated and who suffered violence. Violence is a tool of the wicked—Herod and his soldiers. Herod's moral depravity is on full display throughout the hymn, but the soldiers are also culpable. The hesitation they exhibit in the fifth stanza originates not from moral wavering, but from fear of being ridiculed for attacking infants. Indeed, they ask permission to destroy the whole of Bethlehem to avoid mockery.[28] The children,

---

23 J. H. Barkhuizen argued that Romanos's *On the Massacre of the Holy Innocents* follows the ancient Greek paradigm established by Hermogenes of recounting a battle by separating the narrative into three distinct parts: the pre-battle planning, the battle itself, and the consequence of the battle. Accordingly, stanzas 1–6 are devoted to the pre-battle; stanzas 7–14 summarize the battle; and the remaining stanzas lead the listener through the consequences of battle, focusing not only on those awaiting Herod but humanity as well. See J. H. Barkhuizen, "Romanos Melodos, *On the Massacre of the Innocents*: A Perspective on Ekphrasis as a Method of Patristic Exegesis," *Acta Classica* 50 (2007): 29–50, esp. 31–32.

24 Romanos, *On the Massacre of the Holy Innocents*, stanza 14 (Carpenter, *Kontakia of Romanos*, 32).

25 Romanos, *On the Massacre of the Holy Innocents*, stanza 14 (Carpenter, *Kontakia of Romanos*, 32).

26 Romanos, *On the Massacre of the Holy Innocents*, stanza 10 (Carpenter, *Kontakia of Romanos*, 30).

27 Romanos, *On the Massacre of the Holy Innocents*, stanza 11 (Carpenter, *Kontakia of Romanos*, 30–31).

28 Romanos, *On the Massacre of the Holy Innocents*, stanza 5 (Carpenter, *Kontakia of Romanos*, 28).

of course, truly innocent, are the primary recipients of violence. The parents suffer traumatizing emotional violence, witnessing the savage death of their children firsthand. Unlike many of the hymns of the chantbook chronicling the suffering of Christ, there is no rebounding of violence in Romanos's hymn, no divine retribution of violence upon the violent. Romanos offers no apocryphal accounting of vengeance against Herod or his soldiers.

The kontakion offers an unambiguous explanation for the cause of the violence. In the second, third, and fourth stanzas, Romanos gives voice to Herod's inner thoughts. There one finds a king crippled by paranoia, by fear that he will lose his power to the child prophesized to unseat him. Fear has usurped Herod's stillness of mind, his ability to make sound decisions. Afraid and confused, Herod demands violence, the massacre of all children with the hope of destroying the child who threatens his grip on power. Following a popular contemporary exegetical interpretation of Matthew 2, Romanos suggests that Herod has become so blinded by fear and jealousy that he fails to save his own children from the slaughter. In the thirteenth stanza, the last to focus on Herod, Romanos wrote,

> O depravity, O madness of the king,
>   O pitiless temper which made war
>   On babes and showed no mercy to his own people;
> He was not mindful of his own children
>   Nor of the fact that there is the same nature for all.
> He did not pity his family; but maddened with rage
>   He at first ignored even himself
>   And then all of his brothers,
> As he attacked all people like a wild beast.
>   When it flees from its pursuers who lay snares for it.
> Fathers mourned for their sons and mothers with them;
>   But the shameless man
>   Did not care for them; but one thing alone
>   He considered as he wept
> That his power would soon be destroyed.[29]

---

29 Romanos, *On the Massacre of the Holy Innocents*, stanza 13 (Carpenter, *Kontakia of Romanos*, 31–32). Henry Maguire believes that Romanos in this stanza is drawing on

From a theological perspective, one might conclude from the closing portrayal of Herod that Romanos understands violence as exacerbating a sinner's separation from virtue and thus from God. Killing the children brings Herod no respite from his fear, no return to a longed-for stillness. For Herod, acting violently only extends his own suffering. In this hymn, there is no consideration that violence could be an instrument of good. Instead, violence is an instrument of the wicked, perpetrated against the good.

For the victims of violence and, one would assume, for the Christians who listened to or sang the hymn, the instantiation of violence against the holy innocents actually served as an occasion for hope. Even the mothers who plead to be killed before their children—that is, the survivors most traumatized by the wicked events—affirm that their children will be received in the bosom of Abraham.

> So that each cried bitterly: "Kill them, but the bosom of Abraham
> Will receive them like the faithful Abel."[30]

For Romanos, the endurance of violence is, ultimately, a source of joy.[31] More specifically, in the hands of Romanos, the massacre of the children is presented as one piece in a long but necessary succession of events in the cosmic history of salvation. Romanos anticipates Christ's victory—the victory over death—in the final stanzas, which chronicle the holy family's flight to Egypt, where the mere presence of the Christ child leads to the overthrow of idols.

Elsewhere in Romanos's corpus, one finds an understanding of violence similar to that in *On the Massacre of the Holy Innocents*, especially the contention that the suffering of the virtuous is part of the divine plan for salvation. For example, in *On Peter's Denial*, Romanos dramatizes the numerous ways in which Jesus remains unmoved by the multiple acts of violence perpetrated against him. Christ's stoic-like suffering differentiates him from Peter who, although he

---

the exegesis of Basil of Seleucia, who wrote an extended commentary on the pericope. See H. Maguire, *Art and Eloquence in Byzantium* (Princeton, 1981), 22–23.

30 Romanos, *On the Massacre of the Holy Innocents*, stanza 11 (Carpenter, *Kontakia of Romanos*, 31).

31 Romanos, *On the Massacre of the Holy Innocents*, stanza 11 (Carpenter, *Kontakia of Romanos*, 31).

witnesses these acts, is too weak in faith to affirm his association with Christ.[32] As with *On the Massacre of the Holy Innocents*, only the righteous suffer in *On Peter's Denial*.

On Judas similarly describes Christ's suffering, but it also includes a feature not employed in *On the Massacre of the Innocents*. Near the conclusion, Romanos dramatizes Judas suffering violence in the present, his hanging, and also in the future, his anticipated punishment in hell. In Romanos's hands, Judas's suffering is a plight of his own making.[33] Despite the unrelenting critique of Herod in *On the Massacre of the Innocents*, there is no comparable discussion of any violence that the evil king will himself suffer. Nevertheless, in each of these hymns, violence points to the soteriological endgame of the death and Resurrection of Jesus Christ.

On the Lament of the Mother of God

After *On the Massacre of the Holy Innocents*, *On the Lament of the Mother of God* is the authentic kontakion by Romanos with the most detailed and consistent engagement with themes of violence. This seventeen-stanza hymn recites an imagined conversation between Jesus and his mother at the time of the Passion, including the Crucifixion, to explain the theological purpose of Christ's suffering. Violence is present from the start. The prelude directly refers to the Crucifixion,[34] and the first stanza opens with Mary's grief at the forefront, watching her "lamb being dragged to the slaughter."[35] In fact, every stanza of this kontakion refers to the violence of Christ's Passion, and yet, as Arentzen notes, it is Mary who actually suffers in this hymn, not Christ.[36] The third stanza typifies Mary's grief for her son's pain as well as the way Romanos seeks to differentiate her deep commitment to him from the less enthusiastic commitment of the disciples:

---

32 Romanos, *On Peter's Denial*, esp. stanzas 10–12.

33 Romanos, *On Judas*, stanzas 19–20.

34 Romanos, *On the Lament of the Mother of God*, prooemion (E. Lash, trans., *On the Life of Christ: Kontakia* [San Francisco, 1995], 143).

35 Romanos, *On the Lament of the Mother of God*, stanza 1 (Lash, *On the Life of Christ*, 143).

36 Arentzen, *The Virgin in Song*, 141.

> You are on your way, my child, to unjust slaughter,
> and no one suffers with you. Peter is not going with you, he who said,
> "I will never deny you even though I die."
> Thomas has left you, he who cried out, "Let us all die with him!"
> The rest too, your own and your companions
> who are to judge the tribes of Israel; where are they now?
> Not one of all of them, but you alone, my child,
> one on behalf of all are dying. Instead of them you have saved all.
> Instead of them you have made satisfaction for all,
> > My Son and my God.[37]

It is noteworthy that Romanos's reimagining of the event has erased the presence of the apostles. The Virgin alone is both the witness of and spokesperson for the Crucifixion. She gives voice to the grief of the community, but does so in a particularly feminine and maternal way.

Several themes examined in the chantbook hymns are present in this stanza. For example, the stanza offers an explicit explanation of the purpose of Christ's suffering—the salvation of all. Indeed, as the hymn progresses, Romanos pits Mary's grief against the necessity of Christ's violent death. The voice of Christ insists that his, the savior's, suffering and death are the remedy for death; they are the gift of salvation. While the hymn's theological stress lies in this soteriological maxim, the dramatic emphasis focuses squarely on Mary's grief, a heart-wrenching grief akin to emotional violence. Mary anticipates the loss of her child in real time, an experience that would have been all too common for the individual Christians comprising Romanos's audience.

Mary, who does not want her son to suffer and knows of his power, repeatedly questions why he would allow himself to suffer at the hands of evil men. At one point, Mary asks how it is that Christ can raise the dead and perform all sorts of miracles yet cannot grant salvation to Adam without dying himself.[38] Romanos's Mary speaks not only for herself but for all Christians, and not only for those theologically confused by Christ's suffering, but also those who watch their own children suffer.

---

37 Romanos, *On the Lament of the Mother of God*, stanza 3 (Lash, *On the Life of Christ*, 144).

38 Romanos, *On the Lament of the Mother of God*, esp. stanza 8.

In responding to Mary, Christ lists each of the physical torments that he will endure—the nails, the cloak, the cross, and so on—but simultaneously presents them as medicinal therapies offered for the body and soul of Adam and, by extension, to all of humanity.

> Be patient a little longer, Mother, and you will see
> how, like a physician, I undress and reach the place where they lie
> and I treat their wounds,
> cutting with the lance their calluses and their scabs.
> And I take vinegar, I apply it as astringent to the wound,
> when with the probe of the nails I have instigated the cut, I shall
> plug it with the cloak.
> And, with my cross as a splint,
> I shall make use of it, Mother, so that you may chant with understanding,
> "By suffering he has abolished suffering,
>   My Son and my God."[39]

In the poet's hands, the details of Christ's suffering provide the precise formula for Adam's salvation, which is the salvation of all.

By the end of the hymn, Romanos has achieved his theological and exegetical point—explaining the need for Christ's suffering in terms of the cosmic plan for salvation. It also does something that no previous Greek exegete had done—tell the narrative of the Passion primarily through the witness and voice of Mary, a character virtually ignored in the scriptural accounts of the Crucifixion. What is more, Romanos effectively invents for Greek audiences the notion of Marian lament.[40] Even though Mary consents to her son's will and tacitly accepts his explanation for his own suffering, she never sets aside her grief. Note, for example, the way that Romanos gives voice to this in the final line of the penultimate stanza, when Christ consoles her:

---

39 Romanos, *On the Lament of the Mother of God*, stanza 13 (Lash, *On the Life of Christ*, 148).

40 See Arentzen, *The Virgin in Song*, 144.

"When you see these things, if, as a woman, you are afraid,
　Cry out to me, 'Spare me,
　　My Son and my God.'"[41]

Romanos neither ignores nor belittles Mary's grief as most previous Christian exegetes had done.[42] Rather, through Christ, he instructs her to give her sorrow over to him. Christ's strength, made manifest through his suffering, is sufficient to absorb Mary's grief.

For Arentzen, the conclusion of the hymn suggests that Mary's weeping voice has turned into something powerful. She has become a partner in Christ's death and Resurrection by giving voice to it. Mary does not endure the violence of the cross, but she is its lone spokesperson and, as such, is a participant.[43] The hymn ends by emphasizing both Christ's suffering and his gift of voice to the Virgin:

Like a lamb you took away our sins;
Putting them to death by your slaughter, O Savior, you saved all mankind.
You are, both in suffering and in not suffering.
You are, dying and saving. You granted the honored Lady the freedom
　of speech to cry to you
　　"My Son and my God."[44]

Because Mary's cry is the cry of the refrain, the cry of the people, her empowered voice becomes their own. What began as a cry of grief and despair concludes as a cry of anticipation of the Resurrection. Lament is not forgotten; it is transformed into a sorrowful joy.

One other thing Romanos does in this kontakion is single out the Jewish community as being responsible for the death of Christ, as several idiomela do. For most of the hymn, the dialogue between Mary and Christ maintains a tone of

---

41 Romanos, *On the Lament of the Mother of God*, stanza 16 (Lash, *On the Life of Christ*, 150).

42 C. Sweeney, "Grief and the Cross: Popular Devotion and Passion Piety from Late Antiquity to the Early Middle Ages" (PhD diss., Fordham University, 2019), 171-77.

43 Arentezen, *The Virgin in Song*, 148-49.

44 Romanos, *On the Lament of the Mother of God*, stanza 17 (Lash, *On the Life of Christ*, 150).

universal hope, a sense that Christ's Passion will grant salvation to all the descendants of Adam and Eve.[45] In the fifteenth stanza, however, Mary's lament adopts a tone of anti-Jewish resentment:

> I am conquered, my child, I am conquered by love,
> and truly I cannot bear that I should be in my room, but you on the tree,
> that I should be in my house, but you in a grave.
> I shall look on the monstrous daring of those who honor Moses.
> For it is to avenge him, so they say, that these blind men have come to slay you.
> But Moses said this to Israel,
> "You are going to see life on the tree."
> Life, who it is? It is
>   My Son and my God.[46]

Christ's response in the following stanza continues as the previous ones had with a gentle consolation that his suffering is necessary. This consolation includes a warning of the events that will accompany his death—eclipse, earthquake, and so on—so that she will not be frightened by them. One of the final warnings notes specifically, "The Temple will rend its tunic against those who dare this outrage."[47] Thus, here too, Romanos implies Jewish culpability in Christ's death. What is interesting about these stanzas is that Romanos seems to bifurcate between a narrow historic account of the Passion, wherein the Jews are uniquely culpable, and a proclamation of the mystery of Jesus's death and Resurrection, which promises to restore Adam and all of his descendants. Of note, although the hymn marks the Jews in terms of their culpability and their difference—they are not a Christian community—Romanos's implied conclusion is that all partake in Christ's salvific work.

The engagement of violence in *On the Lament of the Mother of God*, as in *On the Massacre of the Holy Innocents*, follows what one might describe as

---

45 Stanazas 8–14 refer directly to Adam, and several of them include Eve as well.

46 Romanos, *On the Lament of the Mother of God*, stanza 15 (Lash, *On the Life of Christ*, 149).

47 Romanos, *On the Lament of the Mother of God*, stanza 16 (Lash, *On the Life of Christ*, 150).

a traditional account. In the lament, only the unambiguously virtuous suffer violence: Christ willingly suffers physical violence, and Mary endures emotional violence. The virtuous suffer not because the world is unfair, but because it is part of the plan for salvation. Indeed, the exegetical thesis of the hymn is that Christ had to suffer in order to deliver salvation. As with the kontakion on the holy innocents, that on Mary's lament also offers no rebounding of violence or prophecy of future violence for the wicked. In both kontakia, Romanos's presentation of violence is consistently unambiguous.

On the Victory of the Cross

Romanos's *On the Victory of the Cross* is arguably one of the most rewarding of all of his hymns. Likely composed for Good Friday and consisting of eighteen stanzas, the kontakion provides an intriguing dialogue between Hell personified and an anthropomorphic Satan, who are "offstage" at the start of Christ's Crucifixion.[48] Drawing on the classical dramatic element of scene recognition (ἀναγνώρισις), Romanos's hymn effortlessly sketches two simultaneous settings for his audience. One is familiar—Golgotha, the site of the Crucifixion in the four Gospels—while the other is more elusive: an offstage, subterranean area where Satan and Hell engage one another; there is no biblical referent for this encounter.[49] As the kontakion unfolds, the reader moves back and forth between the two scenes and is also made to recall several episodes from the Hebrew Bible. Because Hell and Satan produce all of the dialogue in the hymn, the audience is moved to interpret the familiar (the canonical Gospels) through the lens of the invented (the subterranean conversation). To be sure, Romanos was not the first to contrive an imagined conversation between Hell and Satan—Ephraim the Syrian had introduced the motif to Christianity during the fourth century in his own hymns—but

---

48 During the middle Byzantine period, the hymn was likely performed on the Third Sunday of Lent rather than Good Friday. See Mellas, "Liturgical Emotions in Byzantine Hymns," 63–64.

49 It is possible, of course, that Romanos is playing on his audience's knowledge of Greek mythology in imagining hell as the underworld. He is certainly drawing on themes in the apocryphal Gospel of Nicodemus, which sought to chronicle Christ's "harrowing of hell."

Romanos's account is unique, particularly in its repeated turn to Hebrew prophecy as an anticipatory affirmation of the Crucifixion and the Resurrection.[50]

In addition to speech-in-character and scene recognition, the reversal of circumstance (περιπέτια) is the other obvious plot device that Romanos adopts from Athenian drama. Indeed, the entire kontakion hinges, somewhat farcically, on Satan's transition from failing to see the consequence of the Crucifixion to finally understanding it. Stanzas 1–9 function as an argument between Satan and Hell; stanzas 10–17 offer their shared lament about their change in circumstance. In the final stanza, the eighteenth, Romanos speaks on behalf of the Christian community. In the form of a doxology, the final stanza pledges that all Christians will metaphorically nail themselves to the cross to imitate the violence suffered by Christ—and sing praise to the Lord because, through the cross, humans have been granted eternal life.[51]

On the Victory of the Cross employs three metrically unique prooemia that focus on distinct aspects of the story of salvation.[52] The first describes the cross's destruction of the gate barring entrance to Eden; the second praises the suffering of Christ; the third celebrates Adam's redemption. Situated post-Resurrection, all of them frontload the audience with the knowledge that Christ's suffering on the cross is not only a triumph, but also the linchpin in the long history of salvation.

As noted, the first stanza simultaneously sets both the Golgotha and subterranean scenes and establishes the connection between the two. Just as the crosses rise on Golgotha, Hell is overcome with pain and announces to Satan that he wants to release Adam and his descendants.

> My ministers and powers,
> Who has fixed a nail in my heart?
> A wooden lance has suddenly pierced me and I am being torn apart.

---

50 For a summary of the connection between Ephraim and Romanos, see B. Guevin, "Dialogue between Death and the Devil in Saint Ephrem the Syrian and Saint Romanos the Melodist," *StP* 92 (2017): 113–18. See also G. Frank, "Christ's Descent to the Underworld in Ancient Ritual and Legend," in *Apocalyptic Thought in Early Christianity*, ed. R. Daly (Grand Rapids, MI, 2009), 221–25.

51 Romanos, *On the Victory of the Cross*, stanza 18 (Lash, *On the Life of Christ*, 163).

52 Romanos, *On the Victory of the Cross*, prooemia 1–3 (Lash, *On the Life of Christ*, 155).

> My insides are in pain, my belly in agony,
> my senses make my spirit tremble,
> and I am compelled to disgorge
> Adam and Adam's race. Given me by a tree,
> a tree is bringing them back
>   again to Paradise.[53]

Satan, who cannot see or feel Hell's affliction, criticizes Hell's sudden fear and tries to convince him that Jesus's Crucifixion will be their victorious moment.[54] The discussion between Satan and Hell carries on for several stanzas, with the two of them speaking past one another: Hell remains in agony, while Satan maintains that Hell fears without reason. Throughout these stanzas, Romanos alternates between graphic accounts of Hell's suffering and repeated typological references to a tree or cross paradigm in the texts of the Hebrew Bible. At the midpoint of the kontakion, the debate between Hell and Satan abruptly shifts because the events of Christ's Crucifixion have since unfolded. Satan now understands that the cross has vanquished the power of death. Stanzas ten through sixteen offer Satan's lament at the loss of his power and at his own foolishness for not seeing the multiple prophecies of a triumphant cross in the Hebrew Bible.

Implicit throughout the hymn is the notion that the violence unleashed upon Christ is an essential component of the story of salvation; the implicit is explicit in the second prooemion. What makes this hymn unusual, however, is the relative downplaying of Christ's personal pain as, meanwhile, Hell suffers and does so graphically. Thus, unlike in Romanos's other kontakia, here the perpetrators of violence, rather than the virtuous, come to suffer violence. To be clear, the violence they experience is of their own making; it is not a direct act of divine retribution. Indeed, in the early stanzas, Hell's lament is directly juxtaposed to Satan's efforts to inflict pain on Christ. In a sense, the entire hymn is a dramatic, perhaps comedic, reversal of the violence enacted by Satan but felt by Hell.

Also of note in the hymn, the victory of the cross liberates those one might otherwise expect to suffer. Indeed, the cross that Hell and Satan erect becomes a refuge for "thieves, murderers, and publicans and harlots" who are able to escape

---

53 Romanos, *On the Victory of the Cross*, stanza 1 (Lash, *On the Life of Christ*, 155–56).
54 Romanos, *On the Victory of the Cross*, stanza 2 (Lash, *On the Life of Christ*, 156).

their due punishment and find safe haven in Paradise.[55] The only figures who suffer in perpetuity are Hell and Satan themselves. *On the Victory of the Cross* holds that the whole of "Adam's race" finds redemption in the cross, as *On the Lament of the Mother of God* also recounts.[56]

As is the case with *Massacre of the Holy Innocents*, Romanos's description of violence is vivid as well in *On the Victory of the Cross*. As noted above, in the first stanza, Hell laments being pierced by a wooden lance and "being torn apart," his insides in pain and agony. A nail is fixed in his heart.[57] The *wooden* lance is simultaneously the tree of Eden, the soldier's lance used to pierce Christ, and the cross that pierces Hell. In explicitly anthropomorphic ways, Hell suffers the pain that should be experienced by Jesus. As elsewhere in Romanos's hymns, the dramatization of violence, in this case the Crucifixion, points to the liberation of humanity and brings the divine plan to fruition.

Another noteworthy feature of this kontakion is Romanos's use of military imagery to dramatize the story, as in the opening stanza, where he describes the cross as a lance that pierces Hell's stomach. Even more than that, Romanos leans on Roman imperial structures when he speaks of the cross as the "throne of Christ" and of Christ himself as the "tribune" who advocates for the common citizen against Satan.[58] At least one other hymn among Romanos's authentic kontakia similarly employs imperial and military metaphors—the second kontakion for the patriarch Joseph, which chronicles his efforts to avert the lustful advances of the Egyptian queen. In that hymn, the first stanza frames the entire cosmic plan for salvation as an imperial or military metaphor. As the hymn progresses, Romanos routinely uses martial language, for example, "invisible arrows," to describe the ways in which the queen is conquered by her lust or seeks to conquer with it.[59]

To be clear, although Romanos employs military and imperial language in *On the Victory of the Cross*, it is in the service of the theological assertion that the historical act of Christ's Crucifixion destroyed the power of death over

---

55 Romanos, *On the Victory of the Cross*, stanza 16 (Lash, *On the Life of Christ*, 162).
56 Romanos, *On the Victory of the Cross*, prooemion 3 (Lash, *On the Life of Christ*, 155).
57 Romanos, *On the Victory of the Cross*, stanza 1 (Lash, *On the Life of Christ*, 155–56).
58 Romanos, *On the Victory of the Cross*, stanza 9 (Lash, *On the Life of Christ*, 159).
59 See, for example, the fourth stanza, which states that "invisible arrows torture the soul" of the invisible queen when she looks upon Joseph's youth with "licentious eyes" (critical edition: Maas and Tyrpannis, *Cantica Genuina*, 354–67).

humanity. In contrast to several later hymns, during the Herakleian era and post-Herakleian, there is no equivalence between divine power and imperial power, no equivalence between Satan and the enemies of the empire.[60]

Also in this regard, this hymn, more than any others by Romanos set at the time of the Crucifixion, ascribes special culpability for the death of Jesus to Pilate.[61] Like other hymns, *On the Victory of the Cross* includes denigrating statements about the Jews—for instance, in stanza 2, Satan says that he incited them, and stanza 14 refers to them as "lawless"—but contrary to other hymns, Romanos here places equal, if not more, blame on the Romans for Christ's death.[62] Thus, one should not assume that Romanos's use of Roman imperial themes in this hymn indicates an uncritical elision of Roman and Christian identity, despite his hymns being heard by individuals who had clearly conflated the two as one.[63] Indeed, Romanos subtly uses Roman imperial power as a metaphor for Christ's achievement but also to criticize Roman responsibility for his death. The liturgical poets of the Herakleian and post-Herakleian period either lacked that skill or chose not to employ it. For them, the enemies of the state and the enemies of God were always one and the same.

To be sure, *On the Victory of the Cross* exhibits several unique features. For the purposes here, perhaps the most important one is its status as the only kontakion of the three examined where the enemies of God—Satan and Hell—suffer, even if of their own making. As a kontakion, the hymn emphasizes dramatic

---

60 In one especially moving passage from stanza 16, Satan laments that what he has planted—the tree of the Garden of Eden—has become a "holy" trunk and that under its branches, "thieves, murderers, and publicans and harlots" will reap the sweet fruit of eternal life.

61 Pilate is mentioned by name in the first, fourth, and tenth stanzas.

62 In stanza 14 of *On the Victory of the Cross*, Christ's death and pending Resurrection absolves the Jews because "they know not what they do." By contrast, Hell and Satan know their own evil, and they suffer for it. In other words, Romanos willingly denigrates the Jews and identifies them as "other" vis-à-vis the Christian community, but he does not exclude them from Christ's salvific work.

63 For more on the Roman appropriation of Christian identity and vice versa, see the masterful A. Cameron, *Christianity and the Rhetoric of Empire: The Development of Christian Discourse* (Berkeley, 1994). Of more recent note, see R. S. Falcasantos, *Constantinople: Ritual, Violence, and Memory in the Making of a Christian Imperial City* (Oakland, 2020).

exegesis rather than petition, so singers of it are not so much asking God to punish Hell and Satan as they are being entertained by it.[64] The singers and audience are clearly celebrating Hell and Satan's defeat, the inescapable consequence of Christ's victory on the cross.

Conclusion

In *Homo Sacer*, the Italian philosopher Giorgio Agamben maintains that all state power, from Aristotle to the modern era, has sought to separate political beings (citizens) from "bare life" (mere bodies) to determine which lives are to be incorporated into the political body and which will be excluded, often through public deaths.[65] If Agamben is right about the ancient political relationship between bare life and politics, then Romanos's notion of violence and sacrifice seems to be a reversal or, at the least, an alternative vision of their relationship. Romanos in *On the Massacre of the Holy Innocents* and *On the Victory of the Cross* not only rejects the state's right to violate the body—Herod's slaughter of children and Pilate's crucifixion of Christ—but he celebrates the triumph of bodies sacrificed on behalf of all.

With respect to the first point—Romanos's rejection of the state's authority over life and death—his engagement with "state authorities" in these hymns is with the villains of the Gospels, that is, Herod and Pilate. Although Pilate had been a Roman governor, none of Romanos's hymns explicitly critique the state authority of his own day, and several actually laud the emperor and his soldiers.[66] Nevertheless, it is plausible that some of the citizens who heard Romanos's hymns may have understood his condemnations of Pilate, Herod, and other

---

64 There is a certain similarity here between the way Romanos presents Satan and Hell and the way Athenian dramatists, such as Euripides, were able to lead their audience to sympathize with (or, at the very least, be entertained by) hostile or evil characters.

65 G. Agamben, *Homo Sacer: Sovereign Power and Bare Life*, trans. D. Heller-Roazen (Stanford, 1998).

66 Indeed, Romanos composed two hymns to commemorate the Forty Martyrs of Sebaste, soldiers whose veneration was a Byzantine celebration of their empire being protected by God. The final stanza of the later of the two hymns goes so far as to ask Christ to "grant victory and trophies to the emperor against the barbarians." While it is conceivable that this was written by Romanos, Maas and Tyrpannis, *Cantica Genuina*, 505, consider this particular stanza "dubious" in terms of such an attribution. My thanks to Alexander Lingas for alerting me to this stanza.

biblical villains to be a means by which one could also critique contemporary power structures when state actors acted immorally. More importantly, Romanos's notion of true power is at odds with Agamben's thesis. For Romanos, power—indeed, salvation—flows from suffering violence, not from enacting it. To be sure, this is a theological claim, not a political or philosophical assertion. It is also predicated on a belief in the soteriological significance of the Crucifixion-Resurrection cycle. In Romanos's hands, even the suffering of the children of Bethlehem is typology for the suffering and Resurrection of Christ.

While both the form and content of Romanos's kontakia are fundamentally different from the hymns assessed in the *Jerusalem Georgian Chantbook*, the theological conceptualization of violence is quite similar. In both sets of hymns, violence is typically presented as an instrument of the wicked perpetrated against the good—usually Christ. Even in those instances where Romanos describes violent events other than the Crucifixion, such as the murder of the children of Bethlehem, the enduring of the violence is made holy because of the eventual soteriological impact of the Crucifixion and the Resurrection. No matter how savage or how heart-wrenching the violence, Romanos never wavers from the belief that the violent or emotional suffering of the innocent is made perfect through the cosmic plan for salvation enacted through the death and Resurrection of Jesus Christ.

One might thus conclude that with respect to violence, Romanos parts ways with the chantbook in style rather than substance. His account is more dramatic, more graphic, more psychological. In Romanos, one weeps with the mothers of Bethlehem, feels the Virgin's emotional trauma, revels in Satan's slow realization of being undone by his own wickedness. Like the chantbook hymns, however, one never loses sight of Christ's suffering not only leading to the salvation of all, but also its being a fundamental component of that salvation.

CHAPTER 4

FEAST OF THE EXALTATION OF THE HOLY CROSS

Christians' appropriation of the cross as a physical symbol of Christianity was slow in developing. Although the scriptures and church leaders emphasized the centrality of Christ's death on a cross, it did not mean that the earliest Christians employed crosses as symbols of their faith or identity. There is little evidence that Christians used the cross as a physical symbol prior to the fourth century.[1] In fact, the cross served as a military and imperial insignia before it became a popular symbol of Christian identity. Its eventual popularity as a marker of Christian identity was almost certainly triggered by the Roman emperor Constantine, who incorporated the cross shape into his military standard in the fourth century.[2]

According to Eusebius of Caesarea, Constantine's biographer, the emperor came to Christianity through a pair of miraculous visions, or dreams, shortly

---

[1] On this, see R. Jensen, *The Cross: History, Art, and Controversy* (Cambridge, MA, 2017), esp. 25–48: "Despite the importance of making the sign of the cross in everyday religious practice or in tracing it on the foreheads of the newly baptized, early Christians did not—to any significant degree—incorporate plain crosses in their homes, tomb epitaphs, or even on small personal objects (rings, dishware, clothing)" (44). For much of the twentieth century, some scholars of early Christianity held that the lack of extant crucifix artifacts stemmed from Christians' aversion to the cross as a symbol. For a challenge to that view as well as the art historical consensus that few artifacts survive from the period prior to Constantine, see B. Longenecker, *The Cross before Constantine: The Early Life of a Christian Symbol* (Minneapolis, 2015).

[2] Jensen, *The Cross*.

before the battle of the Milvian bridge, where his victory in 312 gave him control of the western half of the Roman Empire.[3] Inspired by these visions, Constantine commissioned a new battle standard, the labarum, with a cross-shaped central design feature, along with other elements.[4] Eusebius's account asserts a close connection between Constantine's success on the battlefield, his use of the labarum as a battle standard, and the direct intervention of God, who had selected Constantine to be his instrument on earth.[5] For example, in book 2 of *The Life of Constantine*, Eusebius narrates a battle from 321 between Constantine and Licinius, once an ally in the East but now a rival. Eusebius describes Constantine deploying the labarum as though it were a powerful talisman that could transform the success or failure of soldiers on the battlefield simply by its being turned in a different direction.[6]

In the centuries that followed Constantine's conversion, the cross grew in popularity both as a physical symbol of Christian identity and as a symbol of the empire. The legends connecting Constantine's vision of a cross to his supposed divinely sanctioned success on the battlefield emerged as key features in the development of an eventual sacralization of violence through hymnography. The Feast of the Exaltation of the Holy Cross, more than any other liturgical commemoration, became the mechanism through which hymnographers would bring together popular devotion to the cross, the Christianization of empire, and the idea of Rome as New Israel to beseech the Lord for victory on the battlefield.

The hymnography accompanying the development of the Feast of the Exaltation significantly innovated liturgical engagement with violence by envisioning the cross as an object of devotion in its own right. One result of this was

---

3 Eusebius, *Life of Constantine* 1.27–32 (A. Cameron and S. G. Hall, trans., *Eusebius: Life of Constantine*, Clarendon Ancient History Series [Oxford, 1999], 79–82).

4 Silver coins dating to 317 feature the labarum, confirming Eusebius's description of it. An overlapping *chi* and *rho* adorns the top of the cross, and a banner with outlined images of Constantine and his two sons hang from the cross arms.

5 Eusebius, *Life of Constantine* 1.5–6 (Cameron and Hall, trans., *Eusebius: Life of Constantine*, 69).

6 Eusebius, *Life of Constantine* 2.7 (Cameron and Hall, trans., *Eusebius: Life of Constantine*, 98).

hymnography ascribing power to the cross itself, not merely referencing its typological or soteriological attributes. In fact, the feast became the catalyst by which Christian hymnographers began to conceive of the relationship between faith and violence in entirely new ways. This transformation of the presentation of violence accompanied the introduction of an explicit hymnographic association between the community of Christian singers and the political structures of the Roman Empire, especially the emperor.

The Feast of the Exaltation, celebrated in Byzantium on 14 September, developed as a ritual amalgamation of four distinctive commemorations: (1) Christ's Crucifixion; (2) the legendary finding of the cross near Jerusalem, presumably in the early part of the fourth century; (3) the consecration of the Martyrium basilica, the church on the site of Christ's Crucifixion on Golgotha in the fourth century;[7] and (4) the return of the relic of the cross from Persia to Jerusalem, in 630 in March.[8]

The earliest surviving evidence for possessing a relic of the cross comes from Cyril of Jerusalem and dates to the 350s.[9] Cyril makes no mention of how the cross was discovered or how his church came to possess it. The various legends, including the one that ascribes its discovery to Constantine's mother, St. Helena, are subsequent creations.[10] While some of these legends situate the discovery on

---

7 It is not clear whether the church, likely dedicated in 335, was built on the exact spot on Golgotha where Christ was believed to have been crucified or if it was at an adjacent location. The earliest testimony on the fourth-century building program is by Egeria, the pilgrim, who seems to describe a separate, open-air "shrine" of the cross that was distinct from the basilica and the rotunda shrine of the church of the Anastasis (Holy Sepulcher). See Jensen, *The Cross*, 62–63, citing Egeria's *Itinerarium* 48 (P. Maraval, ed., *Égérie: Journal de voyage [Itinéraire]*, SC 296 [Paris, 1997], 316).

8 For the scholarly debates about the likeliest series of events regarding the return of the relics in 630, see J. W. Drijvers, "Heraclius and the *Restitutio Crucis*: Notes on Symbolism and Ideology," in *The Reign of Heraclius (610–641): Crises and Confrontation*, ed. G. J. Reinink and B. H. Stotle (Leuven, 2002), 175–90, esp. 177–78.

9 Cyril mentions the relics three times, in each case stating that he and his listeners are standing in the presence of the relics at Golgotha: Cyril of Jerusalem, *Catechesis* 4.10, 10.19, and 13.4.

10 During the late ancient and medieval periods, three distinctive, legendary accounts explained the finding of the "true" cross. The oldest, attributing the finding to St. Helen, Constantine's mother, finds its first expression in St. Ambrose's funeral oration for the emperor Theodosius, which he delivered in the year 395, roughly sixty years after

13 or 14 September, the initial impetus for celebrating the feast of the cross on 14 September derives from the consecration of the church at Golgotha occurring on 13–14 September, likely in 335.[11] Thus, the earliest verifiable connection between the feast of the cross and a September date is the Jerusalem-centered annual commemoration of the dedication of the basilica on Golgotha.[12]

Multiple sources, the oldest being the pilgrim Egeria in the late fourth century, state that the Encainia, the annual commemoration of the church's founding, included a ritual presentation and veneration of the relic(s) of the cross.[13] As the feast of the church's founding grew during the fifth and sixth centuries, this "lifting," or exaltation, and veneration of the relics of the cross became the principal ritualized aspect of the commemoration.[14] By the mid-sixth century, the liturgical ritual had effectively split into distinct festivals, held on sequential days: the commemoration of the dedication of the church was celebrated on 13 September and a newly established Feast of the Exaltation of the Holy Cross

---

the events he narrates. It is possible, of course, that Ambrose derived this story from other, now-lost sources. The more popular version in the Middle Ages by far, however, is the Judas Cyriacus version, which claims that a Jew assisted Helen in her discovery of the cross and dates to the early fifth century. See J. W. Drijvers, *Helena Augusta: The Mother of Constantine the Great and the Legend of Her Finding of the Cross* (Leiden, 1992); S. Heid, "Der Ursprung der Helenalegende im Pilgerbetrieb Jerusalems," *JbAC* 32 (1989): 41–71; and S. Borgehammar, *How the Holy Cross Was Found: From Event to Medieval Legend* (Stockholm, 1991).

11 On the consecration of the Martyrium, including the accounts of the commemoration preserved in the *Jerusalem Georgian Chantbook*, see G. Shurgaia, "L'esaltazione della croce nello Iadgari antico," in *L'Onagro Maestro: Miscellanea di fuochi accesi per Gianroberto Scarcia in occasione del suo LXX sadè*, ed. R. Favano, S. Cristoforetti, and M. Compareti (Venice, 2004), 137–88.

12 For the complex history of the date of commemoration and how it is tied to the consecration of the Martyrium basilica, the church of the Anastasis, which was part of the same larger Christian complex, and the supposed date of the finding of the cross, see L. van Tongeren, *Exaltation of the Cross: Toward the Origins of the Feast of the Cross and the Meaning of the Cross in Early Medieval Liturgy* (Leuven, 2000), 19–36.

13 Egeria, *Itinerarium* 48.1–2. The display of the relic is also attested in the so-called Armenian Lectionary. See Renoux, *Le codex arménien Jérusalem 121*, 2:362–63.

14 A report from a sixth-century witness, an archdeacon by the name of Theodosius, confirms the public display of the cross during the festivities on 14 September. See van Tongeren, *Exaltation of the Cross*, 36–39.

Feast of the Exaltation of the Holy Cross 93

was held on 14 September.[15] During the mid-seventh century, the feast expanded further to incorporate and celebrate the return of the relic(s) of the cross from Persia. Just as the feast began to include this new element, a new imperial edict by Herakleios instructed clergy throughout the empire to celebrate what had been until that point a Jerusalem-based ritual.[16]

The oldest surviving hymns for the twin celebrations on 13 September and 14 September were composed for the annual commemoration of the Martyrium. The current scholarly consensus dates the hymns to the mid-sixth century, during the reign of Justinian (r. 527–565)—prior to the Persian War (602–628) and the expansion of the feast to include the return of cross relics—which places their composition at roughly the same time as both the Idiomela and the hymns of Romanos the Melodist.[17] Although they were composed in Greek, none of these early hymns survive in a Greek manuscript.[18] Fortunately, like the hymns of the Octoechos, a Georgian translation of these early hymns is found in the *Jerusalem Georgian Chantbook*.[19]

While the majority of these hymns treat violence in much the same way as other hymns analyzed thus far—focusing primarily on the violence that Christ suffered—a cluster of those for 14 September, the feast, claim that divine intervention, through the cross, was responsible for the victory of Christian emperors against their enemies. These appear to be the oldest surviving hymns of Christian

---

15 See van Tongeren, *Exaltation of the Cross*, 37.

16 There is some evidence that a 14 September feast had begun to spread outside of Jerusalem at roughly the same time as the composition of the original hymns for the feast, that is, the mid-sixth century. What is perhaps most noteworthy of the verifiable sources attesting to these commemorations is that each local community celebrating the Exaltation before the reign of Herakleios had its own small relic of the cross. Such is the case with the small Syrian town of Apamea, whose celebration of the Exaltation in 540 is attested by Evagrius Scholasticus, *Ecclesiastical History* 4.26. See van Tongeren, *Exaltation of the Cross*, 37, and A. Frolow, *Le relique de la vraie croix: Recherches sur le développement d'un culte* (Paris, 1961), 184–85.

17 See the Stephen Shoemaker's introductory comments to appendix 1 in this volume.

18 Greek manuscripts that provide evidence of the Palestinian or Constantinopolitan commemorations reflect subsequent liturgical and hymnographic development.

19 I am deeply grateful to Stephen Shoemaker, who completed English translations of these hymns, which appear as appendix 1 in this volume.

composition to connect God to active violence.[20] They are also the oldest surviving hymns to celebrate the reign of Constantine, whose eventual conversion to Christianity after a vision of the cross is heralded as both a sign of God's intervention in human events and his blessing of the empire. These features will prove to be key instruments in the imperialization of hymnography that began to take a more advanced form during the reign of Herakleios.

Hymns for 13 September

The festal section of the *Jerusalem Georgian Chantbook* presents hymns composed for a single day according to a solar calendar, that is, a specific, immovable date; it does not include any of the standard hymns repeated week after week or according to some other pattern, such as the eight-week cycle of the Sunday Octoechos. For 13 September, the chantbook lists 110 hymns for the vesper, matins, and liturgy cycle, most of them for the matins.[21] This service was designed specifically for the Martyrium basilica at Golgotha because the Feast of the Dedication was a celebration of the anniversary of the church's founding. Unsurprisingly, the vast majority of these hymns refer specifically to the basilica or Christ's provision for the building and the sanctifying of church structures.

Nearly every grouping of hymns directly refers to the dedication of the church. Several affirm its apostolic origins, and many turn the commemoration into a plea for continued support or grace. Representative examples from the matins service include the following:

We the believers commemorating the Dedication,
Standing today in his temple,
We praise the Savior and God and say,
Sing to the Lord, for he is gloriously (glorified).[22]

---

20 As noted in the introduction to this volume, several of the psalms make similar requests and were sung by Christians, but they were not Christian compositions.

21 For a critical edition of the 13 September hymns, see E. Metreveli, C. Čankievi, and L. Xevsuriani, *Uzvelesi iadgari* [The oldest chantbook], Żveli kʻartʻuli mcerlobis żeglebi 2 (Tbilisi, 1980), 287–98. Roughly eighty of the 110 hymns are for the matins service.

22 *Jerusalem Georgian Chantbook*, Encainia, matins, first ode, other hymns, no. 2.

Behold, behold the Lord our God,
Who founded his church through the flesh of the apostles,
And in it has taught the believers,
Knowledge of God through the apostles.[23]

Behold, behold, behold the Lord our God,
Who has adorned the church with glory,
And in it you have gathered the believers,
For the observance of the feast.[24]

It is noteworthy that the cross is something of a hymnographic afterthought for the feast. There are hymns that mention the cross, but most of them are included in the final sections of the matins service. Some of the hymns that include the cross refer specifically to its lifting, which likely suggests that they were composed when the dedication and Exaltation were still a single feast.

Given the focus of the Feast of the Dedication, it is not surprising that these hymns offer few references to violence. When they do incorporate violence, it is almost always in reference to the violence that Christ willingly suffers on the cross. In several instances, this violence sanctifies the very ground upon which the basilica has been built. For example, note these hymns from the matins service:

We praise you King, God of all things,
Who have sanctified your church by your glorious blood, Savior,
The shackles of the faithless are shattered,
And even more the holy church has been edified,
And in it believers have received incorruption.[25]

You have sanctified your church,
Christ Savior, by your holy blood,
For you are the Lover of humankind,
And in it you reign and save the believers.[26]

23 *Jerusalem Georgian Chantbook*, Encainia, matins, second ode, other hymns, no. 2.
24 *Jerusalem Georgian Chantbook*, Encainia, matins, second ode, other hymns, no. 3.
25 *Jerusalem Georgian Chantbook*, Encainia, matins, third ode, other hymns, no. 2.
26 *Jerusalem Georgian Chantbook*, Encainia, matins, fourth ode, hymn no. 2.

> By your glorious blood, O Christ our God,
> You sanctified your temple,
> And the new people that you gained,
> Who in it cry out and say while glorifying,
> Grant us your [peace].[27]

> Today the holy altar was established in the holy church,
> On which is offered the body and blood of Christ,
> For forgiveness of sins and life eternal,
> We magnify you with a hymn, the Only Begotten Son.[28]

These hymns present a palpable link between the blood that Christ shed during the Crucifixion and the sanctification of the church that now stands on the very spot. The temple, or church, is holy because of Christ's sacrifice, the site of the shedding of his blood, the site of his death. Its holiness also derives from being the place where his blood is distributed through the Eucharist to those who need it.[29]

In addition to the hymns that draw a direct connection between Christ's blood and the sanctification of a space, a small number of hymns from the matins service for 13 September commemorate other facets of Christ's suffering violence on the cross.

> He who came down from heaven was nailed to the cross,
> By his Resurrection he has crowned the churches.
> Sing to the Lord and exalt him above all, [unto the ages].[30]

> You who are Lord of heaven and earth and Creator of the ages,
> You came and willingly stretched forth your body on the cross,
> And by the cross you destroyed the sin of the first father,

---

27 *Jerusalem Georgian Chantbook*, Encainia, matins, fifth ode, other hymns, no. 4.

28 *Jerusalem Georgian Chantbook*, Encainia, matins, ninth ode, other hymns, no. 2.

29 For more on the multivalence of blood in early Christian theology, see A. Wilson, "The Blood of Christ and Christian Blood: A Model for Interpreting the Concept of Blood in Second- and Third-Century Christian Theology" (PhD diss., Fordham University, 2022).

30 *Jerusalem Georgian Chantbook*, Encainia, matins, eighth ode, other hymns, no. 1.

Feast of the Exaltation of the Holy Cross

> You brought forth from hell those who were dwelling in darkness,
> By which the churches were illuminated.[31]

These hymns share many of the motifs of the Octoechos when referring to the violence that Christ endures. His bodily suffering has the soteriological purpose of destroying sin and grants life everlasting.

The only variation of the presentation of violence in the hymns for 13 September is that a few of them turn the violence away from Christ and toward hell and "the enemy."

> Your church is adorned with praise and glory, O Christ God,
> In which shines the grace of your cross,
> And it shattered the power of hell.[32]

> Your tomb, more gloriously adorned than the sun,
> Has brought complete salvation to the world, O Christ God,
> For before, when your all-holy body was placed in it,
> In that moment, corruption was obliterated,
> And the sting of death was destroyed,
> But on this day of the Dedication,
> The holy churches rejoice,
> For by it joy is bestowed on us,
> And the sinners find forgiveness of sin and great mercy,
> By which you delivered us,
> O Lord, the Merciful and the Lover of humankind,
> Glory to your life-giving Resurrection.[33]

Like the hymns of the Octoechos, this rebounding of violence against hell, death, and the enemy focuses the singers on the soteriological impact of the Crucifixion and Resurrection. Eternal life is possible because death has been destroyed by Christ, who suffered violently, died, and rose again.

31 *Jerusalem Georgian Chantbook*, Encainia, matins, following Ps. 148, other hymns, no. 2.
32 *Jerusalem Georgian Chantbook*, Encainia, matins, following Ps. 148, hymn no. 1.
33 *Jerusalem Georgian Chantbook*, Encainia, liturgy, following petition, first mode.

Hymns for 14 September

Whereas the hymns of 13 September largely followed preexisting patterns when engaging the category of violence, several hymns for 14 September, the Feast of the Exaltation of the Holy Cross, reflect genuine innovation in this respect.[34] Not only are they likely the oldest surviving hymns of Christian composition to link divine favor to military success, they are also the first to celebrate Constantine and to position the emperor as an instrument of God's intervention in history. While it is impossible to date any individual hymn in the collection, given that the Feast of the Exaltation was a subsequent development of the original dedication of the Martyrium, one can reasonably assume that the hymns for 14 September are, on balance, of later composition than those of 13 September. One can also presume that they fall into the later range of the possible dating for the group that approximates the reign of Justinian.[35]

The chantbook contains approximately 160 hymns for the vesper, matins, and liturgy cycle of the Feast of the Exaltation.[36] The majority of the hymns include themes of violence that Christ suffered on the cross to its soteriological purpose—the destruction of death, the granting of eternal life.[37] As one might expect, the 14 September hymns focus more than the 13 September on the actual cross, both the material relic and the theological symbol, with the latter emphasizing the construction of the Martyrium. Over the course of the three services for this feast, this emphasis on the cross takes many forms, including prompts to reflect on the historic act of the Crucifixion. More unique, however, are the injunctions to venerate the material remains of the cross. The following examples illustrate how these two themes were often intertwined:

> We cry out to you, Christ,
> Who by your precious cross,

---

34 For a critical edition of the hymns for 14 September, see Metreveli, Čankievi, and Xevsuriani, *Uzvelesi iadgari*, 298–313.

35 On the dating of the various elements of the chantbook, see Shoemaker, *The First Christian Hymnal*, xv.

36 There are 13 hymns for vespers, approximately 135 for matins, and 11 hymns for the liturgy.

37 See *Jerusalem Georgian Chantbook*, Exaltation of the Holy Cross, vespers, following Ps. 140, hymns no. 2 and no. 3.

Dispelled the fall through the tree,
The debt of sin of our father,
And bestowed resurrection on the believers,
Therefore, Christ, we venerate your precious cross.[38]

The enemy was vanquished, and death was trampled down,
By the elevation of your cross on Golgotha.
The power of death was destroyed,
And the resurrection has been granted to the believers.
Therefore, we venerate your precious cross.[39]

In some instances, the 14 September hymns focus almost entirely on an injunction to venerate the remains of the cross, which of course would have fit well with the specific liturgical festival.[40] Elsewhere, the hymns speak of the cross as potent protection for the faithful:

For a seal has been given to us—the tree of the cross,
On which the Savior willingly suffered,
By the tree he crushed the pride of the enemy,
And granted us the cross as the guardian of our souls,
Let us laud him with praise and give glory to God.[41]

The eternal royal sign, which was given to us, the believers,
To vanquish the enemy, the precious cross,
Priests, bless him,
People exalt him above all, unto the ages.[42]

---

38 *Jerusalem Georgian Chantbook*, Exaltation of the Holy Cross, vespers, following Ps. 140, other hymns, no. 1.

39 *Jerusalem Georgian Chantbook*, Exaltation of the Holy Cross, vespers, following Ps. 140, other hymns, no. 2.

40 *Jerusalem Georgian Chantbook*, Exaltation of the Holy Cross, matins, second ode, other hymns, no. 3; sixth ode, other hymns, no. 4.

41 *Jerusalem Georgian Chantbook*, Exaltation of the Holy Cross, matins, second ode, other hymns, no. 5.

42 *Jerusalem Georgian Chantbook*, Exaltation of the Holy Cross, matins, eighth ode, other hymns, no. 2.

> The people of the believers celebrate today with joy,
> For Christ has raised up among us the cross as a protector,
> By which he destroyed the arrogance of the enemy,
> We who have hope in the cross,
> Worship him, the immortal King,
> We glorify him with a hymn.[43]

This sort of petition can also be found in the Octoechos, even if those hymns were not particularly focused on the physical object of the cross as protection against spiritual threats. What make the hymns of the Feast of the Exaltation distinctive are the ways in which this traditional invocation evolves to more specifically focus on physical threats from other humans, rather than spiritual ones alone.

The following hymns strikingly demonstrate the progression. The first pair of hymns are for the matins service, and at first glance suggest a traditional doxological affirmation of God's protection against "the enemy."

> You who have given us your precious cross,
> For our protection and victory over the enemy,
> Glory to you, O Jesus Son of God.[44]

> You who were raised up on the cross,
> And have illuminated the world,
> And through it you have granted us victory over the enemy,
> Blessed are you, O Lord, God of our fathers.[45]

In the Octoechos, the most obvious way to interpret "the enemy" is as a metaphor for Satan or maybe death, even accounting for the challenge of a double translation from Greek to Georgian and Georgian to English. Several hymns from the Feast of the Exaltation, however, suggest an evolution of epistemic orientation in

---

43 *Jerusalem Georgian Chantbook*, Exaltation of the Holy Cross, matins, ninth ode, hymn no. 2.

44 *Jerusalem Georgian Chantbook*, Exaltation of the Holy Cross, matins, fifth ode, hymn no. 4.

45 *Jerusalem Georgian Chantbook*, Exaltation of the Holy Cross, matins, seventh ode, other hymns, no. 2.

which the enemy might no longer be of a spiritual nature, but could just as easily be human. The following short hymn offers a prime example of the ambiguity concerning the identity of the enemy:

> As a triumphant armament, Christ,
> You have given us your cross,
> And by it we will triumph in combat with the enemy.[46]

This particular hymn is illuminating in efficiently incorporating multiple elements that suggest possibilities beyond spiritual battle. Indeed, the hymn deploys military metaphors throughout: the cross is likened to "triumphant armor," which with the community of singers expects to be victorious in "combat" against the enemy. While one could view the battle as a metaphor for spiritual combat, there are several reasons for deducing that others might have understood this particular hymn to mean more than that. That this hymn, and several others in the collection, focuses on the cross as a physical object, rather than the Crucifixion as an event, as in the Octoechos, implies that the "gift" of the cross is a tangible gift for a physical need. As such, one can reasonably conclude that those singing or hearing these hymns in sixth-century Palestine would have envisioned "combat with the enemy" in terms of real, physical threats to the Christian Roman community.[47]

Militaristic language aside, the way the same body of hymns speaks about the Roman emperor and recounts his God-given victory against enemies is the primary reason to consider interpreting hymns like this one as a recalibration of the perceived enemy as animate rather than spiritual. Note, for example, the way the following hymn for the matins service connects the wood of the cross, as both a symbol and a physical relic, to imperial authority:

> The life-giving and incorruptible sign,
> The wood of the cross, has appeared on the earth,

---

46 *Jerusalem Georgian Chantbook*, Exaltation of the Holy Cross, matins, following Ps. 148, second set of other hymns, no. 1.

47 Historical context at the time of composition, the mid-sixth century, suggests that a Jerusalem-based hymnographer would likely imagine those "threats" to be the Persians, with whom the Romans had been fighting for centuries, or possibly the Jews, with whom Roman communities in Palestine had been skirmishing.

It grants authority to the emperors,
It eliminates deception, it enlightens us all,
Priests, bless him,
People exalt him above all, [unto the ages].[48]

This hymn speaks simultaneously of the spiritual benefits of the cross—it "eliminates deception" and "enlightens"—but it is also a physical instrument that confers authority to emperors and, by extension, to the Roman Empire.

The next hymn in the service reinforces the connection between the cross and imperial authority, offering a potentially subtle double meaning to the "royal sign":

The eternal royal sign, which was given to us, the believers,
To vanquish the enemy, the precious cross,
Priests, bless him,
People exalt him above all, unto the ages.[49]

The "royal sign" might be interpreted to refer exclusively to the divine, just as the cross's ability to "vanquish the enemy" in the subsequent line might be understood to refer exclusively to a spiritual enemy, but such a spiritualizing exegesis of these hymns becomes increasingly difficult as the service continues and the link between the power of the cross, the emperor, and combat with enemies becomes all the greater. Indeed, a few hymns later, the connection between the cross, empire, and divine assistance in warfare is made explicit in a memorialization of the divine favor shown to the Roman emperor, here Constantine:

The triumphant, precious cross,
Which appeared in the Heavens to the invincible emperor,
By which he was granted victory over the enemies,

---

48 *Jerusalem Georgian Chantbook*, Exaltation of the Holy Cross, matins, eighth ode, hymn no. 4.

49 *Jerusalem Georgian Chantbook*, Exaltation of the Holy Cross, matins, eighth ode, other hymns, no. 2.

> He received the cross of Christ with joy,
> Come, O peoples, let us venerate the precious [cross].⁵⁰

There are several noteworthy aspects of this hymn. First, the hymn implies that the "invincible emperor" is the emperor of the congregation. As such, the hymn allows little space for the possibility that the Christian singer or listener has a political identity other than Roman. This is intriguing because Jerusalem was, at that time, a popular pilgrimage destination for Christians from around the ancient world, both Romans and non-Romans. Second, and more importantly, it is through the cross that the emperor "was granted victory over the enemies." While leaving some space for the interpretive agency of individual singers and listeners, the hymn appears to promote the notion that these enemies are human foes.

This hymn profoundly represents a genuine innovation in the way Christian hymnographers imagined the correlation between faith, violence, and God's intervention. No longer was violence imagined exclusively as something that happened to Christ for the benefit of salvation; instead, violence could be voiced to recall God's subsequent intervention for the benefit of the Christian ruler against the enemies of the Christian people. It is noteworthy that this shift occurs in the context of the celebration of the very instrument, the cross, through which Christ most directly suffered violence. It is equally noteworthy that Constantine used the symbol of that same instrument to mark his own military and political identity.

Although the previous hymn refers, without a doubt, to Constantine's miraculous vision of the cross, it does not name him. Another hymn similarly references his mother, Helen, and the legend surrounding her discovery of the cross without naming her.

> Boldness was given to the blessed empress by God,
> With faith she sought the tree of the cross,
> Through a miracle the cross of Christ was discovered,
> Come, O peoples, let us venerate the precious cross.⁵¹

---

50 *Jerusalem Georgian Chantbook*, Exaltation of the Holy Cross, matins, ninth ode, other hymns, no. 3.

51 *Jerusalem Georgian Chantbook*, Exaltation of the Holy Cross, matins, ninth ode, other hymns, no. 4.

One final hymn, near the end of the matins service, references Constantine by name.

> To the servant of God the emperor Constantine,
> The sign of your cross appeared, O Lord,
> And by it he vanquished the armed camp of the enemy,
> With your help, O Lord, and by the appearance of your precious cross,
> His enemies were defeated,
> By this same cross, have mercy on us and save us.[52]

This final hymn explicitly evinces a connection between the cross appearing to Constantine and God's direct intervention on the battlefield. Indeed, the hymn declares that it was through the miraculous vision of the cross that Constantine was able to "vanquish the armed camp of the enemy." The hymn then goes on to add something more with its doxological affirmation that Constantine's enemies were defeated with the Lord's help. In many ways, the hymnographers have equated Constantine's empire with the Jews of old, with the Romans now designated as the people of God. The Roman Empire is New Israel. It would only be a matter of time before hymnographers transitioned from recalling God's previous interventions on earth to invoking God to intervene in the future against the enemies of the people and their emperor.

Conclusion

It should perhaps come as no surprise that the Feast of the Exaltation of the Holy Cross was the catalyst for Christian hymnographers, loyal to the empire, to reconceptualize the relationship between faith and violence in liturgical prayer. The need to create hymns that celebrated the Exaltation and veneration of the relic of the cross prompted liturgical poets to reflect on popular legends associated with the cross as a miraculous instrument in the lives of Christians. For sixth-century Romans, no legends associated with the cross were more popular or potent than those associated with Constantine. Not only had the cross been

---

52 *Jerusalem Georgian Chantbook*, Exaltation of the Holy Cross, matins, following Ps. 148, third set of other hymns, no. 3.

the vehicle by which God revealed himself to the emperor, but Constantine had also chosen the cross as his military standard. Thus Constantine, more than anyone else, was responsible for making the cross a ubiquitous symbol of the empire itself. Of note, the Feast of the Exaltation was the only major Christian celebration that originated through imperial auspices—Constantine's patronage of the Martyrium basilica.

After hymnographers began to mine the legends surrounding Constantine's vision of the cross, they logically incorporated other aspects of the Constantinian legend, popularized by Eusebius among others, especially those directly related to the cross. As noted, Eusebius claimed that Constantine had been victorious on the battlefield because he had deployed his cross-shaped battle standard in ways that curried divine intervention. Some Christians, like Eusebius, not only saw in Constantine a divinely appointed emperor, whose adaptation of the cross symbolized his legitimacy, but also understood Christianity to be linked to the empire in ways previously unimagined. For these Christians, to be Christian was to be Roman, and to be Roman was to be Christian.

The organic development linking the veneration of the cross to Constantine and the empire would have profound implications in creating new possibilities for themes of violence in hymnography. For hymnographers closely linked to imperial interests, the sacralization of violence through liturgy would only increase.

CHAPTER 5

HERAKLEIOS, EXALTATION OF THE HOLY CROSS, AND THE VIOLENCE OF EMPIRE

A small collection of hymns originating with the Feast of the Exaltation of the Holy Cross in Jerusalem provide testimony to two important innovations in Byzantine hymnography. First, the hymns present violence in a new way. Whereas previous hymns focused on the violence that Christ, and the saints, suffered, the Feast of the Exaltation gave occasion for hymnographers to suggest that the relics of the cross not only could protect Christians from violence in this world, but also empowered Christian rulers on the battlefield. Implicit in these hymns is the notion that the cross could be an instrument of sacred violence authorized by God for the protection of the faithful. Second, a few of these hymns positioned the singing community as unequivocally Roman. Such hymns did not simply take the institution of the Roman Empire and the emperor as a given, but cast them as God-given. In the case of the emperor, his personal authority derived from the cross, whose power also aided his victories on the battlefield.

These two tendencies, or themes, developed in distinctive ways as new hymns were added to the Feast of the Exaltation in the differing political and cultural contexts of imperial Constantinople and Arab-controlled Jerusalem. In Constantinople, these hymnographic novelties came to dominate the liturgical commemoration of the feast when the emperor Herakleios ordered its adoption in the imperial capital in the early seventh century.[1] In the Constantinopolitan commemoration of the feast, notions of empire and violence became intertwined.

In Palestine, a new hymnographic form, the kanon, became popular shortly after the Arab conquest (637/638). St. Kosmas the Hymnographer composed a kanon for the Feast of the Exaltation during the early part of the eighth century. Unlike Justinianic- and Herakleian-era hymns for the Feast of the Exaltation, Kosmas's kanons were not composed in a Roman milieu, even if the vestiges of an imperial Christian culture remained key elements in his community and outlook. While these hymns have similarities with the imperial elements of hymns of Constantinopolitan origin, their language of violence predominantly reflects earlier patterns. A comparison of these two sets of hymns for the feast reveals a correlation between a hymnographer's proximity to the imperial court and his willingness to link the feast to the imperial violence.

Historical Interlude: The Persian Sack of Jerusalem, the Arab Conquest of Palestine, and Violence in Hymnography

From the fourth century BCE until the seventh century CE, the Greco-Roman world frequently engaged in war with successive empires based in Persia, modern-day Iran. The prolonged and escalating conflict between the Romans and Sasanians during the sixth and seventh centuries proved to be so economically and militarily devasting to both empires that neither could effectively resist the rise of a new military powerhouse recently united under the banner of Islam and centered in the Arabian Peninsula. Shortly after the Romans and Sasanians brokered a final peace in 628, Arab armies conquered most of Persia as well as a great portion of the Roman territories in the Near East, including Palestine. The military and diplomatic impacts of these wars provide useful contexts for analyzing the new ways in which Greek-speaking Roman Christians began to deploy themes of violence within their hymns.

---

1 Although the two themes are reflected in only a small portion of the hymns for the sixth-century commemoration of the Feast of the Exaltation in Jerusalem (as evidenced by the chantbook), they are the overwhelming perspective of the hymns that developed for the Constantinopolitan commemoration.

The final and arguably most devastating armed conflict between the Romans and Sasanians occurred between 602 and 628. Most of the fighting between the two empires had historically taken place on the frontier running along a north–south axis from present-day Armenia, through eastern Syria, and down through Iraq. For most of the early part of this seventh-century conflict, however, the Sasanians were able to penetrate deep into Roman-held territory, including Palestine. In 614 Persian armies sacked Jerusalem, destroyed a number of Christian churches, including the church of the Anastasis (Holy Sepulcher), and, among other things, looted the relics of the true cross, at the time enshrined in the church for almost three hundred years.[2] There is some question as to whether they carried off the actual fragments of wood—which were housed in gold and silver boxes, according to the late fourth-century pilgrim Egeria[3]—or perhaps seized the large bejeweled cross that the Roman emperor Theodosius II (r. 408–450) had erected at the presumed spot of Christ's Crucifixion on Golgotha, which was part of the larger church complex.[4] Either way, the capture of the cross was a dramatic event; by the early seventh century, there was no more powerful symbol of Christian faith and imperial superiority than the true cross. Its removal and transference to Persia must have caused considerable trauma, even existential angst, for Christians, who likely presumed that they were protected from destruction because of their faith in the one true God. The cross had also become an imperial symbol as much as a Christian one. Since the early fourth-century

---

2 The sack of Jerusalem is recorded in the *Chronicon Paschale*. For an English translation, see M. Whitby and M. Whitby, trans., *Chronicon Paschale, 284-628 AD* (Liverpool, 1989), 156. Cyril of Jerusalem, *Catechesis* 4.10, 10.19, and 13.4, indicates in three different comments that the cross had been enshrined in the church by the 340s.

3 The late fourth-century pilgrim Egeria provides the oldest account of the actual relics as well as the oldest account of the services commemorating the Feast of the Exaltation 14 September. Egeria, *Itinerarium* 37.1 (P. Maraval, ed., *Égérie: Journal de voyage [Itinéraire]*, SC 296 [Paris, 1997]).

4 The ninth-century historian Theophanes Confessor believed the latter had happened: Theophanes Confessor, *Chronicle*, Annus Mundi (hereafter AM) 5920 (C. Mango and R. Scott, trans., *The Chronicle of Theophanes Confessor: Byzantine and Near Eastern History, AD 284-813* [Oxford, 1997], 135-36). Also see J. W. Drijvers, "Heraclius and the *Restutitio Cruxis*: Notes on Symbolism and Ideology," in *The Reign of Heraclius 610-641: Crisis and Confrontation*, ed. G. J. Reinink and B. H. Stolte (Leuven, 2002), 175-90, at 175-76.

era of Constantine, Eusebius of Caesarea and other authors had suggested that Roman generals who used the cross as a military standard were virtually invincible on the battlefield.

When the Roman emperor Herakleios (r. 610–641) attempted to motivate his troops after the advance of the Persians in 614 his approach reflected a further integration of Christian religious themes and imperial and military ideology. Some writers contend that Herakleios's reign introduced the Christian notion of holy war.[5] Although that overstates the case—not least because it requires a very loose definition of what constitutes "holy war"[6]—it is nonetheless clear that Herakleios understood his military activity to be an obligation of his Christian faith.[7] Perhaps even more significantly, he told his troops that should they die, they would win the crown of martyrdom and be rewarded by God.[8] By the end of the campaign, Herakleios became fixated on the return of the cross to Jerusalem, leading to his becoming a key driver in the promotion and expansion beyond the Jerusalem region of the Feast of the Exaltation of the Holy Cross, which began to be celebrated in Constantinople in 628 with what were believed to be relics of the true cross.

In August 636, the Arab armies of the Rashidun caliphate won a decisive battle against a large but beleaguered Roman army just south of the Yarmuk River, at the present-day intersection of Syria, Jordan, and Palestine. This dramatic

---

5 See, for example, G. Regan, *First Crusader: Byzantium's Holy Wars* (New York, 2003). For a more scholarly and sober assessment of Herakleios's military thought, see W. Kaegi, *Heraclius, Emperor of Byzantium* (Cambridge, 2003).

6 On the historiography of the category holy war in the Byzantine period, see T. Kolbaba, "Fighting for Christianity: Holy War in the Byzantine Empire," *Byzantion* 68 (1998): 194–221, and I. Stouraitis, "'Just War' and 'Holy War' in the Middle Ages: Rethinking Theory through the Byzantine Case-Study," *JÖB* 62 (2012): 227–64.

7 For example, the chronicler Theophanes reports that Herakleios fought the Persians because they "threatened Christians" and because they were "infidels." Theophanes, *Chronicle*, AM 6113, 6114 (H. Turtledove, trans., *The Chronicle of Theophanes* [Philadelphia, 1982], 14–16).

8 Theophanes, *Chronicle*, AM 6115 (Mango and Scott, *The Chronicle of Theophanes*, 19): "The Emperor assembled his army and encouraged and exhorted them. He readied them by saying, 'Brothers, do not be troubled by your enemies' numbers for, God willing, one will chase thousands. Let us sacrifice ourselves to God for the salvation of our brothers. Let us take the martyr's crown so the future will applaud us and God will give us our reward.'"

defeat was the last substantial effort by the Byzantines to thwart Arab advances in that part of the Eastern Mediterranean. The defeat also meant the effective isolation of Jerusalem from Roman supply lines and reinforcements. The following year, an Arab army commanded by Abu Ubaidah began a siege of Jerusalem. After six months and little hope of Roman assistance, the patriarch of Jerusalem, Sophronios, surrendered the city to the Rashidun caliph Umar (r. 634–644). The arrangement between Sophronios and Umar granted certain protections to Christians, but it also required them to pay additional taxes and prohibited some public displays of Christian worship. The population of Palestine remained majority Christian for several more centuries, but never again came under the political control of the Roman Empire. With time, the balance between the Muslim and Christian populations would shift toward the former becoming the majority.

The dramatic change in the political context had immediate consequences for local Christians, including those who had ostensibly abandoned the world for ascetic vocations. Most noteworthy for the purposes here is that this new political and religious landscape laid the foundation for the expansion of a distinctive form of Christian hymn that would subsequently be exported to Constantinople and from there to much of the rest of the Eastern Christian world. Within this context, Palestinian hymnographers came to compose hundreds, if not thousands, of hymns still sung in the modern Orthodox Church. Cut off from the political apparatus and security of the Christian Roman Empire, some hymnographers expressed a longing for the restoration of its rule over Palestine or its divinely appointed agents. The isolation from imperial power also served to temper, by comparison, the profound escalation of the imperialization of violence that came to be associated with the Church of Constantinople in the immediate aftermath of military setbacks at the hands of the Persians and Arabs.

The Constantinopolitan Feast of the Exaltation of the Cross

Herakleios ordered an empire-wide commemoration of the Feast of the Exaltation of the Cross at roughly the same time as the conclusion of the Persian War, in 628, making him the person most responsible for its spread beyond Jerusalem. His patronage of the feast can be understood as a continuation of the imperial religious cult of the cross, which had begun decades earlier, in the later part of the sixth century.[9] At that time, a series of Roman emperors significantly expanded Constantine's use of the cross as a military symbol by carrying what they believed to be a piece of the true cross into battle.[10] Mauricius (r. 582–602) is generally believed to be the first Roman emperor to do so.[11] Mauricius's successor, Phokas (r. 602–610), continued the practice of carrying a relic of the cross into battle, as did Phokas's successor, Herakleios. In short, by the early seventh century, a cultic devotion to the cross was developing in the highest circles of the Roman army that presumed a direct link between the relic and success on the battlefield.[12]

The earliest evidence for the Feast of the Exaltation being commemorated in Constantinople is from 628, when a liturgical "exaltation" took place on 14 September for the first time in Hagia Sophia.[13] According to the *Chronicon Paschale*, the sponge presented to Christ during his Crucifixion was acquired by Herakleios from Jerusalem and ceremonially attached to the relic of the cross during its third lifting.[14] Until recently, the general assumption had been that the first celebration had taken place in 614, but Holger Klein has compellingly demonstrated that the folios of the *Chronicon Paschale* were assembled incorrectly during the most

---

9 For an examination of the ideological and political opportunities provided by the emperor's association with the cult of the cross, see Drijvers, "Heraclius and the *Restitutio Crucis*," esp. 182–83.

10 Like other premodern armies, the Romans, both before and after the adoption of Christianity, believed that the religious devotion and religious rites of soldiers played a key role in war. Christian generals, including the emperor, brought multiple religious objects (relics, icons, and so on) into battle with the expectation that they would trigger divine support and increase the likelihood of victory. For the Christianized Roman armies of late antiquity, the cross was the relic par excellence.

11 One contemporary chronicler states that Mauricius put a (presumably small) piece of the cross inside a metal casing on the end of a golden spear and had it carried into battle against the Avars. See Theophylact Simocatta, *Historiae*, ed. C. de Boor (Leipzig, 1887), 5, 16, 11. Also see G. Dennis, "Religious Services in the Byzantine Army," *Eulogema* 17 (1993): 107–17, at 108. Theophylact lived at the same time as Mauricius, but he likely composed his work in 630, twenty-eight years after the emperor's death.

12 When Herakleios overthrew Phokas in 610, he justified it in explicitly religious terms. To present himself as rightful ruler, committed to Christianity, in 611 he erected a large cross atop a column in Constantinople that Phokas had commissioned. For both events, see Whitby and Whitby, *Chronicon Paschale*, 155.

13 Whitby and Whitby, *Chronicon Paschale*, 157.

14 Whitby and Whitby, *Chronicon Paschale*, 157.

recent binding of the document, such that the dates for the early seventh century are out of order.[15] A dating of 628 would be particularly significant because, as noted, that is when Herakleios secured a lasting peace with the Persians, bringing an end to the destructive decades-long war with them.[16] It is generally believed that the actual relic of the cross that the Persians captured when they sacked Jerusalem in 614 was not returned to the city until 630, but it is plausible that Herakleios and the ecclesiastical authorities in Constantinople might have coordinated a local celebration to coincide with the end of the war. This celebration would have likely employed an alternative relic of the cross, rather than the relics seized in Jerusalem. It is also possible that the Exaltation ceremony made use of the relic that Herakleios had carried with him into battle. The oldest surviving hymns of Constantinopolitan origin for the Feast of the Exaltation derive from this period. "Save, O Lord" (*Soson Kyrie*), the main hymn of the feast, was likely composed for the introduction of the celebration in Constantinople.

"SAVE O, LORD"

In the modern (Chalcedonian) Orthodox Church, "Save, O Lord" is the signature hymn for any commemoration of the cross. For the Feast of the Exaltation of the Cross, it serves as the apolytikion, or "dismissal" hymn.[17] Identifying the date and provenance of an anonymously composed, early medieval hymn is a difficult business, but there is good reason to believe that this hymn originated in Constantinople and dates to the inauguration of the Feast of the Exaltation in the capital in 628.

As for the hymn's provenance, none of the earliest Palestinian sources record it. It does not appear in the fixed-feast section of the *Jerusalem Georgian*

---

15 H. Klein, *Byzanz, der Westen und das "wahre" Kreuz: Die Geschichte einer Reliquie und ihrer künstlerischen Fassung in Byzanz und im Abendland* (Wiesbaden, 2004), 34–47. See also B. Pentcheva, "The Glittering Sound of Hagia Sophia and the Feast of the Exaltation of the Cross in Constantinople," in *Icons of Sound: Voice, Architecture, and Imagination in Medieval Art*, ed. B. Pentcheva (London, 2020), 52–100, at 52–53.

16 Although Herakleios won a major victory against the Persians at the Battle of Ninevah in 627, it was not until the Persian ruler Khoshar II was murdered by his son Kavad II, in 628, that the Persians agreed to a peace.

17 Similarly, "Save, O Lord" is the apolytikion for the Third Sunday of Lent, which also commemorates the holy cross.

Chantbook or the Armenian Lectionary.[18] Kosmas the Hymnographer composed a series of hymns as kanons for the matins service of the Feast of the Exaltation during the early part of the eighth century, but "Save, O Lord" does not appear in his collection of hymns. Thus, one can confidently conclude that "Save, O Lord" did not originate in Palestine.

The earliest written evidence for "Save, O Lord" stems from the *Typikon of the Great Church*, the oldest surviving typikon for services performed at Hagia Sophia, the cathedral of Constantinople.[19] In this typikon, "Save, O Lord" first appears for a special service attended by the patriarch on 13 September.[20] After liturgical elements that one would find in a vesper service, on this date the typikon prescribes the singing of "Save, O Lord" in the first tone.[21] It is the only occasional hymn listed for that day. On the following morning, 14 September, the typikon lists six hymns to be sung during the matins service, with "Save, O Lord" second on the list.[22] Given that the earliest attestation for the hymn comes from Constantinople, and given that the hymn itself is so closely associated with imperial interests, one can reasonably conclude that it was composed in the capital.

Scholars date the oldest manuscript of the *Typikon of the Great Church* to the tenth century. Naturally, it reflects liturgical traditions that preceded its composition, but it is impossible to know from the text alone when the various hymns of the Constantinopolitan commemoration of the Feast of the Exaltation

---

18 See G. Shurgaia, "L'esaltazione della croce nello Iadgari antico," in *L'Onagro Maestro: Miscellanea di fuochi accesi per Gianroberto Scarcia in occasione del suo LXX sadè*, ed. R. Favaro, S. Cristoforetti, and M. Compareti (Venice, 2004), 137–88.

19 A typikon is basically an instruction manual to help clerics navigate the various liturgical changes as a result of the overlapping lunar and solar calendars as well as the variations for the eight-week cycle of the Octoechos. Among other things, the *Typikon of the Great Church* includes instructions for special festal ceremonies and the text of hymns sung for those occasions. For a critical edition of the text, see J. Mateos, ed., *Le Typicon de la Grande Église*, 2 vols. (Rome, 1962–1963).

20 Of note, the typikon does not refer to this service specifically as a vesper service even though many of the elements it lists derive from vespers. It also calls for a four-day period of adoration of the cross, beginning on 10 September. Mateos, *Le Typicon de la Grande Église*, 1:24–33.

21 Mateos, *Le Typicon de la Grande Église*, 1:28.

22 Mateos, *Le Typicon de la Grande Église*, 1:28–30.

first came into practice.²³ Bissera Pentcheva has proposed that both "Save, O Lord" and another hymn, "You Who Were Lifted upon the Cross" (*O Ypsotheis en to stavro*), date to the inauguration of the feast in Constantinople, in large part because of the clear association of these hymns with imperial military concerns.²⁴ Given the lack of seventh-century sources, it is impossible to confirm this, but there is no reason to challenge the assumption that this hymn emerged within the context of the creation of the Constantinopolitan feast.²⁵ In fact, the very language of the hymn might suggest a connection to Herakleios. As Irfan Shahid documented fifty years ago, Herakleios was the first Roman emperor to adopt the term *basileus*—the Greek equivalent of the Latin *rex* (king)²⁶—as one of his titles.²⁷ Shahid argued that the genesis of Herakleios adopting the title was his devotion to Christianity and his desire to promote himself with language suitable for a genuinely Christian emperor. On this count, it is worth noting that the Greek translation of the Hebrew Bible, the Septuagint, uses the word *basileus* in reference to ancient Jewish kings. Pro-imperial Christian authors, among them Eusebius, had written of Roman emperors as the basileus, possibly due to the Septuagint.²⁸ "Save, O Lord" includes the term *basileus* in one of its petitions, but it was certainly not the first hymn to do so. A small collection of hymns for

---

23 A. Baumstark, "Denkmäler der Entstehungsgeschichte des byzantinischenritus," *OC* 2 (1927): 1–32, proposes that the seven surviving manuscripts of the typikon derive from two different productions, both originating in the ninth century. Even a ninth-century production of a typikon can reflect older elements.

24 Pentcheva, "The Glittering Sound," 60, 67.

25 For purposes here—a genealogical mapping of the sacralization of violence in Byzantine hymnography—one only needs to be reasonably assured that the hymn's dating is roughly consistent with the shift in the commemoration of the cross inaugurated by Herakleios in Constantinople. It is not necessary to prove that it was composed for the introduction of the feast in 628.

26 As Shahid notes, we should not interpret *basileus* as the Greek equivalent for the Roman *imperator* (emperor), because prior to the reign of Herakleios, the Greek term in use around the empire was always *autokrator*. I. Shahid, "The Iranian Factor in Byzantium during the Reign of Heraclius," *DOP* 26 (1972): 293–320.

27 Shahid, "The Iranian Factor in Byzantium during the Reign of Heraclius," notes that Herakleios did so officially for the first time in 629 through the issuance of an edict.

28 See, for example, Eusebius, *Church History* 8.12.13–14 (E. Schwartz and T. Mommsen, eds., *Eusebius Werke*, vol. 2.2, *Die Kirchengeschichte*, GCS n.s. 6.2 [Berlin, 1999], 776), which refers to Constantine as the *basileus*. My thanks to Stephen Shoemaker for this reference.

14 September in the *Jerusalem Georgian Chantbook* uses a Georgian equivalent in association with the Feast of the Exaltation.[29] Are Herakleios's adoption of the term and its repeated use in the Constantinopolitan hymns for the feast just a coincidence? Perhaps, but "Save, O Lord" provides everything one might expect of a hymn commissioned by a Roman military leader who for the first time uses the term *basileus* at that particular point in his reign.

In regard to form, "Save, O Lord" is best described as a troparion, the earliest and most basic form of Byzantine hymn. The term can be applied to any unique stanza in Byzantine hymnography, whether a kontakion, kanon, or sticheron.[30] Over time, individual troparia became associated with particular feast days, like the Exaltation of the cross. Given the significance of the hymn in the genealogy of the sacralization of violence in the Christian East, "Save, O Lord" is surprisingly short. The Greek original and a literal English translation of the hymn's opening are as follows:

Σῶσον Κύριε τὸν λαόν σου καὶ εὐλόγησον τὴν κληρονομίαν σου, νίκας τοῖς βασιλεῦσιν κατὰ βαρβάρων δωρούμενος καὶ τὸ σὸν φυλάττων διὰ τοῦ σταυροῦ σου πολίτευμα.[31]

Save, O Lord, your people and bless your inheritance, granting victory to the emperors against the barbarians, and protecting the empire through your cross.

Like many hymns, "Save, O Lord" builds directly from one of the psalms. The opening request, that the Lord "save ... your people and bless your inheritance," is from the final line of Psalm 28 (27).[32] This particular psalm operates within

---

As noted in the introduction in this volume, there are several other connections between Herakleios and his imagining of his reign as a continuation of the line of King David.

29 On the 14 September hymns, see chapter 4 in this volume. Romanos the Melodist used the term *basileus* when referring to the emperor Justinian, but that is not the same thing as Justinian using the title for himself.

30 E. Jeffries, "Troparion," *ODB* 3:2124.

31 Mateos, *Le Typicon de la Grande Église*, 1:28.

32 One recension of the typikon section of the *Jerusalem Georgian Chantbook* for 14 September assigns Psalm 28 for the vesper service. Although there is no mention of

a discourse of divine violence. The petitioner in the psalm, traditionally understood to be King David, asks that he not be associated with evildoers. Much of the psalm anticipates, even celebrates, that God will render vengeance upon evildoers: He will "destroy them," and he will "weaken them." The Lord will also "strengthen," "aid," and "save" the righteous, among whom the petitioner hopes to be included. Because the psalm draws a sharp distinction between those who are and those who are not on the side of the Lord, it serves as a useful biblical anchor for "Save, O Lord," which explicitly connects a petition for military victory to a pledge of proper veneration of the cross.

There is, of course, more to this short hymn than the opening reference to the psalm. Among the requests, the most striking are those to grant "victory to the emperors against the barbarians" and to protect the empire "through the cross." Of note, the prayer in its first appeal does not seek protection of the emperor or that he rule for many years—two very common elements of Roman political acclamation—but instead asks that the emperors (plural) be successful warriors. Implicit in this request is the understanding that victory is achieved through violence and the death not only of the enemies of God, but also of those fighting on behalf of the emperors. While it is, of course, possible to spiritualize the hymn toward alternative meanings, the most straightforward interpretation is that this is a hymnographic request for success in war. "Save, O Lord" appears to be the oldest surviving hymn of Christian composition to petition for success in war.[33] Although subtle, what differentiates this hymn from those of the chantbook is that with respect to violence, "Save, O Lord" is petitionary, and the others are doxological. Put another way, "Save, O Lord" asks for future victory while the chantbook hymns give thanks for past victories.

That the emperors' victories come against "barbarians" is another important aspect of the hymn's first request. Byzantine political philosophy, like that of the Romans, effectively divided the world between those living within the empire, the *oikoumene* (the inhabited earth), and those who did not, meaning the "barbarians," who were not considered among the "inhabitants" of the earth.

"Save, O Lord" in the chantbook, the overlap in the use of the psalm in both is intriguing. See Shurgaia, "L'esaltazione della croce," 142.

33 It is possible, of course, that the other hymns created for the Constantinopolitan Feast of the Exaltation are equally as old.

The Byzantines knew that non-Roman civilizations existed beyond the borders of the empire. Indeed, they traded with them, established diplomatic alliances with such groups, engaged in tribute systems with them, and so on. In Byzantine political rhetoric, however, all non-Romans were barbarians.[34] What makes this significant is the sense of Roman political superiority being so succinctly incorporated into the theological assumptions of "Save, O Lord." Thus, in this respect as well, the hymn appears to be an extraordinary innovation in the genealogy of Christian hymnography.[35] Political and religious identity are so intertwined in "Save, O Lord" that the inner logic of it presumes, much like Psalm 28, that the Lord is only the Lord of the petitioners, in this case, the Romans. That said, the hymn does not specifically exclude barbarians from the concern or love of God, though there is little doubt that the hymn presumes that God loves the Romans, or Byzantines, more than all others.

The hymn's second appeal, to protect the empire, is perhaps less explicit about the use of force, but no less significant in its implications. Indeed, the presumed logic of the entire hymn is that the Christian community secures military victory for the emperors and protection of the empire through the proper veneration of the cross by the faithful.[36] The cross preserves the people, it saves them as well, but it does so through the emperors' application of coordinated violence on the battlefield.[37] Absent from this hymn is an explicit affirmation that eternal salvation comes through Christ's willful sacrifice on the cross as well as the notion that the victory of the cross is a victory over death. In its place, the

---

34 For an excellent summary of Byzantine attitudes toward other cultures, see A. Kaldellis, *Ethnography after Antiquity: Foreign Lands and Peoples in Byzantine Literature* (Philadelphia, 2013).

35 Here, too, is a similarity to a small collection of hymns in the chantbook that take the institutions of empire and the emperor for granted. These hymns do not, however, express the rhetorical caricature of non-Romans as "barbarians" or imply the superiority of Romans to other ethnic, cultural, or political groups.

36 In other words, through veneration of the cross the community is assured of military success, which the grammatical and rhetorical structuring of the hymn relates through the opening appeal that the Lord "save your people and bless your inheritance."

37 When the Feast of the Exaltation was introduced in Constantinople, the barbarians were most likely imagined to be the Persians. In the centuries that followed, the barbarians imagined by singers and listeners surely shifted to include other groups, among them Arabs, Slavs, Turks, and crusaders.

violence of the cross is an active violence that, at least implicitly, causes death. With God's approval, the violence of the cross is a violence to be unleashed by imperial armies against their enemies.

THE FEAST OF THE EXALTATION IN THE *TYPIKON OF THE GREAT CHURCH*

As noted, "Save, O Lord" is one of six hymns listed in the *Typikon of the Great Church* for singing during the matins service on the morning of 14 September. By the tenth century, the annual Constantinopolitan commemoration of the Feast of the Exaltation of the Holy Cross had developed into a major civic event, celebrated with as many as five days of public commemoration.[38] The focal point of the nearly week long ritual was the ceremonial lifting of the cross during a special service between matins and the Eucharist.[39] In addition to the typikon, several middle Byzantine texts provide information on the public ceremony, which incorporated both patriarchal and imperial roles. These include the *Book of Ceremonies*, listing details about public imperial protocol, and several illuminated manuscripts with depictions of a patriarch lifting the cross in Hagia Sophia.[40] The only hymn prescribed by the typikon for the lifting service is "Kyrie eleison."[41]

Of the six troparia for the 14 September matins service, three are still sung in today's Orthodox Church.[42] Beyond "Save, O Lord," the most famous of these is "You Who Were Lifted upon the Cross," which is listed last in the sequence for matins. Along with "Save, O Lord," Pentcheva assigns the composition to the inauguration of the Constantinopolitan feast in 628 and presumes the active

38 For a detailed overview of the service as performed in the eleventh century, see Pentcheva, "The Glittering Sound," 55. Also see B. Flusin, "Les cérémonies de l'Exaltation de la Croix à Constantinople au XIe siècle d'après le *Dresdensis* A 104," in *Byzance et les reliques du Christ*, ed. J. Durand and B. Flusin, 61–89, at 87, vv. 48–69; and Porphyrogennetos, *De ceremoniis aulae Byzantinae* 1.1.22 (A. Moffatt and M. Tall, trans., *Constantine Porphyrogennetos: The Book of Ceremonies* [Leiden, 2017], 126–27).

39 According to the typikon, the patriarch ascended a central ambo and lifted the relic of the cross numerous times as the people sang Kyrie Eleison. Mateos, *Le Typicon de la Grande Église*, 1:30–32.

40 The most detailed account of the feast in Constantinople stems from MS Gr. A 104, Sächsische Landesbibliothek, Dresden, a slightly later text than *De ceremoniis* surviving only in this manuscript. See Pentcheva, "The Glittering Sound," 55 (for MS Gr. A 104).

41 Mateos, *Le Typicon de la Grande Église*, 1:30.

42 The three are "Save, O Lord," "The Wood of Your Cross," and "You Who Were Lifted upon the Cross," the second, fifth, and sixth hymns, respectively.

patronage of the emperor Herakleios. Although one cannot know for certain when the hymn was composed, there is little reason to challenge Pentcheva's hypothesis. Indeed, "You Who Were Lifted upon the Cross" is as imperial and militant as "Save, O Lord." The hymn reads,

> You who were lifted upon the cross voluntarily, O Christ God,
> grant your mercies to the new commonwealth that bears your name.
>   By your power, gladden our pious emperors,
> granting them victories over those with whom they war
> so that they may have your alliance as a weapon of peace and
> an invincible trophy.[43]

The typikon describes the hymn as a troparion and lists this stanza alone.[44] The hymn is actually a kontakion that initially included several additional stanzas, which were eventually dropped.[45] More important for the purposes here is the content of the stanza in the Hagia Sophia typika, which connects Christ's willful acceptance of crucifixion to the request of the people that Christ provide the emperor victory in war through the power of the cross, which is paradoxically also a "weapon of peace" and an "invincible trophy." In effect, the hymn not only authorizes but compels imperial violence against the enemies of the state.

More explicitly than "Save, O Lord," this hymn emphasizes the elision between Christian and imperial identity. The first petition of the hymn is that Christ grant mercy to his "new commonwealth" (*kaine politeia*); the second is that the Lord make the emperors learn to trust in divine power. The injunctions for violence that follow flow from these connections between faith and empire, between religious and political identity. While the hymn does not juxtapose the empire to barbarians as "Save, O Lord" does, there is little doubt that it both reflects and reinforces an ecclesiology in which the Christians of the empire enjoy a unique privilege in the divine economy.

One important distinction between "You Who Were Lifted upon the Cross" and "Save, O Lord" is that the former retains the theological and historical claim

---

43 Mateos, *Le Typicon de la Grande Église*, 1:30.
44 Mateos, *Le Typicon de la Grande Église*, 1:30.
45 Pentcheva, "The Glittering Sound," 67–68, notes that the typikon for the Evergetis monastery calls for three stanzas of the hymn to be sung.

that the cross is, first and foremost, the site of Christ's willful sacrifice. The recognition of Christ's sacrifice—he was lifted upon the cross voluntarily—serves as the hymn's doxological framing for the petitions that follow for the empire and the emperor. In this way, the hymn is more anchored to the hundreds of hymns mentioning the cross that predate it, wherein the violence of the cross is primarily a violence that Christ endures. The hymn quickly transitions, however, recalibrating the relationship between the cross and violence such that those who rightly acknowledge Christ's suffering on the cross may now petition the Lord to inflict violence upon their human enemies.

The Hagia Sophia typikon prescribes four additional hymns for the matins service on 14 September:

- troparion 1: The life-giving cross, which you gave to us in your goodness, Lord, we who are unworthy present it to you in prayer: "Save the emperors and the city that entreats you, O only Lover of humanity."
- troparion 3: Venerating you on the cedar, the pine, and the cypress, O Christ God, the church cries out to you: "By the Theotokos, grant victory to the emperors and have mercy on us."
- troparion 4: Today the prophetic word has been fulfilled, for we venerate the place where your feet stood, Lord, and, by receiving the wood of salvation, we have obtained, through the prayers of Theotokos, the liberation of sinful passions, O only Lover of humanity.
- troparion 5: The wood of your cross was only planted, O Christ, but the foundations of death were shaken, Lord. Hades had swallowed you eagerly but with trembling it disgorged you. You have shown us your salvation, Holy One, and we glorify you, Son of God, have mercy on us.[46]

Of these four hymns, troparion 5 remains part of the contemporary service; the others were replaced at some time after the production of the *Typikon of the Great Church* in the tenth century.[47] Of these four hymns, two explicitly petition on behalf on the emperor: troparion #1 asks that the emperor and the city be

---

46 Mateos, *Le Typicon de la Grande Église*, 1:28–30.
47 It is possible that the version recorded in the typikon remained in effect for the cathedral rite for as long as it survived, that is, until 1204 and the Fourth Crusade.

saved, and troparion #3 asks that the emperor be granted victory. Both of these hymns appear to fit well within a discourse of hymnographic sacred violence, but neither is as explicit as "Save, O Lord" or "You Who Were Lifted upon the Cross."

In some ways the fifth matins troparion is the most interesting of this set of six hymns because it is the only one that replicates the theological vision and understanding of violence in the hymns, focusing on the Crucifixion as an act. Like the hymns of the chantbook and the Good Friday Idiomela, this fifth troparion fixes its theological concern on the soteriological impact of Christ's sacrifice on the cross and how that event ultimately destroyed the power of death and granted salvation to humanity. There is no sense in this hymn that the true faith belongs solely to the Romans or that the proper veneration of the cross can be instrumentalized for the destruction of worldly enemies. So, while the Constantinopolitan commemoration of the Feast of the Exaltation transformed the ways in which Christian hymns not only conceptualized violence but also absorbed Roman political ideology within their ecclesiology, it is important to emphasize that elements of the previous hymnographic tradition survived in the Constantinopolitan commemoration of the feast. In addition, in the later kanon of St. Kosmas, that earlier tradition not only survived but thrived in Palestinian commemoration of the Exaltation in the early centuries after the arrival of Islam.

St. Kosmas the Hymnographer's Kanon for the Feast of the Exaltation

Not surprisingly, Greek learning and culture in Palestine went into decline in the aftermath of the Arab conquest of the region during the reign of Herakleios.[48] A century later, however, Christian hymnographers were composing kanons that

---

48 See C. Mango, "Greek Culture in Palestine after the Arab Conquest," in *Scritture libri e testi nelle aree provinciali di bisanzio: Atti del seminario di Erice (18–25 settembre 1988)*, ed. G. Cavallo, G. De Gregorio, and M. Maniaci (Spoleto, 1991), 149–60. For an excellent introduction to the experience of Christians under Islamic rule, see S. H. Griffith, *The Church in the Shadow of the Mosque: Christians and Muslims in the World of Islam* (Princeton, 2008). For an account of the ways in which Christians' veneration of the cross led to accusations of idolatry by their Muslim rulers, see C. Tieszen, *Cross Veneration in the Medieval Islamic World: Christian Identity and Practice under Muslim Rule* (London, 2017).

would be some of the most celebrated hymns of the medieval period.[49] This is not to say that these authors invented the kanon form—new research suggests that it might date to the fourth or fifth century—but simply to note that hymnography using this technique flourished in Palestine in the century after the Arab conquest.[50] The traditional account is that hymnographers at the monastery of Mar Saba were responsible for the development of the kanon form as well the majority of the hymns composed in that style. Although some of the most famous authors who used the format—among them John of Damascus and Kosmas the Hymnographer—spent time at Mar Saba, scholars have begun to question whether Mar Saba was really the hymnographic factory for kanons as long believed.[51] For the current purposes, however, it is not particularly important whether the kanon originated and thrived at Mar Saba per se. Of significance is that one of the monastery's hymnographers, Kosmas, composed a kanon for the Feast of the Exaltation of the Holy Cross during the early part of the eighth century, roughly one hundred years after the Arab conquest. With respect to the presentation of violence, this set of hymns differs dramatically from those employed for the Feast of the Exaltation in Constantinople during this same period.

A kanon, an eight- or nine-ode composition,[52] is typically for the matins service and most commonly associated with the monastic office of Palestine.[53] By the middle Byzantine period, kanons were being composed in a number of places, especially in monastic circles in Constantinople, and they were occasionally composed for services other than matins, including two special akolouthia

49 On the influence of Jerusalem hymnography in Constantinople, see S. S. R. Frøyshov, "The Early History of the Hagiopolitan Daily Office in Constantinople: New Perspectives on the Formative Period of the Byzantine Rite," *DOP* 74 (2020): 351–82.

50 See S. S. R. Frøyshov, "Rite of Jerusalem," *The Canterbury Dictionary of Hymnology*, https://hymnology.hymnsam.co.uk/r/rite-of-jerusalem.

51 For an overview of this issue, see D. Galadza, *Liturgy and Byzantinization in Jerusalem* (Oxford, 2019), 95–97.

52 If the kanon is prescribed for Lent, it consists of nine odes, and if for a non-Lenten time of year, eight. The second of the (eight or nine) odes is performed only during Lent. Typically, each of the eight or nine odes derives from one of the Canticles.

53 Some of the most famous composers of the kanon form did not live in Palestine and were not monks per se, even if they were celibate. Andrew of Crete and Germanos of Constantinople are such examples. Frøyshov, "The Early History of the Hagiopolitan Daily Office in Constantinople."

services related to battle. Each of the odes of a kanon offers a poetic variation on the special feast, biblical reading, or liturgical theme of the day. Each ode has its own heirmos (music-setting melody and rhythm) that serves as the opening stanza. In some kanons, the heirmos is followed by additional musically imitative troparia that continue the same poetic theme, until moving on to the next ode. Because the musical setting for each ode is distinctive, a complete kanon is far more musically diverse than a kontakion, which follows a single melody. The way they employ biblical content also differs significantly. Whereas kontakia take considerable liberty with the biblical text—by adding invented dialogue and imagining the inner thoughts of biblical characters—kanons are more direct in using the actual wording of the scripture, which in the Byzantine period typically led to an internalization of the biblical text or to a doxology based on the biblical referent.[54] Another difference likely derives from initial audience of the different forms: kontakia dramatically retold biblical stories for the lay audience who participated in the cathedral rite, and kanons developed for a more introspective monastic setting.

Kosmas the Hymnographer was born in Damascus circa 675 and died in Maiouma, in Gaza, circa 752. John Damascene's father adopted Kosmas in his youth, and Kosmas and John were educated together by a Constantinopolitan tutor in Damascus. Like John, Kosmas is believed to have entered the monastery at Mar Saba as an adult. In 734 or 735, he was elected bishop of the see of Maiouma.[55] Kosmas composed several kanon cycles for liturgical feasts, including those for the Nativity, Palm Sunday, each day of Holy Week, the Dormition of the Virgin Mary, the Transfiguration, the Entrance of the Christ child into the Temple, and the Exaltation of the Holy Cross.[56] Kosmas's kanon for the Feast of the Exaltation is one of his longest.[57] In addition to the eight heirmoi, which

---

54 The kanon form primarily developed within the context of the monastic rite, whereas the kontakion developed within the cathedral rite of Constantinople. For more on the difference between the kontakion and kanon forms, see J. Grosdidier de Matons, "Liturgie et Hymnographie: Kontakion et Canon," *DOP* 34/35 (1980–1981): 31–43.

55 See A. Kazhdan and N. Ševčenko, "Kosmas the Hymnographer," *ODB* 2:1152.

56 For the full list of works attributed to Kosmas, see PG 98:459–524.

57 For the kanon in Greek, see PG 98:504–9. The English translations of the hymns are my own throughout this section of the chapter. For an English translation of the full matins service for 14 September, see "Digital Chant Stand," Greek Orthodox Archdiocese of

establish the musical setting for each of the eight odes, the kanon includes an additional twenty-six troparia, for a total of thirty-four stanzas. The entire kanon remains a part of the matins service for the Feast of the Exaltation in the modern Orthodox Church.

A dominant theme of Kosmas's kanon for the feast is the numerous ways in which the cross is prefigured in the Hebrew scriptures, through the actions of Moses, Jacob, Joseph, Jonah, the Chaldean children, and others. Because the kanon is too long to assess stanza by stanza, the focus here is on three important elements found throughout it: (1) encouragement of devotion to the cross itself, (2) retention of the early hymnographic treatment of violence that emphasizes the violence suffered by Christ, and (3) occasional emphasis on the cross as an instrument that protects Christians, especially the emperor, from the violence of enemies.

The oldest extant hymns evince Christians singing about Christ's Crucifixion for as long as they have been composing them. Prior to Justinian, however, there is little evidence that Christian hymnography stressed devotion to the cross as a religious object in its own right. It was only after the Jerusalem feast at the Martyrium split into concurrent celebrations for the establishment of the basilica on Golgotha and the Feast of the Exaltation, 13 and 14 September, respectively, that the latter commemoration put greater emphasis on the relic(s) of the true cross. Kosmas's kanon emphasizes this ceremonial dimension of the Feast of the Exaltation much more than the Constantinopolitan commemoration of the feast does.[58] Several hymns emphasize the role of the cross as an object in the economy of salvation,[59] while others refer directly to the ritual of the lifting and encourage veneration/devotion.[60] Kosmas's emphasis on the ceremonial lifting of the relic and devotion to it stem from his writing for Palestinian communities

---

America, https://dcs.goarch.org/goa/dcs/dcs.html, which can be accessed a few months of the year. This is an excellent resource for contemporary church singers but does not always capture the precise language of the original Greek texts, particularly with respect to issues of violence and war.

58 See, for example, the first troparion of ode 5, PG 98:504.

59 For example, the first and second hymns of ode 7, PG 504:505, emphasize the historical role that the wood of the cross plays in the salvation of humanity. The first and second troparia of ode 9 poetically juxtapose the tree from which Adam ate, bringing death to the world, and the tree of the cross, which brought salvation.

60 See, for example, the third troparion of ode 8, PG 98:508.

for whom these rituals were lived realities and central themes to their identity as Christians. For the purposes here, what is most noteworthy about the hymnographic promotion of cultic devotion to the cross is the way in which the hymns link the site of Christ's suffering of violence to their call for devotion to the object itself. For example, the second troparion of ode 8 reads,

> Sing praises, powers of heaven, at the lifting of the wood, which is sprinkled with the blood of the Incarnate Word of God. Celebrate the restoration of mortals. Venerate the cross of Christ, O people, by which resurrection is granted to the world throughout all ages.[61]

The subsequent hymn reads similarly:

> Earthly instruments of grace, with reverent hands lift up the cross on which Christ our God hung, and the lance that pierced the body of the Word of God. Let all nations see the salvation of God and glorify him throughout the ages.[62]

Many of these hymns remind the congregation of the violence that Christ suffered on their behalf. The cross is powerful and worthy of devotion precisely because it functioned as the site of his suffering. With this emphasis, the majority of Kosmas's kanon for the Feast of the Exaltation deploys violence in traditional ways—either as a reminder of Christ's suffering or as an affirmation of the soteriological consequence of that suffering.

Despite these traditional hymnographic presentations of violence, Kosmas's kanon for the Exaltation does incorporate violence similarly to the sacralizing of imperial violence that one finds in the final Georgian hymns for the Feast of the Exaltation. While not as militant or emphatic as the Constantinopolitan "Save, O Lord" or "You Who Were Lifted upon the Cross," six of the thirty-four stanzas either connect the symbol of the cross to divine intervention against worldly enemies or make some reference to a past or present emperor. For example, two stanzas link ancient Jewish military success to actions that prefigured the sign of

---

61 PG 98:508.
62 PG 98:508.

the cross.⁶³ Note, for instance, the way that the second stanza links Moses's use of the sign of the cross to the victory against Amalek:

> The prophet Moses of old prefigured the undefiled passion when he stood between the priests, with his hands lifted up in the form of the cross, he raised a monument of victory, defeating the destroyer Amalek and his soldiers. So let us sing to the Lord Christ our God, for he is greatly glorified.⁶⁴

The third stanza of ode 4 is even a little more explicit with its connection between a Hebrew prefiguration of the cross and the marching of God's soldiers:

> The people of Israel, a sacred army drawn up in four divisions, marched as a type of witness before the Ark, gaining glory for having arranged themselves in the sign of the cross.⁶⁵

These hymns focus their attention on the Hebrew scriptures and offer no direct comparison to the present moment. They also do not indicate any explicit expectation that Christian soldiers bearing the cross will be victorious in battle; in fact, there is no reference to Christian soldiers at all. There is little doubt, however, that the singers and listeners of these hymns might imagine a connection between the veneration of the cross and earthly victories for the people of God.

Perhaps even more intriguing than these references to the Hebrew scriptures are a pair of troparia that imply a connection between the Roman emperor Constantine, the veneration of the cross, and the spread of Christianity. The fourth hymn of the kanon reads,

> The cross that appeared in the sky to the godly minded and pious emperor seemed to be the emblem of victory. It has struck down the raging of hostile foes; deceit has been overthrown; and faith in God has spread to the

---

63 Here too, Kosmas appears to follow a pattern established for the Feast of September 14, which is found in the *Jerusalem Georgian Chantbook*.
64 PG 98:504.
65 PG 98:504.

corners of the earth. So let us sing to the Lord Christ our God, for He is greatly glorified.⁶⁶

This hymn does not directly link the veneration of the cross to success on the battlefield. Instead, it vaguely notes that "raging foes" have been "struck down." The hymn does, however, celebrate Christianity's spread as a consequence of Constantine's reign, which began with the miraculous appearance of the cross.⁶⁷ Both this hymn and final one, which also refers to Constantine, cite actions in the past tense; they do not connect Constantine to the present. So, while these hymns contain some of the same elements found in the Constantinopolitan commemoration of the cross—pious emperors and the presumption that the proper veneration of the cross makes them successful—the presentation of these elements is more muted, more subtle, more akin to an earlier generation of Palestinian hymns reflected in the festal section of the *Jerusalem Georgian Chantbook*.

Two final troparia of Kosmas's kanon, the third of ode 3 and the third of ode 7, are the only two troparia that speak of Christian emperors in general, as opposed to Constantine specifically. They also offer the most explicit expectation that the proper veneration of the cross leads to protection from enemy armies in the present. The third troparion of ode 3 reads,

> When your immaculate side was speared, water and blood came out, inaugurating the covenant and the cleansing of sin, O Savior. And now believers boast in the cross, which for emperors was a strength and a firm support.⁶⁸

The hymn begins in a traditional way, with an affirmation that the cross is the historic site of Christ's suffering and by asserting the soteriological significance of

---

66 PG 98:504.

67 At the end of the kanon, Kosmas offers a more precise link to Constantine. The final troparia reads, "Wishing to show the world that the figure of your Cross is most glorious and should be venerated by everyone, O Lord, you formed it in the sky above resplendently with boundless light, the invincible armor that Constantine the Emperor adopted, which all the hosts of heaven magnify" (PG 98:508–509). While the hymn refers directly to Constantine, it makes no mention of armies, enemies, or battles. It only gestures toward the notion that the cross serves as "armor."

68 PG 98:504. As in the Constantinopolitan hymns, the Greek word *basileus* is used for "emperor."

that suffering, that is, the inauguration of the new covenant and the remedy for sin. The hymn is subtle but affirmed in asserting a link between proper veneration of the cross and the sort of protection that past emperors enjoyed. The third troparion of ode 7 is more direct. In calling those attending to adore and exalt the cross, this hymn more than any other in the kanon links the power of the cross to success on the battlefield:

> Rejoice, faithful Christian emperors, chosen by divine lot. Receiving the precious cross from God, make this trophy-bearing weapon your source of honor, for with it the enemy tribes that rashly seek battle are scattered throughout all ages.[69]

Perhaps most noteworthy about this hymn is that it functions as an exhortation to Christian emperors, rather than to all Christians. It instructs these emperors to use the cross as a "trophy-bearing weapon" and tells them that the cross will scatter those foreign enemies who rashly seek battle. Given the context of Kosmas's writing, one might ask which emperor, or emperors, does he have in mind? At the time and place of composition, there was no emperor to sing the hymn, no singer who lived in the domain of a Christian (Roman) emperor. Indeed, at the time of composition, the Christians of Palestine had been under the rule of caliphs for nearly one hundred years. Thus, the hymn appears to long for a return to a political past, wherein the Christians of Palestine were rightly ruled and protected by faithful Christian emperors, who venerated the cross. The subsequent appropriation of this kanon in Constantinople would, of course, prompt different hermeneutical perspectives for singers and listeners.

Conclusions

The Feast of the Exaltation of the Holy Cross expanded considerably during the seventh and eighth centuries. What had originally been a local cult centered on the ritual lifting of the relic or relics of the cross at the site of Christ's Crucifixion grew into one of the most popular religious festivals in the Byzantine Church. More than any other feast on the Christian calendar, the Feast of the

---

69 PG 98:509.

Exaltation provided an occasion for the promotion of Christianized imperial ideology because of the multiple legends connecting the Roman emperor Constantine to the cross and the cross to his victory on the battlefield. Whether in Constantinople or Palestine, new hymns in this period celebrated and reinforced these connections.

The impetus for the expansion of the feast was the conclusion of a multi-decade war with the Persians, which included the return of the relics of the true cross to Jerusalem in 630. These events prompted the emperor Herakleios not only to bring the festival to Constantinople but to spread it throughout the empire. In the capital, the festival was transformed into a celebration of imperial Christianity. Hymns commissioned for the Constantinopolitan commemoration not only herald the emperor but unambiguously present him as a righteous instrument of divine violence in the world. As with the David Plates produced in Herakleian workshops and court panegyrics that linked Herakleios to King David, the Constantinopolitan expansion of the Feast of the Exaltation celebrated the very notion of a sacred monarchy that presented the Roman Empire as a New Israel. Constantinopolitan hymnographers did not develop these elements out of nothing. Rather, a small collection of sixth-century Palestinian hymns had blended the ancient Hebrew notion of a God-chosen king with popular legends surrounding the emperor Constantine; but whereas the sixth-century Jerusalem hymns were little more than a tangential theme to a ceremony focused elsewhere, the Constantinopolitan celebration emphasized the link between the proper veneration of the cross and the subsequent authority it gave to the emperor to protect the people of God through violence.

The early medieval evolution of the feast occurred according to two distinctive tracks, one in Constantinople and one in Palestine. The Constantinopolitan feast provides perhaps the most explicit example of the ways in which Christian and political ideology and identity became intertwined through liturgy during the period. More than any other surviving Byzantine hymns from that time, "Save, O Lord" and "You Who Were Lifted upon the Cross," both created for the Constantinopolitan commemoration of the Feast of the Exaltation, not only presume an ecclesiology in which God is uniquely the God of the Romans, but also presume that non-Romans lie outside the Christian community. Regarding those on the outside, "the barbarians," the hymns ask that God conquer them by strengthening Christian emperors and their armies through the power of the cross. While some of the hymns of Constantinopolitan origin retain aspects of the ancient hymnographic tradition of seeing violence through the lens of Christ's suffering on the cross, most move beyond that tradition—"Save, O Lord" ignores it altogether—by employing a theology of violence in which violence is an active instrument wielded by Christians against their enemies.

In Palestine, where Muslim Arabs assumed political control in the 630s, Christian hymnographers developed new hymns to address their changing circumstances. The wide berth in biblical interpretation and character analysis enabled by the kontakion form was never really employed in Palestine. There, in the early days of Islam, monastic hymnographers emphasized a more regulated and typological interpretation of the biblical text through hymns of the kanon form. One of the most famous representatives of this hymnographic style, St. Kosmas the Hymnographer, produced an extensive kanon for the Feast of the Exaltation that creatively combined various liturgical conceptions of violence and, at the same time, encouraged devotion to the cross itself. Like the hymns of the Octoechos, several troparia in Kosmas's kanon detail the violence that Christ suffered, but several stanzas in his kanon also incorporate aspects more prevalent in the Constantinopolitan commemoration of the feast, such as the link between the symbol of the cross and military success and the notion that the emperor serves as God's chosen instrument to lead the people. Nothing in Kosmas's kanon is as explicit or ecclesiologically isolating as a hymn such as "Save, O Lord," but of note his kanon employed some of the features of imperial violence found in the Georgian hymns for the Feast of the Exaltation, even though the reality of the empire had long since disappeared for Palestinian Christians.

There is little doubt that the Feast of the Exaltation of the Holy Cross spurred the sacralization of violence in the Byzantine liturgy. In large part, this is because the Feast of the Exaltation was the only major feast of the Byzantine Church with imperial origins. Contributing to the elision of the cult of the cross and the cult of empire were the legendary connections between Constantine's vision of the cross, his mother finding the cross, the construction of an imperial basilica at the site of Christ's Crucifixion, the development of a cross-shaped battle standard, and the decision by sixth-century emperors to carry relics of the cross into battle. This elixir of imperial violence by means of devotion to the cross would continue to develop liturgically throughout the middle Byzantine period. Perhaps most noteworthy about the evidence presented here is the clear correlation between the proximity of the hymnographer to imperial influence and the poetic emphasis on imperial violence. The hymns most closely tied to imperial patronage and interest were the ones most likely to emphasize the sacralization of the empire and of violence. For those hymnographers like Kosmas, for whom the empire was more of a nostalgic memory, the poetic emphasis of their hymns lie in the more ancient tradition of presenting violence primarily in terms of that suffered by Christ, a violence that benefited all humans.

CHAPTER 6

TENTH-CENTURY LITURGICAL RITES BEFORE BATTLE AND AFTER DEATH

Enlisting Christian clergy to serve as chaplains in the Roman army counts among the many changes that the fourth-century emperor Constantine initiated that helped integrate Christianity and Roman culture. According to Eusebius, the emperor instructed Roman soldiers to attend Divine Liturgy every Sunday; even those soldiers who were not Christian were required to recite a monotheistic prayer, possibly composed by Constantine himself.[1] To facilitate worship, Constantine established field chapels in tents that could be moved along with the army.[2] Roman armies, like the armies of their enemies, had performed religious rites and employed religious clerics long before the advent of Christianity, but starting with Constantine, Christian emperors actively promoted religious observance and consistently articulated the view that Roman victory on the battlefield was linked to moral purity among the army's ranks.[3] This view was shared

---

1 Eusebius, *Life of Constantine* 4.18–20. See G. Dennis, "Religious Services in the Byzantine Army," *Eulogema* 17 (1993): 107–17, who evaluates the suggestion that Constantine authored the prayer and the impact of the changes.

2 Sozomen, *Ecclesiastical History* 1.18.

3 See Dennis, "Religious Services." The *Taktika*, the military manual composed by the emperor Leo VI at the turn of the tenth century, insisted that military success depended on genuine religious observance by the troops. G. Chatzelis and H. Harris, trans., *A Tenth-Century Byzantine Military Manual: The Sylloge Tacticorum* (Abingdon, 2017). For

by Roman historians, both before and after Constantine, who routinely attributed events on the battlefield to divine, angelic, or saintly intervention.[4]

One might presume that chaplains were noncombatants, but to remove all doubt, Christian leaders explicitly prohibited clerics from bearing arms.[5] Field chaplains presumably counseled soldiers, attended to the sick and wounded, and performed burial rites for those who died during a campaign.[6] Their liturgical duties likely would have included those of parish settings (vespers, matins, liturgy, and so on), but army chaplains also developed more specialized rites.

There is little evidence of the content of the specialized religious services for soldiers prior to the middle Byzantine period. As George Dennis observed, the first Byzantine military manual to provide any detail about such rituals was the *Strategikon* of the emperor Mauricius (r. 582–602),[7] the first emperor said to carry a piece of the actual cross with him into battle. The *Strategikon* instructs soldiers to recite the Trisagion—"Holy God, Holy Mighty, Holy Immortal one, have mercy on us"—every morning and every evening and directs chaplains to perform "other customary practices," but without enumerating what those are.[8]

The *Taktika* of Leo VI (r. 886–912) provides the earliest surviving detailed information on religious instructions in battle. Among other things, the manual suggests that soldiers take confession and receive the Eucharist prior to battle. It also instructs them to gather for a special prayer service on the evening before a battle.[9] The manual does not, however, provide the text for the service, but one such service that likely dates to the same period has been preserved in a

---

a recent account of Leo's vision of Christian military service, see M. Riedel, *Leo VI and the Transformation of Byzantine Christian Identity: Writings of an Unexpected Emperor* (Cambridge, 2018).

4 In one example, the author of the *Chronicon Paschale* attributes the thwarting of a barbarian advance on Constantinople to the active intervention of the Virgin Mary. See M. Whitby and M. Whitby, trans., *Chronicon Paschale 284–628 AD* (Liverpool, 1989), 180–81.

5 Apostolic Canon 83. The canons, derivative of the *Apostolic Constitutions*, likely date to the late fourth century.

6 See Dennis, "Religious Services," 110.

7 See Dennis, "Religious Services," 111–12.

8 Dennis, "Religious Services," 112.

9 Dennis, "Religious Services," 112.

manuscript.[10] Simply known as Akolouthia before Battle, the service consists of eleven stichera followed by a kanon of forty-six hymns. Agostino Pertusi edited and published an edition of the Greek text in 1948.[11] John Klentos's translation of the service into English appears as appendix 2 of this volume. Sometime after the publication of Leo's *Taktika*, perhaps under Nikephoros II Phokas (r. 963–969), a hymnographer in Constantinople composed a memorial service for soldiers who had died in battle or captivity. Designated for Saturday of the Souls, a customary time for the liturgical commemoration of the dead, this service constitutes the only surviving evidence of a specialized liturgical commemoration of fallen soldiers and captives from the Byzantine period.[12] The Akolouthia for Fallen Soldiers consists of six stichera and a kanon of forty hymns.[13] The text was edited and published with a facing French translation by Theocharis Détorakis and Justin Mossay. An English translation of it appears as appendix 3 of this volume.

These two prayer services represent the most developed expressions of the sacralization of violence that survive from the Byzantine period and express an ecclesiology fundamentally intertwined with imperial ideology. Indeed, in the Akolouthia before Battle, the hymns not only ask God to destroy the enemies of the basileus, but they presuppose that those fighting for the emperor are doing so on the side of God, while those fighting against him are waging war against God. In virtually every case, it is the person of the emperor, rather than the people of the empire, who signals the "side" for which God will inflict violence or offer his protection. The sacralization of violence in the Akolouthia for Fallen Soldiers is of another sort, but equally potent. Its hymns never reference the role of the basileus, but they repeatedly advance the notion that the soldiers who die fighting

---

10 For the dating of the Akolouthia before Battle, see A. Pertusi, ed., "Una akolouthia militaria inedita del x secolo," *Aevum* 22 (1948): 145–68, esp. 149–52.

11 Pertusi, "Una akolouthia militaria inedita del x secolo."

12 In the Orthodox tradition, Saturday of the Souls is the last Saturday before Lent.

13 See the introduction by T. Détorakis and J. Mossay, "Un office byzantin inédit pour ceux qui sont morts à la guerre, dans le Cod. Sin. Gr. 734–735," *Le Muséon* 101 (1988): 183–211, esp. 183–85. As the editors note, there are a few interesting elements in the canon. First, the opening letters of the stanzas of the canon form an acrostic, which translated means "Funeral Song for Defenders of Christians." Second, the anonymous author of the service included a second heirmos, a second set of hymns, for the ninth ode, which demonstrates familiarity with some of the more famous eighth-century Palestinian hymnographers, among them Kosmas.

for the empire are performing a religious act. As such, the hymns straddle the request and expectation that God will forgive the sins of soldiers who die defending the Christian community.

The Akolouthia before Battle

Whereas several hymns composed for the Feast of the Exaltation of the Holy Cross retained the most ancient hymnographic model for engaging violence—focusing on the violence that Christ suffered during the Passion—not a single hymn for the Akolouthia before Battle engages that theme. For this service, the hymnography of violence is an active violence petitioned by the army and its chaplains to ask that God, through his basileus, destroy the enemies of the Romans. The first sticheron sets the tone:

> Savior who gave strength in battle to David the wise, as [he fought] Goliath in the past,
>> destroy those who war against us, Compassionate One, and with your invisible slingshot, Christ, crush their audacity and bad intentions, so that we may praise you in faith.[14]

Just as God had enabled David to defeat Goliath, the army supplicates God to "destroy those who war against [them]" and to crush their audacity and bad intentions with his "invisible slingshot," referencing David's weapon.

Similar exhortations appear throughout the akolouthia. God is asked to "destroy the bow and arrows" of enemies.[15] The Virgin Mary is beseeched to "destroy the walls and cities."[16] "Throwing down the armies and walls of the barbarians by the hands of angels," the Word of God is invoked to grant "complete destruction of the impious and terribly arrogant people."[17] In most cases, the requests for violence are framed in terms of general destruction, but there is the

---

14 Akolouthia before Battle, first sticheron. The translations for the service are provided by John Klentos (appendix 2) and are based on the Greek manuscript published by Pertusi, "Una akolouthia militaria inedita del x secolo."
15 Akolouthia before Battle, third ode, hymn no. 3.
16 Akolouthia before Battle, third ode, hymn no. 5.
17 Akolouthia before Battle, sixth ode, hymn no. 2.

occasional graphic request, like the third hymn of ode 6, which asks Christ to "[burn] up the bodies of the enemies."[18] Similarly, the petitioners ask that God "invisibly [launch] burning arrows" so that "the armies of wicked, pernicious enemies" might be "completely consume[d] with flame."[19] Such phrases represent a degree of active violence unlike anything else in the Byzantine hymnographic tradition.

A line from one of the final hymns encapsulates the perspective running through the entire service: "Make us worthy to see the full destruction of our enemies."[20] That this request is followed immediately by the affirmation "you who are the Lover of humankind," and does so without any sense of inherent contradiction or irony, affirms the extent to which Christian faith and the responsibility of soldiers to engage in ongoing warfare were understood to be mutually reinforcing aspects of Byzantine life. It also indicates an approach to religious identity, not unlike ancient Judaism, whereby God is understood to be the God of a single people—the Romans.

Alongside these requests for active violence are additional petitions that further reflect an epistemic horizon set by the experience of warfare, particularly with respect to plunder. Perhaps the most arresting for modern audiences is the one that presents the Virgin Mary as a victorious plunderer:

> O Lady, as you are a general fighting for riches in war, immaculate one, the army bearing the name of Christ, through you, will defeat people and cities of the arrogant enemies who do not honor you.[21]

This was not the first hymn to apply a gender-bending metaphor of a military general to the Virgin Mary. A notable seventh-century prologue added to the sixth-century Akathist Hymn, *Ti Ipermachon*, refers to the Virgin as a "champion general."[22] The hymn focuses on Mary as protectress of Constantinople, celebrating in verse a popular legend that Mary had delivered the city from

---

18 Akolouthia before Battle, sixth ode, hymn no. 3.
19 Akolouthia before Battle, fourth ode, hymn no. 2.
20 Akolouthia before Battle, first exaposteilarion.
21 Akolouthia before Battle, eighth ode, hymn no. 4.
22 "O Champion General, your city inscribes to you the prize of victory as gratitude for having rescued us from calamity, O Theotokos. But since you have invincible power,

invasion by the Avars in 626.²³ By contrast, the fourth hymn of ode 8 of the Akolouthia before Battle not only presents Mary's military prowess in more of an attack, rather than a defensive, mode, but also seems to establish military plunder as a key objective. The hymn's closing refrain declares that through her intercession, the army will "defeat people and cities ... who do not honor [her]," in effect green-lighting the Romans to plunder such recalcitrant armies and cities. It makes one wonder what differentiates this sort of petition from one the ancient Athenians might have offered the goddess Athena.

Additional hymns in the akolouthia suggest that other saints also enabled military plunder. For example, the fourth hymn of ode 3 invokes the "trophy-bearing martyrs" to "gather and appear to the faithful army and fleet, making an alliance for plundering the enemies." Noteworthy about these hymns theologically speaking is the treatment of theft as something that soldiers ask God to enable, rather than something that soldiers confess to or for which they seek forgiveness. Yet another stanza asks that God grant victory so that land once belonging to "the inheritance of the Romans" might now be returned.²⁴ In all of these hymns, one sees the extent to which the discourse of military life frames the petitions of the liturgy. Military violence and its associated behaviors are not only taken for granted, they are sacralized through liturgy.

Many of the hymns in the akolouthia request protection or deliverance rather than the destruction of others. The fifth sticheron offers a clear example: "O Virgin, bride of God, entreat God who took bodily form to deliver us from the barbarian attacks and every other harm, so that we might glorify you." In the final sticheron, the Virgin is thanked for her past protection. Similarly, the fourth hymn of ode 1 thanks the martyrs for their past protection as it invokes them to accompany sailors. In the surviving sources, this appeal for protection appears earlier than the more active sacralization of aggressive violence elsewhere in this text.

Modern readers might presume a moral distinction between a petition for protection versus a petition for destruction. Even if one could track the genealogical progression from one to the other in Byzantine hymnography, it would still

---

free us from all kinds of perils so that we may cry out to you: Rejoice, O Bride unwedded "J. Mateos, ed., *Le Typicon de la Grande Église*, 2 vols. (Rome, 1962–1963), 1:28.

23 On the siege and the miraculous intervention by the Virgin Mary, see Whitby and Whitby, *Chronicon Paschale*, 180–81.

24 Akolouthia before Battle, seventh ode, hymn no. 1.

be impossible to know whether unnamed, individual hymnographers, singers, or soldiers would have registered much of a difference between the two forms of prayer. The day-to-day reality of warfare in the Middle Ages likely offered a different hermeneutical framing for whether such a distinction mattered. What is more, several stanzas in the akolouthia ask simultaneously for protection as well as for active military assistance.[25]

The only troparion in the Akolouthia before Battle that seeks repentance on the part of the army appears near the end:

> Having the power from God even to bind the enemies, forgive the mistakes of the army, the compassionate Christ forgets [the mistakes] every time they attack the enemy, in order to take with them the glory.[26]

There are several interesting dimensions to this troparion. The hymn affirms that the army's success is God-given. It further suggests that Christ "takes glory" alongside the army, when victorious in battle. The petitions that Christ "forgive" and "forget" the mistakes of the army are offered in the expectation that Christ's mercy in this respect will translate into victory on the battlefield. Of particular note, there is no indication that the "mistakes" of the army have anything to do with its martial raison d'être. Indeed, nothing in the akolouthia suggests any kind of theological ambivalence with respect to violence. There is no sense that inflicting violence on others, no matter how necessary, requires penance on the part of the soldier, as with Basil of Caesarea's prescription, which canonical interpreters repeated throughout the middle Byzantine era. In sum, violence is sacred and God-given.

ENEMIES DESERVING VIOLENCE

One of the most significant ways that the Akolouthia before Battle advances the hymnographic sacralization of violence is by positioning military enemies as the enemies of God, a rhetorical structure that authorizes violence with the

---

25 Akolouthia before Battle, fifth ode, hymn no. 5: "During hard times having as help your protection, Mother of God, and in war we wish we would find you to be fighting on [our] behalf, saving at sea and protecting on land."

26 Akolouthia before Battle, ninth ode, hymn no. 3.

theological language of prayer. By comparison, singers of the hymns associated with the Feast of the Exaltation ask God to grant victory to the emperor against the barbarians, but the precise reason that the barbarians deserved violence is never made explicit; the hymns simply mark the barbarian as the "other." With the akolouthia, however, the enemy is repeatedly presented as one who denies God, is lawless, or lacks faith. More importantly perhaps, the akolouthia consistently describes the enemy as an obstacle to the practice of true religion. For example, in the sixth sticheron, the enemy is one who "blasphemes" the Virgin. In the seventh, the enemy is deprived of the Virgin's help because of its arrogance. The third hymn of ode 4 authorizes violence because the "impious" enemy has broken "holy things." And the fourth hymn of ode 4 describes the enemy as "barbarian atheists" (βαρβάρων ἀθέων). Throughout the akolouthia, such condemnations of the enemy for rejecting religious observance are frequently juxtaposed to the faithfulness of the army fighting for God. Several troparia declare the singers to be an "army bearing the name of Christ."[27] Earlier in the service, the second sticheron asks God to "have mercy on the army that honors you." In the first hymn of ode 9, God is petitioned to destroy the enemy's plots and to "fight [alongside] those who recognize your power." In yet another example, Christ is asked for victory on the basis that "your army . . . agrees that you are the life-giving Son of God."[28]

The sacralization of violence against the enemies of God is developed further still by poetically framing the request for divine intervention in terms of conditional worship. In several troparia, the logic of the petition runs along these lines: if we are granted victory against the enemy, then we will be able to worship you. For example, in the fifth sticheron the Virgin Mary is beseeched to "deliver us from the barbarian attacks and every other harm, so that we may glorify you."[29] Another hymn asks to be made "strong against barbarian evils" so that "we may cry: Glory is due to your might."[30] The final sticheron employs the same theme

---

27 See, for example, Akolouthia before Battle, first ode, hymn nos. 2 and 4; eighth ode, hymn no. 4; ninth ode, hymn no. 2.

28 Akolouthia before Battle, first exaposteilarion.

29 Akolouthia before Battle, fifth sticheron.

30 Akolouthia before Battle, sixth ode, hymn no. 6.

but alters the grammatical structure such that the army gives thanks to the Virgin because they know that it has already "acquired [her] protection."[31]

The demonization of enemies is not unexpected; medieval warfare was brutal and its realities surely presented a pastoral need that these hymns of the Akolouthia before Battle sought to address. Liturgy offered soldiers a means to affirm the virtue of their sacrifice and to offer solace for their fear and suffering. In the late ninth or early tenth century, when the prayer service was composed, Byzantine soldiers frequently fought against non-Christians, especially Muslims. Thus, it is not surprising that the akolouthia depicts the enemy in terms that contrasts Byzantium's imperial Christianity and the religion of the enemy, presenting them as faithless, godless, atheistic, and so on. One, however, wonders whether the chaplains who performed these services ever altered their hymns in anticipation of battle with fellow Christians, especially fellow Byzantines. By the twelfth century, Byzantine armies were more likely to be fighting Christians from the West than confronting anyone else. By the thirteenth century, when the Byzantine political structure splintered and created multiple claimants to the throne, it is plausible that competing armies, believing themselves to be fighting on behalf of the authentic basileus, both performed a similar akolouthia prior to battle. Also, in the thirteenth, fourteenth, and fifteenth centuries, the various factions of Greek Christians repeatedly allied themselves with Western and Turkish forces as they warred against one another.

SACRALIZING THE BASILEUS AND THE IMPERIAL

The aspect of the Akolouthia before Battle most consistent with the Constantinopolitan hymns for the Feast of the Exaltation of the Holy Cross is the extent to which the Roman emperor, the basileus, is presented as a sacred figure for whom all enemies are the enemies of God and all loyal soldiers are the righteous instruments of God. None of the hymns written prior to the feast and examined here explicitly equate the Romans and the Christians; some of the idiomela did, however, distinguish the community of singers vis-à-vis the "lawless Jews." More to

---

31 Akolouthia before Battle, eleventh sticheron. In a slightly different modification, the fourth hymn of ode 7 invokes the assistance of the martyrs on the basis of the fact that the army faithfully honors their memory (unlike the enemy). The army of the martyrs who in the past destroyed the crafty armies of the demons, now destroy the armies of the enemies raging against us who in faith are acting in honor of your memory."

the point, none of the hymns analyzed here even mentioned the emperor,[32] let alone presented him as a sacred figure selected by God to preserve the people through violence. That, however, is precisely what the Akolouthia before Battle does. It presents the basileus as the figure who stands for the cause of moral good in the context of war.

As noted, the akolouthia opens by invoking the legacy of the ancient Hebrew saint King David. It was during the reign of Herakleios that the imperial court deliberately cultivated a connection to David, seeing itself as the rightful continuation of biblical kingship.[33] The Septuagint had used the word *basileus* to refer to David and the other ancient Jewish kings, perhaps the reason for its adoption by the Romans. David, more than any other biblical figure, represents the righteous and wise soldier-king. Not only was he hand picked by God, he had also successfully led the people of God in battle against their enemies.[34] While court panegyric and art presented Herakleios in a David-like way, the hymnography of the Herakleian period—that is, the Constantinopolitan hymns for the Feast of the Exaltation—did not make this connection to the same degree as the Akolouthia before Battle.

Whereas the opening sticheron in the akolouthia might not invoke the emperor directly, the appeal to King David boldly asserts the connection between God and his hand-chosen royal servant. Indeed, the second sticheron points directly to the Roman basileus: "gladden our faithful basileus, destroy the column of the barbarians and have mercy on the army that honors you." Then, in the fourth sticheron, the connection between David and the Roman emperor is made explicit: "Lord, who fought alongside the most gentle David to subordinate the foreigner [ἀλλόφυλον], fight alongside our faithful basileus; and with the weapon of the cross destroy our enemies." The hymn recalls the history of

---

32 See chapters 1–3 in this volume.

33 See the introduction in this volume. The so-called David Plates, held by the Metropolitan Museum of Art, New York, likely commissioned by the emperor Herakleios, provide clear evidence of the efforts of the Byzantine court to tie its legitimacy to the ancient Hebrew king.

34 For the way various emperors, including Herakleios, sought to project themselves as the new David, see J. McGuckin, "A Conflicted Heritage: The Byzantine Religious Establishment of a War Ethic," *DOP* 65/66 (2011–2012): 29–44, esp. 29–31. McGuckin also examines the efforts of their supporters in this endeavor.

divine intervention in war, it affirms the faithfulness of the basileus, it identifies the cross as a weapon, and it asks that God use this weapon to destroy enemies as it implores him to fight alongside the emperor. In short, this single troparion pulls together several different strands in the genealogy of sacred violence to request divine intervention against the enemies of the emperor. Moreover, the specific framing of the troparion presumes that the enemies of the emperor are both the enemies of the singers and, more importantly, the enemies of God.

Approximately half of the fifty-plus troparia in the Akolouthia before Battle directly reference the basileus and petition God on his behalf. Given the length of the service, it constitutes an unprecedented integration of Roman political interest in the liturgy. In most instances, the emperor is referred to as the "faithful basileus."[35] Notably, one of the few times the faithfulness of the basileus is not explicitly proclaimed is during "Save, O, Lord," chanted just prior to the start of the kanon as the tenth sticheron. Of course, the emperor is referenced in other ways without being explicitly called basileus. For example, he is identified more generally as "he who reigns over your army."[36] Linking the imperial "dynasty" to divine selection is another way various troparia both name the emperor indirectly and also provide theological legitimacy for his rule. For example, the final hymn of ode 3 asks God to grant "your dynasty" a defensive weapon, which is enhanced by the intercession of "the trophy-bearing army of apostles and martyrs."[37] Another troparion refers to the emperor as the "God-crowned basileus," who, unlike the enemy, provides for religious festivals that honor God.[38] These and similar troparia cement the legitimacy of the emperor and his family in the context of prayer, and thus authorize him to wage war on God's behalf. These hymns functioned in multiple ways, but there is little doubt that one of the most important was the use of ecclesial singing to build political legitimacy and martial loyalty among the rank-and-file soldiers.

---

35 A typical example is "through divine power strengthen army and fleet against enemies who blaspheme you and give victory through them to your faithful basileus" (Akolouthia before Battle, ode 1, hymn no. 1).

36 Akolouthia before Battle, fourth ode, hymn no. 1.

37 Akolouthia before Battle, third ode, hymn no. 6. In another troparion, the "undefeatable dynasty" is identified as belonging to the Virgin Mary (sixth ode, hymn no. 5).

38 Akolouthia before Battle, seventh ode, hymn no. 3.

The sacralization of violence and the sacralization of the basileus intertwine throughout the hymns of the akolouthia. Note, for example, the interplay between the two themes in the following troparia:

> Make the basileus whom you chose appear as a trophy-bearing victor against the impious enemies, Lover of humankind, making the reins and scepter of his pious rule powerful in his hands.[39]

Another reads,

> Subdue with your divine power the land and people and cities of lawless enemies and tyrants, O King of all, through your faithful basileus for the preservation of your people.[40]

In the first example, the basileus is identified as hand-selected by God. In the second example, the terminology used to refer to God—"King of all" (πανβασιλεῦ)—plays on the akolouthia's principal term for the emperor, *basileus*, further reinforcing his sacred status. Yet, the focus of both hymns lies in the request for divine assistance so that the emperor might be successful against barbarian and lawless enemies.

The sacralization of the basileus indirectly functions as a sacralization of the very notion of empire, a relationship also suggested in a few hymns for the Feast of the Exaltation. Nevertheless, few of the troparia in the Akolouthia before Battle speak of the empire or the people as a whole. For this service, the hymnography focuses primarily on the figure of the basileus, who leads soldiers in battle. There is only one direct mention of "Romans" in the entire service:

> Regally and mightily, he who is master of all creation, make the earth which was taken from the inheritance of the Romans by the barbarian tyranny subject to the basileus who is proud in you, O you who govern everything.[41]

---

39 Akolouthia before Battle, eighth ode, hymn no. 1.
40 Akolouthia before Battle, sixth ode, hymn no. 1.
41 Akolouthia before Battle, seventh ode, hymn no. 1.

Perhaps most interesting about this reference to "Roman inheritance" is that it describes land that has been lost, but which the petitioners are now asking God to return through the military exploits of the basileus, a faithful Christian.

The Akolouthia for Fallen Soldiers

The presentation of violence in the Akolouthia for Fallen Soldiers is wholly different from that in the Akolouthia before Battle. Whereas the prebattle service invokes God's aid for the destruction of enemies and the perseverance of the basileus and his soldiers, in the memorial service, the discussion of violence focuses almost entirely on the sacrifice of soldiers who died defending fellow Christians. The violence of this service is a violence recalled, not solicited. Of the forty-six hymns of the service, only two make reference, in passing, to Christ's empowerment of soldiers against enemies.[42] Although one might expect a memorial service to focus on the sacrifice of soldiers and petitions for their spiritual salvation, the hymns of this service make little effort to typologize or otherwise connect the soldiers' violent death to Christ's Passion. Only one hymn refers to the shedding of Christ's blood, which is presented as an inspiration for soldierly courage.[43] Instead, the hymns that refer to Christ's power invoke his mercy and compassion.[44]

Nearly every troparion in these hymns notes that the soldiers died in the line of duty or in captivity, but there are no instances of graphic descriptions of their deaths. The closest is a reference in the fifth sticheron: "They purified their souls by shedding their blood, they suffered death by the edge of swords, they were reduced to captivity and were happy to pass into the world beyond."[45] This hymn is one of only two that refer to the shedding of blood and it is the only troparion that mentions a weapon. The second sticheron notes that these fallen soldiers were "beaten" and "slaughter[ed]." None of the forty hymns of the kanon deploy anything

---

42 Akolouthia for Fallen Soldiers, fourth ode, hymn no. 2; seventh ode, hymn no. 1.

43 The opening hymn of ode 6 suggests that the soldiers were inspired by Christ's willingness to shed his "immaculate blood." The opening hymn of the second heirmos of ode 9 references Christ's death, but not the violence that caused it.

44 The first hymn of ode 4 entreats Christ that the fallen soldiers might, in death, find union with his Passion.

45 Akolouthia for Fallen Soldiers, sticheron 5.

resembling graphic violence. In this way, too, the violence of the Akolouthia for Fallen Soldiers differs significantly from that of the Akolouthia before Battle.

CHRISTIANS VERSUS BARBARIANS

The Akolouthia for Fallen Soldiers and Akolouthia before Battle align in the presumption that only those soldiers fighting on behalf of the empire are Christians and that all the empire's enemies are "barbarians." Of course, it is no surprise that a Christian memorial service commemorates fellow Christians, but the texts do not simply combine the soldiers' faith and their occupation as mere coincidence; they very much present the soldiers' engagement in armed conflict as a testimony to and consequence of their faith. In fact, the prayer services repeatedly describe the soldiers' military contribution and willingness to die as being offered directly to Christ. For example, the first hymn of ode 1 notes,

> Savior, King of all, we venerate your nature as God immortal and as one subject to death like us; make worthy of joy those of the elect who died on behalf of you.

The third hymn of ode 7 declares:

> Christ, give to the people who honor you harbors of salvation, those who have put forth their souls on the front lines and in captivity. They who died on your behalf, deem them worthy of joy.

In the second hymn of ode 2, the hymnographer grants agency to Christ, who selects the men as his defenders:

> To protect your chosen people from the hands of the barbarians, Christ, you provided brave warriors who died honorably in battle and in captivity.[46]

Hymns like these declare that a soldier's service—not only his death on behalf of the community, but also the act of carrying out his duties—is a service to Christ himself. As a result, they aver that military service is a religious act, a sacred act.

---

46 Akolouthia for Fallen Soldiers, second ode, hymn no. 2.

Like the hymns of the Akolouthia before Battle and some of the Constantinopolitan hymns for the Feast of the Exaltation of the Cross, the Akolouthia for Fallen Soldiers routinely juxtaposes the Christian soldiers and the barbarians. In the first hymn of ode 2, the hymnographer also references the soldiers' Christian faith versus the barbarism of the enemy: "The descendants of Rome, a flock of the holy shepherd, by confessing you they faced the cruel barbarians and, although they died, they obtained life."[47] "Rome" is mentioned only this one time, but the contrast between Christian soldiers and barbarians runs throughout the text. Because the Akolouthia for Fallen Soldiers never mentions the basileus and defines the soldiers as the "protectors of Christians," rather than protectors of the empire, the juxtaposition of the fallen soldiers and the barbarians more explicitly stresses the religious identity of the soldiers compared to their treatment in the Akolouthia before Battle. This latter service was designed exclusively for soldiers and likely reinforced for them that the basileus had been appointed by God and that their loyalty to him was therefore a service to God. Akolouthia for Fallen Soldiers, however, presupposes the presence of civilian churchgoers and emphasizes the bond of Christian faith between them and the dead soldiers.

SOLDIERS' SACRIFICE, THE ATONEMENT OF SIN, AND THE SACRALIZATION OF VIOLENCE

The most dynamic and arresting aspect of the Akolouthia for Fallen Soldiers is the extent to which the hymns repeatedly gesture toward the idea that the soldiers' sacrifice should serve as an expiation for their sin. In many cases, as illustrated by the following examples, this is framed as a petition for salvation on behalf of fallen soldiers and captives:

> Jesus, purify your most valiant soldiers, who as youths threw themselves into the fray against the enemies, along with those who were taken prisoner, for on your behalf they bathed in blood.[48]

---

47 Akolouthia for Fallen Soldiers, second ode, hymn no. 1.
48 Akolouthia for Fallen Soldiers, first ode, hymn no. 3.

Christian troops, most faithful and steadfast, who died for your people, may their souls be received by you, only King, with sweet-smelling incense.[49]

Savior, show them to be members of the illuminated camp of remitted sin those faithful who perished while fighting or in prison. Accept their piety.[50]

My Savior, with your name as a protective wall, your army routed the barbarian masses. Encamp their souls in your luminous fortress.[51]

Spreading wide their hopes in you, the ones whose bravery lies in your power saved the lives of the whole Christian people. Compassionate one, grant them rest in the abodes of the righteous.[52]

Immortal and unique one, having power over all flesh, judge as worthy of the light those who for the sake of your flock were destroyed in battle or in prison at the hands of the barbarians.[53]

This pattern also characterizes the forty hymns of the kanon. As already noted, many of these hymns affirm that a soldier's service and sacrifice were acts of faith. It is with this presumption in mind that the petitioners beseech Christ's mercy on behalf of their fallen brethren. Indeed, many of the hymns present their case as a kind of soteriological quid pro quo—because the soldiers were x, did y, or endured z, Christ should grant salvation to them.

Perhaps even more intriguing is a pair of hymns that frame the prospects for salvation not so much as a petition, but as an expectation:

The souls of your faithful soldiers, Christ, have been transported as virgins into your divine bridal chamber, still imprinted by the wounds and massacres of which they were victim.[54]

---

49 Akolouthia for Fallen Soldiers, second ode, hymn no. 3.
50 Akolouthia for Fallen Soldiers, sixth ode, hymn no. 2.
51 Akolouthia for Fallen Soldiers, fourth ode, hymn no. 2.
52 Akolouthia for Fallen Soldiers, eighth ode, hymn no. 1.
53 Akolouthia for Fallen Soldiers, ninth ode, hymn no. 1.
54 Akolouthia for Fallen Soldiers, third ode, hymn no. 2.

Having been marked by the drops of your immaculate blood, divinely shed, Jesus, your servants died reducing the strength of the enemies and so they came happily to make camp near you.[55]

Neither hymn explicitly declares that a soldier's death in service to fellow Christians automatically grants salvation, but they do appear to take that belief for granted. In the first hymn, the hymnographer suggests that the souls of fallen soldiers will enter the afterlife, poetically described as Christ's bridal chamber, as virgins but bearing the markings of military wounds. In the second hymn, the metaphors work differently. Here, the soldiers received their miraculous "markings" (that is, the drops of Christ's immaculate blood) in life. Emboldened by those markings they fought valiantly. So, now, in death, they are able to "make camp" near Christ.

While no hymn in the memorial service directly compares fallen soldiers to martyrs, the first hymn of ode 5 creates an imaginative space bringing the soldiers and martyrs into communion through a common bond to the "firstborn" (that is, the holy innocents slaughtered by Herod): "King of all, your soldiers faced danger on behalf of the faith and your name. Place them in the abodes of the firstborn, as being the equals of martyrs." The hymn is remarkable and presents a clear example of the way the service sacralizes military service. Like several other troparia in this akolouthia, it affirms that the memorialized soldiers had acted on behalf of their faith and in service to God. Like many others, it functions as a petition and therefore does not take the salvation of soldiers for granted; rather, it asks for it. The hymn effectively requests that God equate the soldiers' sacrifice to that of the holy innocents, who are themselves comparable to the martyrs. I know of no other hymn in the Byzantine tradition that comes so close to declaring death in military service to be act of martyrdom. Over the course of the Byzantine period, the Eastern Christian traditions did come to identify certain religious qualities or acts of piety, especially heroic asceticism, as grounds for thinking of a saint as being "equal to the martyrs." The early Egyptian ascetics provide the most obvious example. This hymn, however, is distinctive in being the only one to propose military service in the name of God as a quality akin to martyrdom in the way

---

55 Akolouthia for Fallen Soldiers, sixth ode, hymn no. 1.

that the pious asceticism of a St. Anthony or St. Pachomius can be considered akin to martyrdom in the scheme of Christian sanctity.

Scholars have long pointed to a supposed showdown between the emperor Nikephoros II Phokas and Patriarch Polyeuktos over the issue of whether soldiers who died fighting Muslims should be regarded as martyrs by the church.[56] Only one account, written a century later by the chronicler John Skylites, offers details on the conflict. According to Skylites, the patriarch, along with his synod, rejected the emperor's request on the basis of its being inconsistent with the view advanced by St. Basil that killing in war resulted in spiritual pollution. Meredith Riedel has questioned whether the "showdown" actually occurred, at least the way Skylites presents it.[57] She also goes on to propose that the question regarding fallen soldiers must have been ongoing at the time—especially in light of the church having declared a group of executed prisoners to be martyrs—and points to the Akolouthia for Fallen Soldiers as evidence of this. Among her most insightful observations about the akolouthia is that σφαγῆς, an ancient word with religious overtones that the hymns of the service typically use for "death," implies a kind of blood sacrifice.[58] Such a classicizing poetic gesture simply reinforces the extent to which the hymnographer, like others around him, understood soldiering in defense of the Christian community to be a religious act, a sacred act.

---

56 See the introduction, in this volume, and P. Stephenson, "About the Emperor Nikephoros and How He Leaves His Bones in Bulgaria: A Context for the Controversial Chronicle of 811," *DOP* 60 (2006): 87–109; G. Dagron and H. Mihaescu, eds., *Le traité sur la guérilla (De velitatione) de l'empereur Nicéphore Phocas (963–969)* (Paris1986), 284–186; McGuckin, "A Conflicted Heritage," 43; and P. Viscuso, "Christian Participation in Warfare: A Byzantine View," in *Peace and War in Byzantium: Essays in Honor of George Dennis*, ed. T. S. Miller and J. Nesbitt (Washington, DC, 1995), 33–40, at 37–39.

57 M. Riedel, "Nikephoros II Phokas and Orthodox Military Martyrs," *Journal of Medieval Religious Cultures* 41.2 (2015): 121–47. Riedel's challenge to the reliability of Skylites account has merit, even if some of her justifications are misplaced. For example, there is no reason to believe that the military manuals and the canon law tradition would necessarily be aligned or that Nikephoros's "Orthodoxy" would have been entirely consistent with the tradition just because he was pious and ascetic. Moreover, whereas Riedel sees the appeal to Basil of Caesarea on this particular question as odd and thereby historically unlikely, his canon remains the single most obvious authoritative source within the tradition to reject a sacralization of military violence, which is what the proposal entailed.

58 Riedel, "Nikephoros II and Orthodox Military Martyrs," 138. As she notes, the Septuagint uses the word to describe sacrificial slaughter.

In short, even if the Akolouthia for Fallen Soldiers stops short of explicitly declaring these men to be martyrs, there is little reason to doubt that these hymns constitute a sacralization of the violence endured and, by extension, enacted by Christian soldiers in defense of their fellow Christians. The text may not be invested in the sacralization of the emperor in the way that the Akolouthia before Battle is, but it is no less invested in the sacralization of the Christian soldier. One wonders if the text never caught on—it did not become part of the Byzantine Triodion tradition (the Lenten service book, which includes the Saturday of the Souls service)—because it went too far regarding the sacralization of military service and the sacralization of violence. The age of Nikephoros II Phokas clearly pushed the Byzantine Church to consider whether military service constituted a pious or sacred act. Although some were clearly eager to advance this notion, their movement did not gain wide adherence and was, in the end, rejected by the church.

Conclusion

It has been commonplace among Orthodox Christian scholars to juxtapose Orthodox theological reflections on war and violence to those of the presumably more militant Islamic and crusader communities with which the Byzantines regularly fought in the Middle Ages.[59] For example, Father Stanley Harakas, a pioneer in Orthodox theological ethics, suggested that the Orthodox East never sacralized violence the way the medieval Western Christian tradition did.[60] While it may be true that Byzantine theologians never developed a doctrine of penitential violence like the proponents of the Crusades, the Akolouthia before Battle and the Akolouthia for Fallen Soldiers demonstrate decisively that some Byzantine hymnographers did, in fact, sacralize violence through liturgy. These were specialized services designed to accommodate the pastoral needs of the army and those close to it. The Akolouthia before Battle was not designed for

59 See, for example, P. Hamalis and V. Karras, eds., *Orthodox Christian Perspectives on War* (Notre Dame, IN, 2017); A. F. C. Webster, *The Pacifist Option: The Moral Argument against War in Eastern Orthodox Theology* (San Francisco, 1998), whose position evolved over time; and A. F. C. Webster and D. Cole, *The Virtue of War: Reclaiming the Classic Christian Tradition East and West* (Salisbury, MA, 2007).

60 S. Harakas, "The Teaching on Peace in the Fathers," in *Wholeness of Faith and Life: Orthodox Christian Ethics*, pt. 1 (Brookline, MA, 1999), 137–61, at 153–54.

broad usage, and no evidence suggests the adoption of these types of hymns in a parish or monastic environment. In addition, the memorial service does not appear to have been adopted beyond the apparently intended broader Constantinopolitan audience. It also failed to survive in the Orthodox liturgical tradition. Nevertheless, the hymns offer an arresting juxtaposition to all the other groups of hymns examined in this genealogy. The most ancient pattern for engaging violence through hymnography—focusing on the Crucifixion and Passion of Christ—does not appear in these services. Rather, these services were designed as supplications to God, through the saints, that the emperor and his soldiers be victorious on the battlefield and, in the aftermath of battle, that the soldiers who gave their lives find eternal salvation.

These texts represent the most developed expression of a sacralization of violence that survives from the Byzantine period, and this sacralization reflects an ecclesiology fundamentally intertwined with imperial ideology. The Akolouthia before Battle especially presupposes that those who fight for the emperor are fighting on the side of God and those who fight against him are fighting against God. In virtually every case, it is the person of the emperor, rather than the people of the empire, who signals the "side" for which God will inflict violence or offer his protection. What is more, throughout the service, the singers and their enemies are divided, respectively, into those who do and those who do not properly reverence God. As a result, the singers prayerfully hope for victory for their side and that their enemies burn alive. The Akolouthia for Fallen soldiers is less invested in the emperor's divine sanction but no less invested in the notion that soldiering on behalf of the Christian community—the empire—is an act of religious devotion, one worthy of the remission of sin.

CONCLUSION

In the waning centuries of the Byzantine Empire, the Church of Constantinople revised the matins service for Holy Saturday morning.[1] The most distinguishing feature of this revision was the introduction of short hymns, or encomia (lamentations), interspersed among individual verses of Psalm 118 (119), the longest of the psalms. The first mention of the encomia appears in thirteenth-century manuscripts, but the oldest surviving repertoire of the actual hymns is in a 1522 printing of the Triodion, a liturgical typikon for the services of Lent and Holy Week.[2] The number of lamentations varies in subsequent printings. In the modern editions of the Triodion, there are 185 verses interspersed throughout the psalm.[3] The dirge-like pace of the singing in the modern church makes this the longest service of the liturgical year.[4]

---

1 In the modern Orthodox Church, this service is typically performed on Friday evening, after sundown, which would make it Saturday according to the Orthodox liturgical calendar. In the Greek Orthodox Church in the United States, this is the most attended service of the year.

2 See A. Calivas, "Great and Holy Saturday," Greek Orthodox Archdiocese of America, https://www.goarch.org/-/great-and-holy-saturday/.

3 The number of verses has grown since the 1522 Triodion.

4 Mother Mary and K. Ware, *The Lenten Triodion*, vol. 2, *The Service Books of the Orthodox Church* (South Canaan, PA, 1994), 622–61, reproduces the entire service, which most service books do not contain.

Given the scheduling of this service between Good Friday and Easter, it comes as no surprise that the encomia emphasize the death of Christ and the Resurrection.[5] In general terms, the content of the hymns is similar to that of the ancient eight-week Sunday cycle in the *Jerusalem Georgian Chantbook* and the Idiomela for Good Friday. Because the individual lamentations reflect on the psalm's verses, the psalm itself largely dictates engagement with violence. For example, the opening lamentations speak to the death of Christ but do so in general terms, without significant reference to violence and typically focusing on the soteriological outcome of the Passion and Resurrection. As the content of the psalm shifts, introducing what Christians would interpret as prophetic statements about the Crucifixion—the text of the psalm includes a spear, a cross, and a "lifeless corpse"—the encomia follows with more pronounced reflections on the violence that Christ endured. By the middle of the encomia, some of the verses become graphic, but not as graphic as the hymns by Romanos the Melodist. Like Romanos's hymns, the encomia frequently invite the singer to lament the death of Christ by reflecting on Mary's grief and, occasionally, by the singers intoning as Mary, which of course heightens the emotional toll.

The encomia serve as a compelling anecdote with which to begin the final assessment of violence in Byzantine hymnography. The first reason for this concerns the texts' treatment of the Jews. The Good Friday Idiomela had been among the first Christian hymns to identify and critique the Jews as being responsible for Jesus's death.[6] That change reshaped the Christian idea, evident in the Octoechos cycle, holding all of humanity responsible for his death because it needed Christ to die to attain eternal life. The encomia largely follow the path established in the anti-Jewish Idiomela by portraying the Jews as a discrete group singularly responsible for Christ's death. As in the Idiomela, the encomia dramatize the Jewish betrayal of Christ with a series of rhetorical questions designed to emphasize their culpability. More so than the Idiomela, the encomia specifically link the violence that Christ suffers, especially the loss of blood, to the Jews:

---

5 One of the more interesting features of the encomia is that the first and second (of three) sets of hymns express post-Resurrection perspectives. The hymns "lament" Christ's suffering and death but celebrate the soteriological meaning of the events. The final section, however, is from a pre-Resurrection point of views.

6 On this, see chapter 2 in this volume.

O arrogant Israel, O people guilty of blood, why have you set free Barabbas but
delivered the savior to be crucified?[7]

O bloodthirsty people, jealous and vengeful, may the very graveclothes and the napkin put
you to shame at Christ's Resurrection.[8]

Be ashamed, O Jews, for the Life-giver raised your dead, but you slew him out of envy.[9]

Although the encomia deploy a greater degree of anti-Jewish rhetoric than the Good Friday Idiomela, they never reference the Jews outside of the saving work of Christ's death and the Resurrection.[10]

The second noteworthy feature of the encomia is that the lengthy set of hymns contains no trace of the imperialized violence that began with the Feast of the Exaltation of the Holy Cross. In large part, this is because the encomia make no mention of the basileus or contain elements of an exclusive Roman identity on the part of the singers (apart from the othering of the Jews by negation; that is, the singers are not Jews). This means the solemn ceremonies of Holy Saturday do not lend themselves to exploitation by imperial propagandists the way some other religious commemorations might. Hymnographic reflection on the death and Resurrection of Christ long predate the conflation of Christian and Roman identity, and the encomia implicitly presume that faith in the Resurrection frames the boundaries of the singing community. The actual presentation of violence in the text revives ancient patterns, wherein violence is

---

7 Mother Mary and Ware, *The Lenten Triodion*, 629. This translation is lightly edited and modernized throughout.

8 Mother Mary and Ware, *The Lenten Triodion*, 630.

9 Mother Mary and Ware, *The Lenten Triodion*, 638.

10 In fact, the encomia provide a compelling data point in the Orthodox debate concerning the possibility of universal salvation, in that they consistently presume that the whole of humanity (including the Jews) will be saved through the death and Resurrection of Jesus. Even those few verses that suggest that Judas is condemned can be explained by the fact that they occur in the third stasis, where the point of view is one in which the Resurrection has not yet occurred.

presented exclusively as something that Christ suffers; it is never requested on behalf of the community. Even the most rhetorically invective statements against the Jews in the encomia avoid any kind of petition for retribution against them or their descendants.

Caution is advised against attempting to draw firm conclusions about the whole of late and post-Byzantine hymnography based on the treatment of the Jews and the lack of imperial violence in the encomia. Although it is clear that some Byzantine hymnographers in the sixth and seventh centuries began to conflate the Christian community with the Roman community and began to sacralize violence in their hymns, older patterns of hymnography remained operational, even commonplace, throughout the Byzantine and post-Byzantine liturgy.

The preceding six chapters illustrate the variety of ways in which Byzantine hymnographers engaged the category of violence. Chapter 1 discusses how in the Octoechos cycle of Sunday services, the oldest surviving hymns, violence features prominently in Christian reflection on the suffering and death of Jesus Christ. Understanding this violence in terms of its soteriological outcome—the suffering and death of Christ led to the salvation of humans—emerged as one of the most common ways for Christian poets to reflect on it. Occasionally, the hymns advance the language of violence and suffering metaphorically, speaking of Christ's victory over death as the destruction of death or the death of the enemy. In these instances, the hymns of the Octoechos portray violence deployed against the enemies of Christ, but the violence afflicting the enemies is precisely the violence that they themselves had set upon Christ, thus falling victim to a rebounding of their own attacks.

Chapter 2 explores the Good Friday Idiomela, the oldest surviving hymns composed exclusively for the commemoration of Christ's Crucifixion during Holy Week. The twelve hymns engage violence in much the same way as in the Octoechos. Violence is something that Christ suffers so that humanity might be saved. Two features of the Idiomela are largely absent, however, from the Octoechos. The first is the use of the literary technique of speech-in-character, in which the singer sings from the perspective of another person—in this case, Christ or St. Peter. By taking on the persona of Christ and by narrating the toll of betrayal, these hymns introduce emotional violence, making

Conclusion 157

the Good Friday hymns all the more dramatic and evocative. The second innovation of the Idiomela is its isolation of an outsider community, the Jews, as being primarily responsible for the suffering and death of Christ. Whereas the Octoechos hymns implicitly hold all humans guilty for Christ's death, prodding Christians to repent, five of the twelve Idiomela hymns suggest that only those who denied Christ were responsible for it. That marks a profound and theologically problematic shift in the understanding of the Passion, death, and Resurrection sequence. In addition to highlighting this change and explaining its theological significance, the chapter also proposes a historical explanation for the emergence of such anti-Jewish rhetoric in Palestine in the mid-sixth century: it emerged in response to recent Jewish violence against Christian communities that was itself a reaction to anti-Jewish legislation promulgated by the emperor Justinian.

Chapter 3 examines the great Constantinopolitan hymnographer Romanos the Melodist and the ways in which violence featured in his renowned kontakia. Because he employed speech-in-character and greatly expanded on biblical texts to include imagined conversations and extrapolated inner thoughts of biblical heroes and villains, Romanos's kontakia truly stand apart from the hymns examined in the other chapters. His singular skill enabled him to do things that other liturgical poets could not fathom or manage to do. Romanos employed violence in traditional ways—presenting it as something that Christ and the saints suffered—but his hymns introduced conceptions of virtuous suffering not previously found elsewhere. For example, in *On the Lament of the Mother of God*, he explores Mary's agony at the death of her son by imagining the last conversation between them. Mary speaks for all Christians, who question why Christ must die—or perhaps why any innocent person must die—only to have Christ gently reproach her for failing to understand his master plan. In *On the Massacre of the Holy Innocents*, Romanos offers a shockingly graphic account of the murder of Palestinian children as well as a glimpse into the tormented mind of Herod, who ordered their death. In so doing, Romanos provides one of the most impressive examples of the way a hymnographer can take the traditional account of violence, that of Christ's Passion, and extend it to other saintly or innocent persons as a kind of typology for Christ himself.

The first steps toward the sacralization of active violence in Byzantine hymns are explored in chapter 4 through a look at the origins of the Feast of the

Exaltation of the Holy Cross. The feast began in conjunction with an annual two-day commemoration of the dedication of the Martyrium basilica, built by the emperor Constantine on Golgotha. A confluence of factors contributed to the outsized imperial dimension of the hymns for the feast: imperial patronage, circulation of the Eusebian narrative that a miraculous vision of the cross prompted Constantine's conversion to Christianity, and the later appropriation of a legendary account of the emperor's mother, Helen, rediscovering the true cross. With time, commemoration of the church's founding and the ritualistic lifting of a relic of the cross were separated into two distinct feasts held on 13 and 14 September, respectively. The imperial character of the original dedicatory feast continued and even expanded with the development of the separate Feast of the Exaltation. A small set of the oldest surviving hymns for the latter commemoration, likely dating to the reign of Justinian, introduced the first elements of the eventual hymnographic sacralization of violence.

The important ways in which the Feast of the Exaltation expanded in the early seventh century are examined in chapter 5. These include an imperial injunction to commemorate it in all the churches of the empire as well as the introduction of new hymns in Constantinople that not only conflated Christian identity with Roman identity, but also petitioned God to assist the emperor in the destruction of the enemy on the battlefield. The chapter also shows that the subsequent development of the Feast of the Exaltation in Palestine during the early eighth century—when no longer under direct Roman control—drifted away from the vision of imperialized violence without completely abandoning memorialization of Constantine.

Chapter 6 examines two rather different collections of hymns: a prayer service for soldiers prior to battle and another for fallen soldiers. The Akolouthia before Battle catered to the specific pastoral needs of soldiers soon to be surrounded by violence and death. Given the political structure of Byzantium, it is unsurprising that a service such as this would also pray for the basileus and present his cause as morally just. Even with this context in mind, this akolouthia is remarkable in the way it engages notions of violence, imperial legitimacy, and divine activity. The Akolouthia for Fallen Soldiers does not sacralize the imperial office, but it might go even further in sacralizing military life by suggesting that military service should function to expiate sin. Simply put, these texts evince a Byzantine liturgical sacralization of violence.

What Difference Did Hymns Make?

The outset of this volume proposed that a careful examination of select Byzantine hymns might alter, confirm, or refine current knowledge of Byzantine attitudes toward violence, and indeed, this genealogy of violence in Byzantine hymnography has brought to light several important aspects of Byzantine Christianity that otherwise would not have been known. Of particular interest, they reveal that Christian hymnographers began to treat violence in profoundly new ways between the middle of the sixth and middle of the seventh century. Whereas earlier hymns had explored violence almost exclusively in terms of the violence that Christ and the saints suffered at the hands of evildoers, some hymns began to reverse the parameters of violence such that the righteous did not suffer violence but exacted it. Not only did hymns in the Herakleian age begin to ask God to inflict violence on others, they also positioned Christians, through God's assistance, as the ones who would righteously inflict that violence on their enemies. There is no comparable shift in Byzantine theological texts during the same period. In fact, no major theological reflection on war and violence survives from the time.

Another salient discovery is that the Feast of the Exaltation of the Holy Cross served as the occasion by which this hymnographic transformation first took place. Unlike Easter, Christmas, Epiphany, and other major feasts of the church, only the Feast of the Exaltation in the Orthodox Church does not focus on a biblical event or personality. Rather, its origin stems from the annual commemoration of the construction of an imperial basilica, the Martyrium, at the site of Christ's Crucifixion, on Golgotha. Thus, the Feast of the Exaltation is atypical in being a celebration of imperial beneficence from the start. As the feast expanded from a commemoration of the Martyrium's dedication to a celebration of its most prized possession, a relic of the true cross, its imperial dimensions only increased. Memorialization of Constantine as the church's benefactor transformed into a celebration of the emperor as a patron of the cross based on three aspects of his life and legend: his choice of a cross-shaped battle standard, forever marking Roman armies with the symbol of Christ's Passion and death; his conversion to Christianity, prompted by a miraculous apparition of the cross; and his mother's supposed discovery of the true cross during a pilgrimage to Jerusalem. By the mid-sixth century, all these elements combined to make the hymns of the Feast of the Exaltation, at the time still a Jerusalem-centered event, the most imperial of any early Byzantine Christian celebration.

During the early seventh century, the feast underwent its most significant transformations, introducing an unprecedented sacralization of violence into Byzantine hymnography as Roman armies faced their greatest threats—first from the Persians and then from the Arabs. In Jerusalem, the annual festival of 14 September added a commemoration of the return of the relic of the cross from the Persians to the event. In Constantinople, the emperor Herakleios decreed celebration of the Feast of the Exaltation in the capital and ordered all churches throughout the empire to do the same. Also in Constantinople, newly commissioned hymns for the occasion petitioned God for the destruction of the enemies of Christ. Of equal importance, these particular hymns were unambiguously connected to imperial ideology, centered on the figure of the basileus. It was not by happenstance that Herakleios was the first Roman emperor to adopt the title of basileus for himself, be styled as King David by a court panegyrist, and commission artwork linking his reign to David's.

Yet another consequential discovery is the narrowing of the distance between empire and Christian identity. As a general rule, most Byzantine hymns, apart from the language of their composition, offer no implicit or explicit indication of the Christian community being of any particular political, cultural, or ethnic affiliation. The often explicit presumption of the Christian community as Roman and only Roman emerged as one of the most important features of the shift in the hymnographic treatment of violence during the early seventh century. It is within this framework that some hymns ask God to inflict violence on the enemy. More often than not, the emperor, the basileus, is identified as God's chosen instrument and the leader of the Christian cause. In this context, the Akolouthia before Battle frames righteousness before God in terms of loyalty to the basileus. The army of the basileus is God's army. The enemy of the basileus is God's enemy.

The majority of hymns composed after the seventh century, whether in Constantinople, Palestine, or elsewhere, did not adopt the militant and pro-Roman aspects of the Feast of the Exaltation, the Akolouthia before Battle, or the Akolouthia for Fallen Soldiers. The majority of new hymns drew on ascetic or moral lessons from the scriptures or celebrated the lives of individual saints.[11]

---

11 On the ascetic aspect of middle Byzantine hymnography, see D. Krueger, *Liturgical Subjects: Christian Ritual, Biblical Narrative and the Formation of the Self in Byzantium* (Philadelphia, 2014).

There is, however, little doubt that the feasts or special liturgical ceremonies most connected to imperial memory or imperial interests after the seventh century continued to inspire hymns that employed imperialized violence. One must therefore conclude that a thread within Byzantine ecclesial tradition not only tolerated but also celebrated violence through liturgy and that this bent was predicated on a narrowing of Christian identity that reflected imperial ideology. This was not the dominant thread in Byzantine liturgical life or ecclesial life more broadly, but it was more prominent than most assessments of the Byzantine Church have acknowledged.

Consequences of the Liturgical Sacralization of Violence

There is little doubt that the premodern world was a violent place. Ordinary citizens often found themselves at the mercy of local military strongmen and passing armies. If liturgy and, especially, hymnography are the meeting place between theological conviction and lived religious experience, and hymnographers continuously tested new forms and expressions to meet changing realities, then it is not surprising that hymnographers would seek to address the pastoral needs of communities exposed to the pervasive brutality of violence. To be more specific, in the Roman Empire after the legalization of Christianity, it probably made good pastoral sense for hymnographers to occasionally expand their treatment of violence from exclusively focusing on the violence that Christ and the saints suffered to also acknowledge the spiritual needs of Christian communities besieged by enemies. Perhaps more pertinently, they might seek to affirm the belief that God and his saints have the power to intervene in the course of human history to protect the faithful. One can easily understand how a religious festival like the Feast of the Exaltation of the Holy Cross, at least initially, prompted a set of hymns to celebrate that God had made things better for the Christian community through a figure like Constantine, who not only legalized Christianity and built churches, but who also protected Christians from their enemies, if more so in the collective memory than in historical fact.

As this genealogy demonstrates, one can confidently explain and even rationalize the historical progression of transitioning from the production of hymns that met the pastoral needs of the Christian community, while maintaining the theological traditions that proceeded it, to the production of hymns that not only authorized violence but also celebrated it to a degree perhaps unrecognizable to earlier generations of Christians. Ascertaining the precise point at which this happened, however, is more difficult, but it appears to have occurred for the first time in the early seventh century, during the Herakleian era.

The sacralization of violence that began in Constantinople at that time and reached greater maturity during the ninth and tenth centuries is theologically problematic in at least three ways. First, the sacralization in Byzantine hymnography was an imperialized violence that equated the imperial cause with the Christian cause and vice versa. The presumption of Byzantine identity and subservience to the basileus is so pronounced that it makes some hymns incompatible with the universality of the Christian theological claim: that Christ came for all humans, that the Christian community is broader than the divisions of the world, and that God loves all people equally. There is simply no way to affirm Christian universalism when the prevailing assumption is that the Christian cause belongs exclusively (or even primarily) to a single ethnic, cultural, or political community.

Second, the sacralization of violence against others in hymns confuses—and, indeed, seems to completely contradict—Christianity's core message that the birth, death, and Resurrection of Jesus Christ provides eternal life. Rather than emphasizing the wholeness, salvation, and everlasting life made possible by Christ's sacrifice, hymns that sacralize violence against others detract from that message and appear to celebrate the very opposite—that is, death. While it is understandable that Christian hymnographers would need to develop hymns for the pastoral needs of the faithful facing constant threats of violence, it was clearly possible to do so without calling for, let alone celebrating, the death and destruction of others. As one colleague said to me following a presentation of this study while it was still in progress, "Would it not be better to pray for the conversion of enemies rather than their destruction?"[12]

Third, the sacralization of violence in hymns like "Save O, Lord" and "You Who Were Lifted upon the Cross," used in the Constantinopolitan commemoration of the Feast of the Exaltation, usurp the original theological and eschatological vision of the liturgical feast for worldly, political ends. Rather than celebrate

---

12 I would like to thank Lidiya Lozova for her thoughtful reflections and exchange while I was working on this project. As a Ukrainian national, she has experienced violence and reflected on its religious implications in ways I simply have not.

the role of the cross in the cosmic history of salvation, or the construction of the church at Golgotha as an event in the history of salvation, such hymns replace Christian teaching for an imperial ideology that co-opts the Christian message of salvation by situating it within the discourse of imperial power and authority. The celebration of the cross is superseded in these hymns by an affirmation of imperial power and adoption of the emperor's enemies as one's own.

This book began with an anecdote about the construction of a new cathedral dedicated to the Russian armed forces. Without overstating the case, it is only an anecdote; such a church could not be possible in the modern Orthodox world had it not been for the gradual sacralization of violence in liturgy that began to mature in Byzantium between the seventh and tenth centuries. Indeed, it was through hymnography, more than any other ecclesial source, that Byzantine authors first began to sacralize the role of soldiers loyal to the basileus; that the human enemies of the empire were first condemned by the church; and that the figure of the emperor was first tied to important liturgical feasts.

In addition to the theological reasons that such changes were problematic, there are at least two long-term historical consequences for the family of Eastern Christian jurisdictions today. First, the liturgical sacralization of violence that occurred in the middle Byzantine centuries, even if only occasional, provides a powerful historical and liturgical precedent for political opportunists and their supporters, such as Patriarch Kirill of Moscow, who seek to present a military conflict as a moral obligation for a community of Orthodox Christians. Second, and related, the sacralization of violence provides a kind of liturgical precedent for religious nationalism. In the same way that Byzantine hymnographers close to imperial power presented the political cause of the basileus or the empire more broadly as God's cause, so too modern proponents of religious nationalism can look to these hymns as a millennium-long liturgical tradition for authorizing violence against minorities, migrants, refugees, or historical enemies. In all of the above ways, it would seem that the Orthodox Christian world has drifted rather far from the hymns of the Octoechos Sunday cycle, which presents violence exclusively in terms of the violence that Christ suffered for its benefit.

APPENDIX 1

HYMNS FOR THE FEASTS OF THE ENCAINIA AND THE EXALTATION OF THE HOLY CROSS FROM LATE ANCIENT JERUSALEM

STEPHEN J. SHOEMAKER, UNIVERSITY OF OREGON

The following translations were made from the so-called *Jerusalem Georgian Chantbook*, an ancient collection of hymns for the ecclesiastical year reflecting the practice of early Christian Jerusalem. The collection presently survives only in Old Georgian, in a translation called the Iadgari. There are two versions of the chantbook in Georgian, however: the Old Iadgari and the New Iadgari. The latter collection is also known in the original Greek and in this case is called the Tropologion. The New Iadgari was compiled and introduced to the church of Jerusalem in the beginning of the seventh century, at which time it replaced the older collection of hymns in use, the Old Iadgari. Unfortunately, the older collection has been lost in Greek, having been fully supplanted by the revised hymnal. Thus, both the old and new collections survive in Georgian, and thanks to knowing that the newer hymnal was introduced in the early seventh century, one may take some confidence that the Georgian Old Iadgari preserves the hymnography of the Jerusalem church from the period prior to 600. The witness of the Old Iadgari is all the more valuable because most of its unattributed hymns were not carried forward into the new chantbook, but instead were largely replaced by new hymns ascribed to authors of the seventh century.¹ This ancient collection, therefore, preserved only in Old Georgian, affords a truly unequaled window into the world of Christian worship at the end of antiquity, though most scholars of early Christianity scarcely know of its existence.

The translations for this appendix were made from a single manuscript, Sinai Georgian 18, which in the current state of scholarship is considered the best witness to the hymnography of late ancient Jerusalem's cathedral rite—that is, its parish liturgy rather than monastic practice.² The basis for the translations is the major critical edition of the Old Iadgari published in Tbilisi in 1980,³ along with, even more importantly, high resolution photographs of the manuscript itself, which Father Justin of St. Catherine's monastery in Sinai generously provided through the invaluable mediation of Father Daniel Galadza. The translation for this appendix forms part of a larger project currently underway that will ultimately realize a complete translation of the festal hymnography from late ancient Jerusalem as represented in the *Jerusalem Georgian Chantbook*. For those who

---

1 S. S. R. Frøyshov, "The Early Development of the Liturgical Eight-Mode System in Jerusalem," *SVThQ* 51 (2007): 139–78, at 144; S. S. R. Frøyshov, "The Georgian Witness to the Jerusalem Liturgy: New Sources and Studies," in *Inquiries into Eastern Christian Worship: Selected Papers of the Second International Congress of the Society of Oriental Liturgies, Rome, 17–21 September 2008*, ed. B. Groen, S. Hawkes-Teeples, and S. Alexopoulos (Leuven, 2012), 227–68, at 237; E. Metreveli, C. Čankievi, and L. Xevsuriani, *Uzvelesi iadgari* [The oldest chantbook], Żveli k'art'uli mcerlobis żeglebi 2 (Tbilisi, 1980), 793–808. The latter is summarized in English in A. Wade, "The Oldest *Iadgari*: The Jerusalem Tropologion, 4th to 8th Centuries, 30 Years after the Publication," in *Synaxis katholikē: Beiträge zu Gottesdienst und Geschichte der fünf altkirchlichen Patriarchate für Heinzgerd Brakmann zum 70. Geburtstag*, ed. D. Atanassova and T. Chronz, 2 vols. (Vienna, 2014), 2:717–50.

2 See C. Renoux, trans., *Les hymnes de la Résurrection*, vol. 3, *Hymnographie liturgique géorgienne, introduction, traduction, annotation des manuscrits Sinaï 26 et 20 et index analytique des trois volumes*, PO 52, fasc. 2, no. 232 (Turnhout, 2010), 325–26, which summarizes the differences between the manuscripts. See also C. Renoux, trans., *Les hymnes de la Résurrection*, vol. 1, *Hymnographie liturgique géorgienne: Textes du Sinaï 18*, Sources liturgiques 3 (Paris, 2000), 10–13, and the brief remarks in P. Jeffery, "The Earliest Octōēchoi: The Role of Jerusalem and Palestine in the Beginnings of Modal Ordering," in *The Study of Medieval Chant: Paths and Bridges, East and West; In Honor of Kenneth Levy*, ed. P. Jeffery (Woodbridge, 2001), 147–209, at 200–201, which supposes a developmental typology on the basis of these differences that is not entirely warranted.

3 Metreveli, Čankievi, and Xevsuriani, *Uzvelesi iadgari*.

might be interested, I previously published a bilingual edition of the ancient Jerusalemite hymnography for the Sunday services as found in this chantbook's Octoechos on the basis of Sinai Georgian 18.[4] In regard to the hymns translated for the present volume, readers who would like to compare them with another early transmission may also consult French and Italian translations published primarily on the basis of another important early manuscript, Tbilisi H 2123.[5]

The decision to translate from a single manuscript, rather than a critical edition, owes itself to liturgical traditions' often fluid transmission histories, which generally make it impossible to create an edition that recovers some now-lost archetype.[6] For this reason, there is no hard-and-fast guarantee that every single word of these hymns or even every single hymn transmitted in this collection goes back to the actual practice of sixth-century Jerusalem. Nevertheless, research on these traditions has established a sound basis for assuming that the general themes and vocabulary of these hymns, particularly as they are repeated across the collection, do in fact reflect the patterns of worship in late ancient Jerusalem.[7] Put otherwise, one would not want to rest any argument too much

---

4 S. Shoemaker, *The First Christian Hymnal: The Songs of the Ancient Jerusalem Church; Parallel Georgian-English Texts*, Middle Eastern Texts Initiative 10 (Provo, UT, 2018).

5 C. Renoux, trans., *L'hymnaire de Saint-Sabas (V^e-VIIe siècle): Le manuscrit géorgien H 2123*, vol. 2, *De la Nativité de Jean-Baptiste à la Liturgie des défunts*, PO 53, fasc. 3, no. 237 (Turnhout, 2015), 589–631; G. Shurgaia, "L'esaltazione della croce nello Iadgari antico," in *L'Onagro Maestro: Miscellanea di fuochi accesi per Gianroberto Scarcia in occasione del suo LXX sadè*, ed. R. Favaro, S. Cristoforetti, and M. Compareti (Venice, 2004), 137–88. The latter article has the hymns for the Feast of the Exaltation of the Holy Cross but not for the Feast of the Encainia.

6 This is perhaps stated most classically in P. F. Bradshaw, "Liturgy as 'Living Literature,'" in *Liturgy in Dialogue: Essays in Memory of Ronald Jasper*, ed. P. F. Bradshaw and B. Spinks (Collegeville, MN, 1995), 139–54.

7 See, for example, Frøyshov, "The Early Development of the Liturgical Eight-Mode System in Jerusalem"; see also Frøyshov, "Georgian Witness," 233–38; A. Wade, "The Oldest Iadgari: The Jerusalem Tropologion, V–VIII c.," *OCP* 50 (1984): 451–56, at 451; H. Métrévéli, "Les manuscrits liturgiques géorgiens des IXe–Xe siècles et leur importance pour l'étude de l'hymnographie byzantine," *BK* 36 (1978): 43–48, at 47; H. Métrévéli and B. Outtier, "Contribution à l'histoire de l'Hirmologion: Anciens hirmologia géorgiens," *Le Muséon* 88 (1975): 331–59; G. Peradzè, "Les monuments liturgiques prébyzantins en langue géorgienne," *Le Muséon* 45 (1932): 255–72; and Renoux, *Les hymnes de la Résurrection*, 1:85–86.

on a single isolated phrase or even a lone hymn from this collection, but themes and expressions that recur across the corpus, such as those adduced in the present study, are indeed highly likely to derive from the liturgical practices of late ancient Jerusalem. In this broader, more general sense, then, these hymns form an invaluable and unparalleled witness to the piety and devotion expressed by and formative of the Christians of late ancient Jerusalem during their regular worship services.

On an editorial note, readers will notice at the end of many strophes words and phrases enclosed in curly brackets: { }. These expressions are not actually in the manuscript, but are otherwise known to have been part of the hymn in question. They have been added, therefore, for completeness and as an aid to the reader.

13 September, Encainia[8]

VESPERS

At: "O Lord, I cried out to you . . . " [Ps. 140]

1. On the rock of the gospel you have established your church, Christ,[9]
   You built a wall around it and said,
   The gates of hell will not prevail against it [Matt. 16:18],
   And it will endure unto the ages,
   For it has you, who took on flesh, in it,
   O Lord, have mercy on us.
2. We who observe the Feast of the Dedication,
   We glorify you and pray to you Lord, the giver of salvation,
   Sanctify this our refuge of souls and bodies,
   Through the intercessions of the Theotokos and your holy apostles,
   Merciful One and Lover of humankind.

---

8 *Encainia*, a Greek word meaning "the dedication," is the common name for the feast held 13 September in the Jerusalem liturgy. This feast commemorates the dedication and consecration of the church of the Anastasis (Holy Sepulcher) on the day before the Feast of the Exaltation of the Holy Cross. Here the manuscript transliterates the Greek word, but in the hymns, the Georgian word სატფურება is used, which is translated here as "the Dedication."

9 This troparion is also extant in Greek and Armenian. See E. Follieri, ed., *Initia hymnorum ecclesiae Graecae*, 5 vols., Studi e testi 211–215 bis (Vatican City, 1960), 1:358; and *Dzaynk'agh Sharakank'* [Modal hymns] (Venice, 1907), 443.

Appendix 1

3. You have caused your Holy Spirit to descend,
    Lover of humankind, on this temple,
    You have purified it and revealed it as a place of healing,
    For those who hasten to your glory,
    We commemorate its Dedication and cry out,
    Save us, O our God, for you are alone the Holy one,
    And you sanctify all things.

Other Hymns

1. We offer you the evening sacrifice, O Christ God,
    You who sent the Holy Spirit from Heaven to the apostles,
    And filled the catholic church with grace,
    Wherein you have granted us forgiveness of sins through your divinity.
2. We offer you the evening sacrifice, O Christ God,
    You who through divinity illuminated the apostles,
    And through them have glorified the church upon the rock,[10]
    Wherein you have granted us forgiveness of sins through your divinity.
3. Long ago Solomon made a dedication of living beasts,[11]
    He offered a burnt offering as a sacrifice [cf. 3 Kgdms. 8:63;
        2 Chron. 7:5],
    But when it pleased you, Savior, to reject the image,
    And make known the true bloodless sacrifice,
    All the ends of the earth offer you praise,
    You reign over all things,
    You have sanctified all things through your All-Holy Spirit,
    Have mercy on us.
4. Come O peoples, nations, and languages,
    Do not listen, as in the plain of Dura, to carnal praise,
    Nor bend faithless knees to a golden image [cf. Dan. 3:1],
    But, in the most holy temple,
    Let us sing as with spiritual voices,

---

10 That is, the Rock of Calvary.
11 This troparion is also extant in Greek: Follieri, *Initia hymnorum*, 3:260. In MS B however, unlike in other early versions, the temple is not specifically mentioned.

Let us cry out to Christ God,
To send peace upon the earth,
And great mercy for the sake of our souls.

Psalm, Fourth Tone
Let all the earth . . . [Ps. 65:4–5]
Response: "Let us cry out to God, all . . . " [Ps. 65.1]

MATINS
At: "Sing . . . " [Ode 1; Exod. 15:1–19], First Mode
1. We the believers glorify this day, the Feast of the Dedication,
   Let us praise the Savior and God and say,
   Sing to the Lord, {for he is gloriously glorified}.
   Standing today in your temple,
   We sing to you, O Christ God,
   Grant us forgiveness of sins,
   Through the intercessions of the one who gave you birth.
2. In commemorating the assembly of the Dedication,
   Let us the believers celebrate with faith,
   Let us praise the Savior of all and say,
   Sing to the Lord, {for he is gloriously glorified.}

Other Hymns
1. Let us sing to God, the Creator,
   Who sent his Son for the salvation of the world,
   And by him the holy apostles were made known,
   By whom the holy church was established,
   To boast in the orthodox faith,
   Sing to the Lord, for he is gloriously {glorified.}
2. We the believers commemorating the Dedication,
   Standing today in his temple,
   Let us praise the Savior and God and say,
   Sing to the Lord, for he is gloriously {glorified.}
3. In the innumerable assembly,
   We have become worthy to sing and worship,

> We who cry out with ceaseless voice and say,
> Sing {to the Lord, for he is gloriously glorified.}

At: "Take heed, . . . " [Ode 2; Deut. 32:1–43]
1. Take heed, O Heaven,
   Let us speak and sing to God,
   The Only One.
2. Glory to you, glory to you, O King of glory,
   Who by the Holy Spirit perfected the holy apostles,
   And through them you have adorned the church with faith.

Other Hymns
1. Behold, behold the Lord our God,
   Who founded the holy church on the rock of faith,
   And in it the torments of illness are healed.
2. Behold, behold the Lord our God,
   Who founded his church through the flesh of the apostles,
   And in it has taught the believers,
   Knowledge of God through the apostles.
3. Behold, behold, behold the Lord our God,
   Who has adorned the church with glory,
   And in it you have gathered the believers,
   For the observance of the feast.

At: "It was made strong . . . " [Ode 3; 1 Kgdms. 2:1–10]
1. O Lord, strengthen your church,[12]
   {Which you have built through the power of your cross,
   By which you put Satan to shame,
   And illuminated the entire world.}
2. Through faith, O Lord, you have established your church as a rock,
   And you have granted, to those who believe, forgiveness of sins.

---

12 Only the incipit appears in the source manuscript. The complete hymn is translated from the full text that appears in the chantbook's kanon for the deceased: Metreveli, Čankievi, and Xevsuriani, *Უzvelesi iadgari*, 328, lines 32–34.

3. You have revealed, O Lord, this day of Dedication,
    As a joy for the believers,
    On which we sing to you all together, the Merciful Lord.

Other Hymns
1. No one is holy as Christ our God,
    Who established the holy church,
    And in it made the believers worthy to praise him.
2. We praise you King, God of all things,
    Who sanctified your church by your glorious blood, Savior,
    The shackles of the faithless are shattered,
    And even more the holy church has been edified,
    And in it the believers have received incorruption.

At: "O Lord, I have heard . . . " [Ode 4; Hab. 3:2–19]
1. Your grace has shone in your temple,
    And we all gathered together sing to you,
    You have given us your peace, O Christ our God.
2. You have sanctified your church,
    Christ Savior, by your holy blood,
    For you are the Lover of humankind,
    And in it you reign and save the believers.
3. You have sanctified the temple,
    As a house of worship for us,
    Wherein we offer prayer to you,
    O Lord our God, save our souls.

Other Hymns
1. The prophets proclaimed your birth to us, Savior,
    You who revealed humanity with divinity to the world,
    And through the believers you have magnified the holy church,
    Great glory to your majesty, O King of all the ages.
2. Zion rejoices and the holy church is greatly renewed,
    On the Feast of the Dedication,

At which feast the people of the believers also rejoice,
Great glory to your majesty, O King of all {the ages.}
3. Today your believers are filled with joy, O Christ our God,
For in this glorious temple you have made them worthy,
To celebrate the feast and to cry out to you,
Great glory to your majesty, O King of all {the ages.}
4. We praise you, O uncorrupted Virgin, blessed and pure,
For God, whom heaven cannot contain,
Was contained in your womb as a human being,
And from you the Sun of Righteousness,
Took on flesh . . . [13] according to his will,
We cry out all the more and say,
Save us who hope in you, O King of all the ages.

At: "In the night . . . " [Ode 5; Isa. 26:9–20]
1. In the night we rise up early,
We offer you glory, O Lord our God.
You have given us your peace on the day of the Dedication,
And you have saved our souls.
2. The light of salvation has shone upon us in your temple, O Lord,
For by it you purify your believers,
And we all sing to you, O Lover of humankind, our Savior.
3. Having come to your temple, O Lord,
We offer you a plea,
O Lover of humankind, our Savior,
All-Merciful, save our souls.

Other Hymns
1. We rise up early for you, O Christ our God,
You who truly rose up early,
Who firmly and unshakably established,
The holy and most glorious dwelling place of the Holy Spirit,
As a refuge for the believers, for you are the Merciful.

13 There is an illegible word here in the manuscript.

2. Just as you granted peace and steadfastness to the church,
   So also to those who glorify your temple,
   Which the apostles founded,
   O Christ our God, have mercy on our souls, O All-Merciful.
3. The heavens rejoice and the people of the believers are joyful,
   The holy church rejoices with them,
   Which you established as the dwelling place of the Holy Spirit,
   For you are the All-Merciful.
4. By your glorious blood, O Christ our God,
   You sanctified your temple,
   And the new people that you gained,
   Who in it cry out and say while glorifying,
   Grant us your [peace].[14]
5. You have granted us the dew of peace,
   We who glorify your temple,
   And you brought the fruit of truth to your believers,
   For you are the Merciful.

At: "I cried out . . . " [Ode 6; Jon. 2:3–10], First Plagal Mode
1. I cried out in affliction,
   To God the Merciful,
   {He sent} the Word [cf. Ps. 106:19–20].[15]

---

14 Here, again, a word is illegible in the manuscript, although the word ܕܝܠܟ (your), which the editors fail to note, is clearly visible. The word *peace*, here in brackets, completes an expression found elsewhere across the hymns and also fits with the opening line of the following strophe. Nevertheless, the word *mercy* is also a strong possibility, which would keep with the final emphasis on God as the Merciful One at the end of the other hymns in this set. Nevertheless, the exact expression "grant us your mercy" does not occur elsewhere in the festal hymns.

15 Similar versions of this same strophe occur throughout the chantbook, including in its Octoechos, for this same ode in the same tone, allowing the final missing word to be supplied. See Shoemaker, *The First Christian Hymnal*, 164–65. A similar hymn also exists in Greek: S. Eustatiades, Ειρμολογιον: Μνημεια Αγιολογικα, Agioreitike Bibliotheke 9 (Chennevieres-sur-Marne, 1932), 198.

2. Your temple has appeared utterly glorious, O Lord,
   Wherein we sing to you with praise,
   O Lord, the Lover of humankind.
3. On the day of the Dedication, O Lord,
   Your people celebrate with faith and rejoice,
   And they glorify you, the Only One, the Compassionate Lord.

Other Hymns
1. Today the dwelling places of the idols have become destitute,
   And the holy church has been greatly increased,
   Wherein we sing to you, Lord, the Lover of humankind.
2. Today all the believers rejoice,
   And the holy church is crowned,
   Because the Holy Spirit dwells in it.
3. Today joy has been bestowed upon the believers,
   And grace upon the churches,
   For with the angels they have become full of hope,
   And they sing to the Holy Trinity.
4. On this day the holy churches rejoice,
   And the multitude of the believers rejoices,
   And they sing to you, the Only One, Christ.
5. Nevertheless, we the believers of your holy temple,
   Offer you praise and cry out, Glory to you, Christ,
   Who has delivered the world from suffering.

At: "Blessed are you . . . " [Ode 7; Dan. 3:26–56]
1. Blessed are you unto the ages.
2. In your temple we sing to you,
   O Lord, God of our fathers.
3. In the church we bless you,
   O Lord, God of our fathers.
4. In commemorating the assembly of the Dedication,
   We the believers glorify you,
   O Lord, God of our fathers.

Other Hymns

1. Come, O peoples rooted in the faith,
   Bless the Son with the Father and with the Holy Spirit,
   Who has today made us, the believers, worthy,
   To glorify him in his temple and to say,
   You who are God before the ages, you are blessed.
2. We sing to you O God, we who stand in your temple,
   Which you have established as a refuge of souls and bodies,
   We who sing <to> you in the assembly of the Dedication,
   With thanks we celebrate and say,
   You who are God before the ages, you are blessed.
3. With spiritual voices we offer you the angelic song, O church of God,
   You who were established as the boast of humankind,
   And by the Holy Spirit the believers will become enlightened,
   Therefore today we cry out and say on account of your consecration,
   You who are {God} before {the ages, you are blessed.}
4. O Lord of our fathers, O Savior and Creator of all things,
   Grant peace to those who sing of you,
   We whom you have shown as worthy,
   To praise you together with the angels in this holy temple,
   You who are God before the ages, you are blessed.
5. To the undivided, consubstantial Trinity,
   We sing with one mouth and say,
   You who are {God before the ages, you are blessed.}

At: "Bless . . . " *[Ode 8; Dan. 3:57–88]*

1. We offer you the hymn of angels as the youths,
   {In the most holy temple, we exalt you and say,
   All the works of the Lord, bless the Lord.}
2. We bless you, Christ, for you are the Merciful,
   In the most holy temple, we exalt you and say,
   All {the works of the Lord,} bless {the Lord.}
3. We celebrate the Dedication of the altar of your mystery,
   We exalt you and say,
   {All the works of the Lord,} bless {the Lord.}

Appendix 1

Other Hymns

1. He who came down from heaven was nailed to the cross,
   By the Resurrection he has crowned the churches,
   Sing to the Lord and exalt him above all, {unto the ages.}
2. He who established the church on the rock of faith,
   Fortified it with the armor of the cross,
   Sing to the Lord and exalt him above all, unto the ages.
3. He who sent down the grace of heaven to his temple,
   To illuminate the believers,
   Sing to the Lord and {exalt him} above all, {unto the ages.}
4. He who as Trinity and consubstantial,
   Is glorified in the highest, God.

At: "Magnify . . . " [Ode 9; Luke 1:46–55]

1. O all-praised and glorious Theotokos,
   You who {are behind the second veil of the temple,
   Which is called the Holy of Holies [cf. Protev. 8],
   We magnify you with a hymn.}[16]
2. You who are praised by the angels in heaven and in the church,
   God, the Only One, the Lord of all,
   We magnify you with a hymn.
3. You our Sanctifier and Dispenser,
   In the temple that you have glorified, Savior,
   In which we magnify you, the Lord of all things, with a hymn.

Other Hymns

1. Today the King of Kings and Lord of Lords is revealed to us,
   In the holy church where the Holy Spirit is glorified,
   And the multitude of the angels rejoices,
   We magnify you with a hymn, the Merciful Father.

---

16 This hymn is incomplete in MS Sinai Georgian 18 and is only able to be completed based on its complete presentation in MS Sinai Georgian 40.

2. Today the holy altar was established in the holy church,
   On which is offered the body and blood of Christ,
   For forgiveness of sins and life eternal,
   We magnify you with a hymn, the Only Begotten Son.
3. Today Christ sent forth the holy apostles,
   To illuminate the world, to establish churches,
   And to convert those who have gone astray,
   We magnify you with a hymn, the Holy Spirit.
   Let them omit fourth plagal mode: For the Lord was pleased.
   Fourth plagal mode: this is third mode.[17]

At: *"Praise . . . "* [Ps. 148]
1. Your church is adorned with praise and glory, O Christ God,
   In which shines the grace of your cross,
   And it shattered the power of hell.
2. Like light your church shines, O Christ God,
   As the dwelling place of your holy apostles,
   Wherein the Holy Spirit is glorified,
   And the multitude of the angels rejoices.
3. The earth is full of your glory, O Lord,
   Which you created with your right hand,
   The apostles rejoice, the gospel is confirmed,
   The church is greatly exalted,
   Sinners find mercy from you.
4. O peoples come to Zion and surround it,
   Give glory to God in it,
   For it is the mother of all churches,
   In which the Holy Spirit {dwells.}[18]
5. The Lord, my Light, the Lord, my Savior,
   Who illuminated the world with glory,
   And founded the churches by his precious cross.

---

17 The meaning of these instructions, which are unique to this manuscript, is not clear.
18 This word is missing from the manuscript but is found in the others. It seems necessary here to complete the sense of this line.

Appendix 1

6. Rejoice, holy church, the assembly of the multitudes,
   Wherein the Holy Spirit appeared and said to the apostles,
   Raise the voice of your praise in Zion,
   And give glory to God in it.
7. We offer you an angelic voice, holy church of God,
   You whom the holy apostles founded,
   Rejoice, O Cause of Joy, the Lord is with you,
   Christ has established you in peace,
   The Only Begotten, the eternal King.

Other Hymns

1. You who dwell in inaccessible light,
   And the angels stand around,
   You the Beneficent God came down with humility,
   You were born from the holy Virgin without change,
   You revealed to the world the Incarnation,
   By which the churches were illuminated.
2. You who are Lord of Heaven and earth and Creator of the ages,
   You came and willingly stretched forth your body on the cross,
   And by the cross you destroyed the sin of the first father,
   You brought forth from hell those who were in darkness,
   By which the churches were illuminated.
3. You who with a word established the heavens,
   And founded the earth upon the waters,
   And established the church upon the rock,
   Zachariah proclaimed regarding Zion,
   The gates of Zion have been opened,
   And grace from Heaven has been spread forth by the Holy Spirit,[19]
   Today the church is adorned.

---

19 To my knowledge, this citation is not found in the book of Zachariah or attributed to the father of John the Baptist.

LITURGY

Petition,[20] *First Mode*

    Your tomb, more gloriously adorned than the sun,
    Has brought complete salvation to the world, O Christ God,
    For before, when your all-holy body was placed in it,
    In that moment corruption was obliterated,
    And the sting of death was destroyed,
    But on this day of the Dedication,
    The holy churches rejoice,
    For by it joy is bestowed on us,
    And the sinners find forgiveness of sin and great mercy,
    By which you delivered us,
    O Lord, the Merciful and the Lover of humankind,
    Glory to your life-giving Resurrection.

Psalm, First Plagal Mode

    All the nations, . . . [Ps. 85:9]
    Refrain: For to you, Lord, kind and . . . [Ps. 85:5]

Alleluia, First Plagal Mode

    We are filled . . . [Ps. 64:5]

The Washing of Hands, First Mode

    The word of your prophets Isaiah and David
    Has been fulfilled, O God, when they said,
    All nations will come and bow down before you [Ps. 85:9; cf. Isa. 60:14],
    For behold, Compassionate One, in your courts,

---

20 For some reason, and without explanation, Renoux includes this hymn at the end of matins, rather than at the beginning of the liturgy. Nevertheless, the Georgian rubric that introduces it, მბოძა (petition), generally indicates a hymn used for the entrance of the Divine Liturgy. See Renoux, *L'hymnaire de Saint-Sabas (V^e-VIIe siècle)*, 603. Also of note, this hymn is in the manuscript despite the failure of the edition to indicate its presence.

The people will be filled by your grace,
They beseech you, for you endured the Crucifixion,
And by your life-giving Resurrection preserved and pardoned us.

14 September, The Exaltation of the Holy Cross
VESPERS

At: "O Lord, I cried out to you . . . " [Ps. 140], Fourth Mode

1. Wondrous is the light of your face on us, O Lord,
   And all the ends of the earth say to you, singing,
   Glory to you, O God.
2. At the place of the skull you were crucified, Christ,
   And you shattered the power of death,
   And you freed the human race,
   Glory to you, O God.
3. You were raised up on the cross, O Conqueror,
   And you took hell captive, O Mighty One,
   And you raised us up, Merciful One,
   Glory to you, O God.

Other Hymns

1. We cry out to you, Christ,
   Who by your precious cross,
   Dispelled the fall through the tree,
   The debt of sin of our father,
   And bestowed resurrection on the believers,
   Therefore, Christ, we venerate your precious cross.
2. The enemy was vanquished, and death was trampled down,
   By the elevation of your cross on Golgotha,
   The power of death was destroyed,
   And the resurrection has been granted to the believers.
   Therefore we venerate your precious cross.
3. You were laid down on the hewn rock,
   You, the sturdiness of mountains,
   And you raised the dead who were in hell,
   And brought them forth into the light,

And bestowed on them your kingdom.
Therefore we venerate {your precious cross.}

Petition, First Plagal Mode

You will find many arranged on 7 May.[21]

Psalm, Second Plagal Mode

The Lord will sit as King forever... [Ps. 28:10]
Response: Worship the Lord... [Ps. 28:2]

MATINS

At: "Sing..." *[Ode 1; Exod. 15:1–19]*

1. He who brought us forth from the gates of death,[22]
   Let us sing to him, Christ,
   For he is gloriously glorified unto the ages.
2. He who went up on the cross for us,
   With mercy for our salvation,
   Let us sing to him, Christ,
   For he is glorified unto the ages.
3. He who crushed the pride of the enemy,
   And has raised up the cross among the believers,
   Let us sing to him, {Christ,
   For he is glorified unto the ages.}
4. He who stretched forth his hands,
   For all of us on the cross of life,
   Let us sing to him, {Christ,
   For he is glorified unto the ages.}
5. Today let us celebrate the exalted cross,
   Let us bless the King of all things,
   Let us glorify Christ,
   For he is glorified unto the ages.

---

21 This is the day of the Feast of the Apparition of the Cross in Jerusalem.

22 This strophe, or heirmos, is attributed to John of Damascus. See Eustatiades, Ειρμολογιον, 103, ode 4.

Other Hymns

1. Let us sing to the Lord, the Most High,
   The God of glory, the merciful Father,
   Who by angels and humankind is ceaselessly glorified,
   Let us sing to him with a new song,
   For {he is} gloriously {glorified.}
2. Let us sing to the Only Begotten Son,
   And the Word of God, the Savior of Israel,
   Who for us took on flesh from the holy Virgin,
   His name is Lord,
   For he is gloriously glorified.
3. He who by the precious cross shattered the strength of death,
   And took Hell captive by the power of God,
   And saved the world from the violence of the enemy,
   Let us sing to him, Christ, the merciful King,
   Let us sing to him with a new song,
   For {he is} gloriously {glorified}.
4. He who by his holy Resurrection illuminated the world,
   And saved Adam, the first created, from corruption,
   And bestowed on those who believe in him the Spirit of his salvation,
   On account of which we cry out and say,
   Let us sing to the Resurrection of Christ with a {new} song,
   {For he is gloriously glorified.}

At: "Take heed, . . . " [Ode 2; Deut. 32:1–43]

1. Take heed, O Heaven,
   Let us speak and sing to Christ,
   For {he is} gloriously {glorified.}
2. Protect us who hope in you,
   Who endured suffering on the tree for our sake.
3. Righteous and holy is the Lord our God,
   Who by the cross granted salvation to those who believe in him.
4. Behold, behold, for he is God and human,
   Who rose from the dead and renewed Adam.

5. Glory to you, glory to you, O King of glory,
   Who by the precious cross freed us from enslavement to the enemy.
6. O most holy Virgin, intercede for us,
   To God who was born from you, that he will save our souls.

Other Hymns

1. The prophet Moses prefigured the image of the cross,
   When he stretched forth his hands on the mountain,
   And turned back Amalek [Exod. 17:11–13],
   But Christ has given us a sign, the tree of the cross,
   Let us laud him with praise and give glory to God.
2. When Christ went up on the cross,
   And was wounded by the infidels with a lance,
   Then the veil of the temple was rent,
   And all creatures said with astonishment,
   Let us laud him with praise and give glory to God.
3. Come, O believers, let us worship the cross of Christ, our hope,
   By which [the Devil][23] was cast out,
   And the cross that was given to us to vanquish the enemy,
   Let us laud him with praise and give glory.
4. For by the cross Christ destroyed the enemy,
   By the precious cross he shattered the gates of bronze,
   And gave us the cross as a guide to paradise,
   Let us say to him all together,
   Let us laud him with praise and give glory to God.
5. For a seal has been given to us—the tree of the cross,
   On which the Savior willingly suffered,
   By the tree he crushed the pride of the enemy,
   And granted us the cross as the guardian of our souls,
   Let us laud him with praise and give glory to the God.
6. Glory to the infinite patience of the Savior,

---

23 "The Devil" is missing from this manuscript but is present in the other witnesses. It seems necessary here for the sense of the passage.

For he endured everything, he was crucified like a thief,
By the light of his divinity he separated us from the darkness,
And gave us, the believers, paradise,
Let us say to him all together,
And let us laud him with praise {and give glory to the God.}

At: "It was made strong . . . " [Ode 3; 1 Kgdms. 2:1–10]

1. My heart was made strong by the Lord my God,
   For Christ has conquered by the cross,
   And those who were in darkness,
   He has brought forth to the light,
2. You have confirmed your church in truth,
   Among the believers, O Lord,
   And in it you raised up the victorious cross,
   The assurance of humankind.
3. Our enemy, the adversary,
   You have trampled down by the cross, O Christ,
   And by your Resurrection, you have illuminated the world.
4. Unto eternity, O Lord, the memory of your life-giving cross,
   Has assembled all the ends of the earth for your praise.
5. O most holy Theotokos,
   Pray to the one who is seated upon the cherubim,
   And took flesh from you,
   That he will deliver us from temptation.

Other Hymns

1. Strengthen us, Christ, who was born from the Virgin,
   Confirm us in you,
   And lead us to the light of your knowledge,
   For no one is holy apart from you, O Lord
2. Come, O believers, to God who gives strength,
   The enlightener of our souls,
   Let us all glorify him with worship,
   For through his salvation, he has saved the whole world.

3. The sign of your cross, Christ, the deified tree,
   By your heavenly light you made it shine on the earth,
   Through which its ends have been renewed,
   And all the gentiles have come to believe in your salvation,
   They will come and worship before you, O Lord,
   And praise your name.
4. You who brought forth immortality for us by your burial,
   And called those who were in hell to the light of salvation,
   And filled all the ends of the earth with joy,
   Save us, who sing of your cross and Resurrection,
   O Only One, the All-Merciful.
5. You have defeated the enemies of your life-giving cross,
   And of the Theotokos,
   Give us the peace of your salvation,
   For you are the Only One, the Compassionate,
   And deliver our souls, we pray to you, from temptation.
6. O all-praised, Holy Mary the Theotokos,
   Offer prayers for those who hope in you,
   Before your Son so that by your intercession,
   He will forgive us our sins,
   O Holy Mother of Christ our God.

At: "O Lord, I have heard . . . " [Ode 4; Hab. 3:2–19]

1. I have heard of your renown, O Lord,
   For you were raised up on the cross,
   And we glorify your power.
2. By the tree you destroyed sin, O Lord,
   And by your Resurrection,
   You saved the human race from corruption.
3. You who by your precious cross slayed death,
   You raised us up to the light,
   We who glorify {your power.}

Appendix 1

Other Hymns

1. I have heard of your renown, O Lord,
   And I have been seized by fear,
   I have considered your works,
   For you have come to free us from the bonds of death.
2. You have revealed the true Word from heaven,
   You have come into the world, a mysterious plan,
   You took on flesh from the Virgin,
   And saved the human race, for you are God.
3. Through your coming, Christ, you have crowned the churches,
   And you have made the tree of our salvation shine forth,
   Your cross, O Lord,
   By which we the believers all are saved.
4. It pleased you to go up on the cross, Christ,
   For the salvation of the first-created,
   And you freed us from the curse of the law,
   By your precious blood,
   For by your wounds we have all been healed [cf. 1 Pet. 2:24],
   Glory to your power, O Lord, who came for our salvation.
5. You who for the love of humankind,
   Were willingly placed in the tomb,
   And as King by the power of divinity,
   Shattered the shackles of death,
   And by your Resurrection,
   Took hell captive and renewed Adam,
   You granted resurrection to us all,
   Glory to your power, O Lord, {who came for our salvation.}

At: "In the night . . . " [Ode 5; Isa. 26:9–20]

1. You who made the light to shine,
   Who illumined the dawn and made the day shine,
   Glory, glory to you, {O Jesus Son of God.}
2. You who made the light to shine,
   And were born from the Virgin,
   Through her intercessions save our souls, O Jesus Son of God.

3. You who gave incorruption to the human race,
   And forgiveness of sins by your cross,
   Glory, glory to you, O Jesus Son of God.
4. You who have given us your precious cross,
   For our protection and victory against the enemy,
   Glory, glory to you, O Jesus Son of God.
5. You who were crucified, buried, and destroyed hell,
   And rose on the third day,
   Glory, {glory to you, O Jesus Son of God.}
6. With angelic voice we cry out to you,[24]
   O most holy Virgin, {rejoice, O Cause of Joy,
   O unwed Mother of Jesus the Son of God.}

Other Hymns

1. For you we rise up early, O Christ God,
   A true early rising to glorify and praise your name,
   Let us sing ceaselessly to the sign of your cross,
   Which you have given us as an armament for victory.
2. O Lord our God, you have given us your peace,
   And you have guarded us through the protection of your cross,
   You do not disregard the supplications of your people,
   For there is no other God before you.
3. You who nailed to the cross our sinful contract [cf. Col. 2:14],
   And brought forth the fallen Adam from the gates of death,
   And changed our mortality into immortality,
   For your commandments are a light [cf. Prov. 6:23].
4. We boast in your cross, Christ,
   And we sing and declare your holy Resurrection,
   Have mercy on us, O Lord, who sing to you,
   Through the intercessions of your incorruptible Mother,
   O Lover of humankind.

24 Only the first half of this strophe appears in the manuscript, but a complete version is found in some manuscripts in the Octoechos, in the fourth mode for the fifth ode, allowing for the full translation here. See Metreveli, Čankievi, and Xevsuriani, *Užvelesi iadgari*, 427.

At: "I cried out . . . " [Ode 6; Jon. 2:3–10]

1. In the depths of my sin I have fallen, and I cry out,
   O Lord, O Lord, help me.
2. You who preserved the Virgin as a virgin even after birth,
   And freed us by your cross,
   O Lord, O Lord, {help me.}
3. You who stretched forth your hands upon the cross,
   And took hell captive,
   O Lord, O Lord, help me.
4. You who by the cross trampled down death,
   And granted resurrection to us all,
   O Lord, O Lord, {help me.}
5. You who were raised up on the cross, Christ
   And made light to shine upon the world,
   O Lord, O Lord, {help me.}
6. You who condemned Hell by your cross,
   And illuminated those who were in darkness,
   O Lord, {O Lord help me.}

Other Hymns

1. I cried out in my affliction to God the Merciful,
   He heard me on his holy mountain [cf. Ps. 3:4],
   He sent the Word and saved me, the Most High,
   And brought my life up out of corruption.
2. He who became human in the fullness of time,
   And made light to shine upon the world,
   And dispelled the reign of the evil enemy,
   And delivered us from corruption and death, the Lord.
3. He was sent from heaven by the Father,
   The Word became flesh,
   He willingly endured crucifixion,
   He was buried in the heart of the earth for three days and three nights,
   He arose inevitably, since he is God,
   And has granted resurrection to us all.

4. Come, O peoples, let us sing to the Lord with praise,
   Let us cry out to God our Savior,
   Let us venerate the life-giving cross,
   For he has saved us from our transgressions,
   The holy Lord Jesus,
   Who revealed resurrection to us.
5. As your prophet Jonah, I cry out to you, O Lord.
   From the depths of our sins you have saved us,
   By your cross, O Christ God,
   For you are the Only One, the Merciful, the Lover of Humankind.

At: "Blessed are you . . . " [Ode 7; Dan. 3:26–56]
1. You who conversed with Moses on the mountain [cf. Exod. 19],[25]
   And {revealed} the figure of the Virgin {by the bush [cf. Exod. 3:2],[26]
   Blessed are you, O Lord, God of our fathers.}
2. You who deliberately nailed to the cross our sinful contract [Col. 2:14],
   And by it transformed the transgression into incorruption,
   Blessed are you, O Lord, God of our fathers.
3. The first created was expelled from the place of delight,
   But by the cross you call us to say with the thief,
   Blessed are you, O Lord, God {of our fathers.}
4. You who raised up among us the all-protecting cross,
   And by it delivered the world from error, O Giver of Life,
   Blessed are you, O Lord, God of our fathers.

---

25 Only the first part of this hymn appears in the manuscripts, but the complete version is known from the chantbook's Octoechos, fourth mode, seventh ode, and forms the basis for the complete hymn here: Shoemaker, *The First Christian Hymnal*, 127. The hymn is also known in Greek: Eustatiades, Εἱρμολογιον, 104.

26 The burning bush is a common type of the Virgin Mary, in that it held the divine presence without being consumed by it.

Appendix 1

Other Hymns

1. You who were born from the Virgin,
   Because you are God and human,
   You suffered in the flesh on the cross,
   And you saved us,
   Blessed are you, O Lord, God {of our fathers.}
2. You who were raised up on the cross,
   And have illuminated the world,
   And through it you have granted us victory over the enemy,
   Blessed are you, O Lord, God of our fathers.
3. To the consubstantial Father, the Only Begotten Son,
   With the Holy Spirit we give glory,
   Blessed are you, O Lord, {God of our fathers.}

At: "Bless . . . " [Ode 8; Dan. 3:57–88]

1. All the works of God and every creature,
   Bless the Lord.
2. For the salvation of humankind has appeared on earth,
   And has illuminated all the ends of the earth,
   And granted life eternal to us all,
   {Priests,} bless him,
   {People exalt him above all, unto the ages.}
3. A great and guarded mystery, buried in the earth,
   Has shone forth in the heavens,
   The triumphant cross has appeared to us as an armament,
   {Priests,} bless him,
   {People exalt him above all, unto the ages.}
4. The life-giving and incorruptible sign,
   The wood of the cross, has appeared on the earth,
   It grants authority to the emperors,
   It eliminates deception, it enlightens us all,
   Priests, bless him,
   People exalt him above all, {unto the ages.}

Other Hymns

1. We the believers celebrate,
   The feast of your life-giving cross of salvation,
   And we cry out together and say,
   Priests, bless him,
   People exalt him above all, unto the ages.
2. The eternal royal sign, which was given to us, the believers,
   To vanquish the enemy, the precious cross,
   Priests, bless him,
   People exalt him above all, unto the ages.
3. The deified tree of the great divine economy,
   Has been brought forth from the earth for our salvation,
   By the Word of God, the precious cross,
   Priests, bless him,
   People exalt him above all, {unto the ages.}

At: "Magnify . . . " [Ode 9; Luke 1:46–55]

1. Let us sing to the glorious one,
   Who is exalted with the Most High,
   We who confess you after birth as the Theotokos,
   Most holy Virgin Mary,
   We glorify you with a hymn.
2. The people of the believers celebrate today with joy,
   For Christ has raised up among us the cross as a protector,
   By which he destroyed the arrogance of the enemy,
   We who hope in the cross,
   Worship him, the immortal King,
   We glorify him with a hymn.
3. The Lord has revealed his salvation,
   For the deliverance of humankind,
   Since by the cross he freed us from the curse,
   And by his side he granted us the saving forgiveness,
   We who hope {in the cross,}
   Worship him, the immortal King,
   {We glorify him with a hymn.}

Appendix 1

Other Hymns

1. Through you, O Virgin Mary, Christ has shone forth for us,
   Who willingly endured suffering on the cross,
   And nailed our sins to the cross,
   And granted us all eternal life.
2. Blessed is Christ our God,
   Who brought forth those who were in darkness to the light,
   And who gave us the saving cross as an armament,
   Come, O peoples, let us venerate the precious cross.
3. The triumphant, precious cross,
   Which appeared in the Heavens to the invincible emperor,
   By which he was granted victory over the enemies,
   He received the cross of Christ with joy,
   Come, O peoples, let us venerate the precious {cross.}
4. Boldness was given to the blessed empress by God,
   With faith she sought the tree of the cross,
   Through a miracle the cross of Christ was discovered,
   Come, O peoples, let us venerate the precious cross.

At: "Praise . . . " [Ps. 148]

1. We praise Christ God, the King,
   Who for our sake was raised up on the cross,
   And triumphantly took hell captive.
2. We praise you Christ, who were born from the Virgin,
   And by your birth you renewed humankind,
   By the cross you slayed death,
   And saved those who believe in you.
3. We worship you, Christ, who for our sake,
   Became a human being, was crucified,
   Buried, and rose on the third day,
   By the cross you slayed the enemy,
   And saved those who believe in you.

4. The precious cross shone with light,
   On which the Savior stretched forth his hands,
   He destroyed the sins of the world,
   And granted resurrection to us all.

Other Hymns
1. You who by the cross revealed to us the light,
   And made us depart from darkness,
   You made known your invisible magnificence,
   And illuminated the world,
   We ceaselessly venerate the precious cross,
   And sing to your Resurrection,
   O Christ God, have mercy on us.
2. You who transformed our corruption into incorruption,
   And brought forth Adam the first created from the gates of death,
   And transformed our mortality into immortality,
   We ceaselessly venerate the precious cross,
   {And sing to your Resurrection,
   O Christ God, have mercy on us.}
3. You who by your cross shattered the brass gates,
   And brought forth to the light those who were in it,
   And bestowed on us the light of your divinity,
   We ceaselessly venerate the precious cross,
   {And sing to your Resurrection,
   O Christ God, have mercy on us.}

Other Hymns
1. As a triumphant armament, Christ,
   You have given us your cross,
   And by it we will triumph in combat with the enemy.
2. As a sign for those who fear you, O Lord,
   You have given your precious cross,
   By which you dissolved the dominion, the reign of darkness,
   And you have restored us to the original blessing,

Appendix 1

　　　On account of which we acclaim the economy of your love of humankind,
　　　O Jesus, the Almighty, Savior of our souls.
3. Your cross has become a rampart for us,
　　　O Jesus our Savior,
　　　For we the believers have no other hope than you,
　　　Who were nailed to it in the flesh,
　　　And have bestowed great mercy to all.
4. The sign of your cross has been raised up, O Lord,
　　　Which was triumphant in the face of the enemy,
　　　The holy church has been confirmed,
　　　And your holy name is glorified.
5. The light of your face, O Lord, has appeared to us,
　　　By the power of your precious cross,
　　　Therefore we pray and beseech you,
　　　Have mercy on us, your creatures,
　　　For you are the Only One, the Compassionate.

Other Hymns

1. You came for the salvation of all, O Christ God,
　　　Through the will of the Father and the Holy Spirit,
　　　You put on humanity from the Virgin,
　　　In order to call the gentiles to a new song,
　　　By your holy cross save us,
　　　And by your Resurrection have mercy on us.
2. The divinely adorned, lordly tree of your cross, O Lord,
　　　Which appeared to us in the heavens at Golgotha,
　　　By which the creatures were illuminated,
　　　And became worthy of the original blessing,
　　　By this same cross, have mercy on us and save us.
3. To the servant of God the emperor Constantine,
　　　The sign of your cross appeared, O Lord,
　　　And by it he vanquished the armed camp of the enemy,
　　　With your help, O Lord, and by the appearance of your precious cross,
　　　His enemies were defeated,
　　　By this same cross, have mercy on us and save us.

4. The wondrous and brilliantly adorned cross of Heaven,
   Which appeared at Golgotha,
   When it was seen reaching as far as the Mount of Olives,
   Shining more brilliantly than the sun.
   By this {same cross, have mercy on us and save us.}
5. Today your cross, O Lord, is exalted to the highest,
   Hidden in the earth, it is discovered,
   And it renews again the Resurrection of Christ,
   The power of the enemy is bound,
   And the world is saved from deception,
   And the ends of the earth rejoice,
   In the feast of your precious cross,
   By this same cross, have mercy on us,
   And by your Resurrection {save us.}

LITURGY

Petition[27]

> The seal of Christ has saved us all,
> The salvation {and resurrection of our souls.}[28]

Psalm, Fourth Plagal Mode

> Save, O Lord, your people and bless . . . [Ps. 27:9]
> Refrain: The Lord is the strength of his people . . . [Ps. 27:8]

Alleluia

> Be still, and . . . [Ps. 45:11]

The Washing of Hands, Fourth Plagal Mode

> O God, the word of your prophet Moses has been fulfilled, which he said,
> See, before your eyes your salvation hanging on a tree [cf. Deut. 28:66],

---

27 The edition indicates a rubric here referring to 7 May, but there is no such note at this point in the manuscript. The edition also indicates a different hymn for the petition that is not in this manuscript.

28 Completed on the basis of MS C.

For today the cross is exalted and the world is delivered from deception,
Today the Resurrection of Christ is renewed, and the ends of the earth
    rejoice,
We offer the praise of David and say while singing,
O God, you have worked salvation in the midst of the earth [Ps. 73:12],
Through the Resurrection and have illuminated the world,
O Lord, the Merciful and the Lover of Humankind, glory to you.

APPENDIX 2

AKOLOUTHIA BEFORE BATTLE

TRANSLATION BY JOHN KLENTOS

Order chanted upon the army's departure and alliance to our Lord Jesus Christ, the most holy Theotokos, the bodiless [angels], the apostles, and the martyrs.[1]

Stichera
TONE 1

1. Savior who gave strength in battle to David the wise, as Goliath in the past, destroy those who war against us, Compassionate One, and with your invisible slingshot, Christ, crush their audacity and bad intentions, so that we may praise you in faith.
2. O Son of God, Life-giver, through the prayers of your mother, through the sacred petitions of angels, apostles, victorious martyrs, gladden our faithful basileus, shatter the column of the barbarians, and have mercy on the army that honors you.
3. He who showed to Constantine, the first basileus of Christians, the sacred cross and declared from heaven "be courageous by this victory," you are

---

[1] This translation is based upon the Greek text published by A. Pertusi, "Una akolouthia militaria inedita del x secolo," *Aevum* 22 (1948): 145–68.

the God of the cross with strength, and now give victory and strength and truly divine power to your army, as the compassionate one.

4. Glory ... both now ... Lord, who fought alongside the most gentle David to subordinate the foreigner, fight alongside our faithful basileus; and with the weapon of the cross destroy our enemies; O Compassionate One, show to us the ancient things, have mercy; and let them truly know that you are God.

TONE 2 PLAGAL

5. O Virgin, bride of God, entreat God who took bodily form to deliver us from the barbarian attacks and every other harm, so that we may glorify you.
6. Pure birth-giver of God, now quickly bring to naught the designs of the enemies who blaspheme you, through the intercessions of the apostles, angels, archangels, and of the victorious labor-bearers.
7. O Virgin, as you gave birth to the creator of the world, greatly shame and show as weak the arrogant army, burning with rage, heavily armed, lacking your help.

Glory, in the same tone

8. O Cross of Christ, the hope of Christians, guide of wandering people, harbor for the tempest-tossed, victor in times of war, support of basileis, healer of sick people, the resurrection of dead people, have mercy on us.
9. Because we have you, O Theotokos, as hope and protection, we do not fear the plots of the enemies, because you protect our souls.

APOLOTIKION, TONE 1

10. Save, O Lord, your people, and bless your inheritance, grant victory to the basileus against the barbarians, and guard your commonwealth through your cross.

THEOTOKION

11. We who have acquired your protection, O Undefiled, and through your petitions have been saved from sufferings, who have been protected in every way by the cross of your Son, obliged, we all magnify you piously.

Appendix 2

Kanon

ODE 1

1. O Three-sun unity, O three-hypostasis nature, who holds all things, through divine power strengthen army and fleet against enemies who blaspheme you and give victory through them to your faithful basileus.
2. You who established through your will the spiritual company of angelic armies and fire-bearing generals, O King of all, through their divine alliance make victorious against the enemies the army bearing the name of Christ.
3. O Bridegroom of the souls, who showed the wise disciples escorts of the bride [which is] the church and now through their intercessions give to your army the trophies of victory on the earth and sea, as Lover of humankind.
4. Firm soldiers of much-contending martyrs, direct the advances of the army bearing the name of Christ and the pious fleet by your petitions making the sea calm and restoring the earth before their face.

ODE 3

1. Giving force to the God-bearing basileus through your cross, O Christ, give strength against the lawless enemies to the undefeated army which was gathered [by the basileus].
2. Like a chariot and horseman of the army, appear from on high, O Michael, commander-in-chief, with armies of angels fighting against hostile enemies.
3. You who are powerful in times of war, now destroy completely the bows and arrows of the adversaries, in cooperation with the apostles, who were sent as arrows into the world.
4. The whole army of trophy-bearing martyrs of Christ, gather and appear to the faithful army and fleet, making an alliance for plundering the enemies.
5. It is the work of your strength, O all-pure one, to destroy the walls and cities and insolence of the adversaries, O Theotokos, for the preservation of your people.

Kathisma, Fourth Plagal

6. Powerful and mighty in war, the same one, by nature good and compassionate, grant your dynasty as defensive weapon, O Savior, to the people bearing the name of Christ, through the intercessions of the Theotokos, as the good one bringing to light the trophy-bearing army of apostles and martyrs and of the bodiless divine ministers who honor you, O Son of God.

ODE 4

1. As before you glorified Moses the Lawgiver by introduction into the mysteries and by military leadership, O Lover of humankind, and now by the prizes of the best and bravest make completely radiant, O Christ, he who reigns over your army.
2. The fire-bearing power of flame-bearing armies and the work of the squadron commanders invisibly launching burning arrows, completely consume with flame, as grass, the armies of wicked, pernicious enemies.
3. The best are blasphemed by the arrogant enemies and the holy things are broken by the impious, disciples who cleaned the entire earth from error and hatred, now completely shatter their scorn.
4. With the trophies of victory and through the brave actions make radiant against the barbarians[, who are] atheist, the countless-suffering army of very radiant, very brave people, the fleet of the God-thinking basileus, cavalry, and infantry.
5. As one more excellent than the angels and mistress of the creation, making them more powerful than the enemies, now keep those fighting on behalf of your people free from attacks and ill-treatment.

ODE 5

1. Impious people disrespected you lawlessly, but they have to know your dynasty, O Master, through which they will now come under treaty, and they are going to become slaves for those who know you well.
2. Unbelievably you destroyed the numerous army of Assyrians through the hand of the angel, through whom you destroy the barbarian tribes and through the victories make happy the faithful basileus, O Master.

3. Apostles of the faithful, first you became leaders and then show yourselves to be governors of the fleet and army; now we ask you fervently to be sailing together [with them] in the sea and escorting them on land.
4. First expel the noetic and palpable enemies through powerful struggle, formerly arriving as athletes become champions together with us, expelling the armies of the hostiles.
5. During hard times having as help your protection, Mother of God, and in war we wish we would find you to be fighting on [our] behalf, saving at sea and protecting on land.

ODE 6

1. Subdue with your divine power the land and people and cities of lawless enemies and tyrants, O King of all, through your faithful basileus for the preservation of your people.
2. Throwing down the armies and walls of the barbarians by the hands of angels, now, O Word, grant easily complete destruction of the impious and terribly arrogant people.
3. Initiates into the mystery of Christ, appearing first as joyful lamps of all the world, before the face of the Orthodox people through your supplications ignite enlightening fire, now burning up the bodies of the enemies.
4. Through the successful deeds of all the martyrs you were respected, Compassionate One, distribute to your people from on high strength of alliance battling against enemies who do not honor you.
5. Let the nations that do not know God know, O Theotokos, your undefeatable dynasty through which you guard your people, who honor you from every assault.

Kontakion, Fourth Plagal

6. Make us strong against barbarian evils, mighty, powerful, only Lord, through the intercession of the Theotokos, who gave birth to you, of the apostles, archangels, and martyrs, and liberate us from various difficulties, so that we may cry: Glory is due to your might.

Oikos

7. Let us cry out fervently to the Master today, the Christian system being in dangerous situations and sorrows, look down upon the people who from infancy place their hopes in you, and destroy completely the raging fierceness of the arrogant enemies through the prayers of the one who gave you birth, of the immaterial ministers, and of the preachers of God, victorious martyrs, for upon going out to war we invoke you as our helper, the only one powerful in wars; for completely trusting in you and in you we are proud crying out: glory is due your dominion.

ODE 7

1. Regally and mightily, he who is master of all creation, make the earth which was taken from the inheritance of the Romans by the barbarian tyranny subject to the basileus who is proud in you, O you who govern everything.
2. The many-named multitude of heavenly orders, the alliance of the faithful soldiers, be attentive to them all together, showing as defeated the armies and columns of the enemies.
3. O apostles, make powerful through the victories against the adversaries the God-crowned basileus who magnifies your shining festivals by candle-lit sacred and popular feasts.
4. The army of the martyrs who in the past destroyed the crafty armies of the demons, now destroy the army of the enemies raging against us who in faith are acting in honor of your memory.
5. The ends of the earth saw the Word who came from you before salvation, pure one, now let them know by action, all-immaculate, that you save your slaves through the hand of the basileus who desired you.

ODE 8

1. Make the basileus whom you chose appear as a trophy-bearing victor against the impious enemies, Lover of humankind, making the reins and scepter of his pious rule powerful in his hands.
2. Extreme chief of the martyrs of Christ, the so-called Rock of the Faith, lift up the horn of the faithful and destroy the audacity of the lawless enemies who do not honor God whom you proclaimed.

3. Twelve-in-number chorus of apostles, many-numbered multitude of victors, who were excellently steady and who destroyed the audacity of the tyrants, now become allies of the army.
4. O Lady, as you are a general fighting for riches in war, immaculate one, the army bearing the name of Christ, through you, will defeat people and cities of the arrogant enemies who do not honor you.

ODE 9

1. Destroy the enemies' bad intentions against us, the thoughts, treacheries, ways, cunning works, words, arrogance, and audacity, making them unable to act; through your providence, O Word, fight with those who recognize your power.
2. Swords and war of the enemies the arrows and power of the bows destroy, through the alliance of divine angels; through your intervention, Savior, guard the army of the portion bearing the name of Christ, giving to it a trophy of victory.
3. Having the power from God even to bind the enemies, forgive the mistakes of the army, the compassionate Christ forgets every time they attack the enemy in order to take with them the glory.
4. Send now from on high like strong arrows your brave generals for the help of your faithful people who are ready for war to fight against enemies who do not respect your power, for we do not believe in any other except you.
5. Show us to be victors, magnify those who always magnify you, make strong the scepters of the basileis who fervently respect your offspring and richly decorate their army with crowns of victory, O virgin Mother.

Exaposteilarion, Fourth Tone

1. Make us worthy to see the full destruction of our enemies, Merciful One, who loves humankind, through the intercessions of the Theotokos, angels and archangels, martyrs and apostles, and make powerful your army, which agrees that you are the life-giving Son of God.
2. The Savior, the joy, the truth came, and those in darkness and shadow let us see the great light of enlightenment, our God, glory to you.

3. The grace was now given to all of those who bear the name of Christ from Christ the preeminent and world-saving Word and our only God.
Glory to you, our God, glory to you, we thank you, holy Trinity,
glory to you. Amen.

APPENDIX 3

AKOLOUTHIA FOR FALLEN SOLDIERS

TRANSLATION BY GEORGE E. DEMACOPOULOS

For the Saturday of Apokreas, the day of the reposed, especially for those generals, officers, and soldiers who died in combat or as prisoners of war.[1]

Stichera

SECOND TONE PLAGAL

1. Let us come together, people of Christ, and complete the memorial of our brothers who died fighting and those who died in unbearable captivity, let us be troubled on their behalf.
2. Lover of humanity, your servants were heroic, even to the point of slaughter. Receive those who persevered while they were ruthlessly beaten as prisoners. Lover of humanity, may these things become an expiation for their souls.
3. You who alone exist without sin, concerning those you have called to yourself—notable generals, leading officers, and valiant soldiers—deem them worthy to find rest near you.

---

1 This translation is based on T. Détorakis and J. Mossay, "Un office byzantine inédit pour ceux qui sont morts à la guerre, dans le Cod. Sin. Gr. 734-735," *Le Muséon* 101.1 (1988): 183–211.

FOURTH TONE PLAGAL

4. You proclaimed as allies of your people, almighty Christ, those who keep firm their faith and commitment to you as well as those holding firm who are willing to die for you or to endure many years of captivity without denying you, the living Lord; rank them among the choirs of the saints and among the spirits of the righteous.
5. They proved themselves to be the foundation of their country and of their entire race by despising life here below as but fleeting; they purified their souls by shedding their blood, they suffered death by the edge of swords, they were reduced to captivity and were happy to pass into the world beyond; Christ Master, grant rest to their souls in the bosom of Abraham.
6. May your servants see the glory of your saints, Christ, and may they be noetically filled with your joy; may the light of your face and your tenderness shine in them, for they served you only, and they protected your people, having received death or captivity in warfare in return; have mercy on them, grant them joy and rest in you.

Kanon for Those Soldiers Who Died Fighting or in Captivity

ODE 1

1. Savior, King of all, we venerate your nature as God immortal and as one subject to death like us; make worthy of joy those of the elect who died on behalf of you.
2. O depth of rich wisdom, how could you deliver into the hands of those who reject you, the faithful ones who reveal the firmness and purity of soul by enduring an unjust slaughter?
3. Jesus, purify your most valiant soldiers, who as youths threw themselves into the fray against the enemies, along with those who were taken prisoner, for on your behalf they bathed in blood.

Theotokion

4. You fill the world with joy by your childbearing, you who lifted the curse against the first mother; for it was through you that all things were renewed, that God became flesh and lived among us.

ODE 2

1. The descendants of Rome, a flock of the holy shepherd, by confessing you they faced the cruel barbarians and, although they died, they obtained life.
2. To protect your chosen people from the hands of the barbarians, Christ, you provided brave warriors who died honorably in battle and in captivity.
3. Christian troops, most faithful and steadfast, who died for your people, may their souls be received by you, only king, with sweet smelling incense.

Theotokion

4. What is, bride of God, the immense wealth of your goodness? What is the secret design of the mystery? For, through you, the God who became human renews those who are perishing.

ODE 3

1. Here are the divinely chosen people, soldiers of the Lord who died for his inheritance. May their mystical sacrifices be worthy of redemption.
2. The souls of your faithful soldiers, Christ, have been transported as virgins into your divine bridal chamber, still imprinted by the wounds and massacres of which they were victim.
3. Having conquered the enemies by fighting valiantly and lifting trophies from their remains, or having been imprisoned in dungeons, let us be judged worthy of the divine glory which is in you.

Theotokion

4. Theotokos, embellished by the beauty of your virtues, you gave birth and nursed in an ineffable way Jesus, the one who makes beautiful the ugliness of nature.

ODE 4

1. It is lawful, compassionate one, to enlist those who suffered greatly while doing their duty as good and virtuous soldiers, so that in their deaths they might enjoy union with your Passion.

2. My Savior, with your name as a protective wall, your army routed the barbarian masses. Encamp their souls in your luminous fortress.
3. Nature could not bend nor wealth seduce the soldiers of Jesus Christ to prefer an inglorious life to a glorious death; but after dying in battle or captivity they enjoy rest.

Theotokion

4. O Virgin, the might of the envious one was insufficient because the power that the Father encamped in your bosom empowered mortals against him.

ODE 5

1. King of all, your soldiers faced danger on behalf of the faith and your name. Place them in the abodes of the firstborn, as being the equals of martyrs.
2. May the memory be honored for all those admirable lieutenants, the commanding officers of the godly soldiers of Christ, all those who were willing to die in prison or battle on behalf of the Christians.
3. Purified by a desire for Christ, they gave no thought to the harsh violence of the barbarians, those bright towers of Christians who refused submission, worthily they are honored every year.

Theotokion

4. He lovingly lowered the heavens from their highest height to those on earth when he came to dwell in the flesh, being born of a pure virgin, he who regulates all things with a simple nod.

ODE 6

1. Having been marked by the drops of your immaculate blood, divinely shed, Jesus, your servants died reducing the strength of the enemies and so they came happily to make camp near you.
2. Savior, show them to be members of the illuminated camp of remitted sin those faithful who perished while fighting or in prison. Accept their piety.

3. Creator, you alone are not subject to suffering. As you therefore know that [human] nature is perilous and subject to suffering, grant rest to those who died on the front lines.

Theotokion

4. O limitless ocean of goodness, how did you, who are invisible God, humble yourself to take on the form of a servant and be born from the virgin womb of a maiden? This is beyond comprehension.

ODE 7

1. The most stubborn arrogance of the barbarians did not weaken your power. But after you battled against them with courage and firmness, you not only overthrow the enemy but strengthened the Christians.
2. You have been accepted by the Christians as a propitiatory and most sacred offering, for it is you who have freed them from the painful damage of the barbarians. And now, as a worthy exchange, you are the object of their memorial.
3. Christ, give to the people who honor you harbors of salvation, those who put forth their souls on the front lines and in captivity. They who died on your behalf, deem them worthy of joy.

Theotokion

4. Mediatress without reproach, by your birth-giving of the one who became incarnate from you, you reconcile with the Father those who had been rejected, appearing as a propitiation for those who have fallen, and a safe harbor for those who seek refuge in you.

ODE 8

1. Spreading wide their hopes in you, the ones whose bravery lies in your power saved the lives of the whole Christian people. Compassionate one, grant them rest in the abodes of the righteous.
2. The noble defenders of your divine flock were presented to you as sentient offerings, having welcomed those who received the [military] brand, station them now in your indestructible tents.

3. You who know the slipperiness of nature, O Compassionate One, give rest to these generals, officers, and the divine regiments of imprisoned soldiers who have now left this earth.

Theotokion

4. The Word became flesh in you, all blessed one, and goes forward bearing two natures united in the mystery of a single hypostasis, according to the faith of the Incarnation.

ODE 9

1. Immortal and unique one, having power over all flesh, judge as worthy of the light those who for the sake of your flock were destroyed in battle or in prison at the hands of the barbarians.
2. On behalf of the noble soldiers who renounced this earthly existence by offering their lives for Christ and his inheritance and for the faithful as well, we ask that their souls now find rest.
3. Today, let us honor faithfully the memory of those who died a good and honorable death in prison or combat for the sake of the people and the race of Christians.

Theotokion

4. Pure mother, appearing husbandless, you were perceived to be a supernatural mother to the virgins, for you conceived without planting and gave birth to God, who reveals in you things that surpass nature.

AN ADDITIONAL HEIRMOS

1. Christ, death has long feared you. And because of your death, death for men is now called sleep. Without fear, the band of soldiers who hope in you were slaughtered in the battle with the barbarians. Give them rest in you.
2. My savior, be gracious to our compatriots who died on your behalf in battle or captivity, and give them release from their shortcomings on account of our prayers and be appeased by our spotless sacrifices offered for them.
3. Among men, no one is pure of all defilement, except you, the pure God and only compassionate one. Therefore, allow yourself to be swayed by

our supplications and for those who died in service for you here below, enlist them in the armies above.

Theotokion
4. The laws of nature yield before you, Panagia, for you brought into the world while remaining a virgin the one who created and shapes nature, Christ, the one who makes known to all that the authority of his power rests in you as both mother and the all-pure one.

BIBLIOGRAPHY

Abbreviations

BK	*Bedi Kart[h]lisa*
BMGS	*Byzantine and Modern Greek Studies*
BSl	*Byzantinoslavica*
BZ	*Byzantinische Zeitschrift*
CCSG	Corpus christianorum, Series graeca
ChHist	*Church History*
DOP	*Dumbarton Oaks Papers*
JbAC	*Jahrbuch für Antike und Christentum*
JEChrSt	*Journal of Early Christian Studies*
JÖB	*Jahrbuch der Österreichischen Byzantinistik*
JPOS	*Journal of the Palestine Oriental Society*
JQR	*Jewish Quarterly Review*
JR	*Journal of Religion*
OC	*Oriens christianus*
OCP	*Orientalia christiana periodica*
ODB	*The Oxford Dictionary of Byzantium*, ed. A. Kazhdan et al. (New York, 1991)
PG	Patrologiae cursus completus, Series graeca, ed. J.-P. Migne (Paris, 1857–1866)
PO	*Patrologia orientalis*
SC	Sources chrétiennes
StP	*Studia patristica*
SVThQ	*St. Vladimir's Theological Quarterly*
TM	*Travaux et mémoires*

Works Cited

Agamben, G. *Homo Sacer: Sovereign Power and Bare Life*. Translated by D. Heller-Roazen. Stanford, 1998.

Alexander, P. "The Strength of Empire as Seen through Byzantine Eyes." *Speculum* 37.3 (1962): 339–57.

Allen, P., and Datema, C., trans. *Leontius, Presbyter of Constantinople: Fourteen Homilies*. Brisbane, 1991.

Anatolios, K. *Deification through the Cross: An Eastern Christian Theology of Salvation*. Grand Rapids, MI, 2020.

Anderson, G. "King David and the Psalms of Imprecation." *Pro Ecclesia: A Journal of Catholic and Evangelical Theology* 15 (2006): 267–80.

Arentzen, T. *The Virgin in Song: Mary and the Poetry of Romanos the Melodist*. Philadelphia, 2017.

Avi-Yonah, M. *The Jews under Roman and Byzantine Rule: A Political History of Palestine from the Bar Kokhba War to the Arab Conquest*. New York, 1976. Reprint, Jerusalem, 1984.

Azar, M. "Prophetic Matrix and Theological Paradox: Jews and Judaism in the Holy Week and Pascha Observances of the Greek Orthodox Church." *Studies in Christian-Jewish Relations* 10.1 (2015): 1–27.

Baldwin, B. "Romanos the Melode." *ODB* 3:1807–8.

Barkhuizen, J. H. "Romanos Melodos, *On the Massacre of the Innocents*: A Perspective on Ekphrasis as a Method of Patristic Exegesis." *Acta Classica* 50 (2007): 29–50.

Baumstark, A. "Denkmäler der Entstehungsgeschichte des byzantinischen Ritus." *OC* 2 (1927): 1–32.

Boersma, H. "The Church Fathers' Spiritual Interpretation of the Psalms." In *Living Waters from Ancient Springs: Essays in Honor of Cornelis Van Dam*, edited by J. Van Vliet, 41–56. Eugene, OR, 2011.

Borgehammar, S. *How the Holy Cross Was Found: From Event to Medieval Legend*. Stockholm, 1991.

Bradshaw, P. F. "Liturgy as 'Living Literature.'" In *Liturgy in Dialogue: Essays in Memory of Ronald Jasper*, edited by P. F. Bradshaw and B. Spinks, 139–54. Collegeville, MN, 1995.

Brock, S. "From Ephrem to Romanos." *StP* 20 (1989): 139–51.

Bucur, B. G. "Anti-Jewish Rhetoric in Byzantine Hymnography: Exegetical and Theological Contextualization." *SVThQ* 61.1 (2017): 39–60.

Calivas, A. "Great and Holy Saturday." Greek Orthodox Archdiocese of America. https://www.goarch.org/-/great-and-holy-saturday/.

Cameron, A. "Byzantines and Jews: Some Recent Work on Early Byzantium." *BMGS* 20 (1996): 249–74.

———. *Christianity and the Rhetoric of Empire: The Development of Christian Discourse.* Berkeley, 1994.

Cameron, A., and S. G. Hall, trans. *Eusebius: Life of Constantine.* Oxford, 1999.

Carpenter, M., ed. *Kontakia of Romanos.* Vol. 1, *On the Person of Christ.* Columbia, MO, 1969.

Chatzelis, G., and J. Harris, trans. *A Tenth-Century Byzantine Military Manual: The Sylloge Tacticorum.* Abingdon, 2017.

Dagron, G. "L'Église et la chrétienté byzantines entre les invasions et l'iconoclasme (VIIe–début VIIIe siècle)." In *Évêques, moines et empereurs (610–1054)*, edited by G. Dagron, P. Riché, and A. Vauchez, 9–91. Paris, 1993.

———. "Judaïser." *TM* 11 (1991): 359–58.

Dagron, G., and V. Deroche. "Juifs et Chrétiens dans l'Orient du septième siècle." *TM* 11 (1991): 17–273.

Dagron, G., and H. Mihaescu, eds. *Le traité sur la guérilla (De velitatione) de l'empereur Nicéphore Phocas (963–969).* Paris, 1986.

Datema, C., and P. Allen, eds. *Leontii Presbyteri Constantinopolitani Homiliae.* CCSG 17. Turnhout, 1987.

Delehaye, H. *Les légendes grecques des saints militaires.* Paris, 1909.

Demacopoulos, G. E. "Constantine, Ambrose, and the Morality of War: How Ambrose of Milan Challenged the Imperial Discourse on War and Violence." In *Orthodox Christian Perspectives on War*, edited by P. T. Hamalis and V. A. Karras, 159–94. Notre Dame, IN, 2018.

———. *Five Models of Spiritual Direction in the Early Church.* Notre Dame, IN, 2007.

———. "Patriarch Kirill's Crusade." *Public Orthodoxy*, 30 September 2022. https://publicorthodoxy.org/2022/09/30/patriarch-kirills-crusade/.

Dennis, G. "Defenders of the Christian People: Holy War in Byzantium." In *The Crusades from the Perspective of Byzantium and the Muslim World*, edited by A. Laiou and R. P. Mottahedeh, 31–39. Washington, DC, 2001.

———. "Religious Services in the Byzantine Army." *Eulogema* 17 (1993): 107–17.

———, trans. *The Taktika of Leo VI.* Washington, DC, 2010.

Déroche, V. "La polémique anti-judaïque au VIe au VIIe siècle." *TM* 11 (1991): 284–90.

Détorakis, T., and J. Mossay. "Un office byzantine inédit pour ceux qui sont morts à la guerre, dans le Cod. Sin. Gr. 734-735." *Le Muséon* 101.1 (1988): 183–211.

Diehl, C. *L'Afrique byzantine: Histoire de la domination byzantine en Afrique*. Paris, 1896.

"Digital Chant Stand." Greek Orthodox Archdiocese of America. https://dcs.goarch.org/goa/dcs/dcs.html.

Drijvers, J. W. *Helena Augusta: The Mother of Constantine the Great and the Legend of Her Finding of the Cross*. Leiden, 1992.

———. "Heraclius and the *Restitutio Crucis:* Notes on Symbolism and Ideology." In *The Reign of Heraclius (610–641): Crises and Confrontation*, edited by G. J. Reinink and B. H. Stotle, 175–90. Leuven, 2002.

Dunkle, B. *Enchantment and Creed in the Hymns of Ambrose of Milan*. Oxford, 2016.

Dzaynk'agh Sharakank' [Modal hymns]. Venice, 1907.

Ericksen, U. H. "The Poet in the Pulpit: Drama and Rhetoric in the *Kontakion* 'On the Victory of the Cross' by Romanos the Melodist." *Transfiguration: Nordic Journal of the Arts* (2010/2011): 103–23.

Eustratiades, S. Ειρμολόγιον: Μνημεία αγιολογικά. Agioreitike Bibliotheke 9. Chennevieres-sur-Marne, 1932.

Falcasantos, R. S. *Constantinople: Ritual, Violence, and Memory in the Making of a Christian Imperial City*. Oakland, 2020.

Flusin, B. "Les cérémonies de l'exaltation de la croix à Constantinople au XIe siècle d'après le *Dresdensis* A 104." In *Byzance et les reliques du Christ*, edited by J. Durand and B. Flusin, 61–89. Paris, 2004.

Follieri, E., ed. *Initia hymnorum ecclesiae Graecae*. 5 vols. Studi e testi 211–215. Vatican City, 1960.

Foucault, M. *The Archaeology of Knowledge*. Translated by A. M. Sheridan Smith. New York, 1972.

Frank, G. "Christ's Descent to the Underworld in Ancient Ritual and Legend." In *Apocalyptic Thought in Early Christianity*, edited by R. Daly, 211–26. Grand Rapids, MI, 2009.

———. "Romanos and the Night Vigil in the Sixth Century." In *Byzantine Christianity: A People's History of Christianity*, edited by D. Krueger, 59–78. Minneapolis, 2006.

Frolow, A. *La relique de la vraie croix: Recherches sur le développement d'un culte*. Paris, 1961.

Frøyshov, S. S. R. "The Early Development of the Liturgical Eight-Mode System in Jerusalem." *SVThQ* 51 (2007): 139–78.

———. "The Early History of the Hagiopolitan Daily Office in Constantinople: New Perspectives on the Formative Period of the Byzantine Rite." *DOP* 74 (2020): 351–82.

———. "The Georgian Witness to the Jerusalem Liturgy: New Sources and Studies." In *Inquiries into Eastern Christian Worship: Selected Papers of the Second International Congress of the Society of Oriental Liturgies, Rome, 17–21 September 2008*, edited by B. Groen, S. Hawkes-Teeples, and S. Alexopoulos, 227–68. Leuven, 2012.

———. "Rite of Jerusalem." *The Canterbury Dictionary of Hymnology.* https://hymnology.hymnsam.co.uk/r/rite-of-jerusalem.

Gager, J. G. *The Origins of Anti-Semitism: Attitudes toward Judaism in Pagan and Christian Antiquity*. New York, 1983.

Galadza, D. *Liturgy and Byzantinization in Jerusalem*. Oxford, 2019.

Goodman, M. *Mission and Conversion: Proselytizing in the Religious History of the Roman Empire*. Oxford, 1994.

Griffith, S. H. *The Church in the Shadow of the Mosque: Christians and Muslims in the World of Islam*. Princeton, 2008.

Groen, B. "Anti-Judaism in the Present-Day Byzantine Liturgy." *Journal of Eastern Christian Studies* 60 (2008): 369–87.

Grosdidier de Matons, J. "Liturgie et Hymnographie: Kontakion et Canon." *DOP* 34/35 (1980/1981): 31–43.

———. *Romanos le Mélode et les origins de la poésie religieuse à Byzance*. Paris, 1977.

Guevin, B. "Dialogue between Death and the Devil in Saint Ephrem the Syrian and Saint Romanos the Melodist." *StP* 92 (2017): 113–18.

Haldon, J., ed. *Byzantine Warfare*. Aldershot, 2007.

Hamalis, P. T., and V. A. Karras, eds. *Orthodox Christian Perspectives on War*. Notre Dame, IN, 2018.

Harakas, S. "No Just War in the Fathers." *In Communion*, rev. 15 August 2003. https://incommunion.org/2005/08/02/no-just-war-in-the-fathers/.

———. "The Teaching on Peace in the Fathers." In *Wholeness of Faith and Life: Orthodox Christian Ethics*. Pt. 1, *Patristic Ethics*, 137–61. Brookline, MA, 1999.

Harvey, S. A. "Bearing Witness: New Testament Women in Early Byzantine Hymnography." In *The New Testament in Byzantium*, edited by D. Krueger and R. Nelson, 205–20. Washington, DC, 2016.

———. "Liturgy and Ethics in Ancient Syriac Christianity: Two Paradigms." *Studies in Christian Ethics* 26 (2013): 300–316.

———. Review of M. Doerfler, *Jephtha's Daughter, Sarah's Son: The Death of Children in Late Antiquity*. IOTA Forum: Reviews, 28 June 2021. https://iota-web.org/2021/06/28/doerfler-jephthahs-daughter-sarahs-son/.

———. "Revisiting the Daughters of the Covenant: Women's Choirs and Sacred Song in Ancient Syriac Christianity." *Hugoye: Journal of Syriac Studies* 8 (2009): 125–49.

———. *Song and Memory: Biblical Women in Syriac Tradition*. Milwaukee, 2010.

Heid, S. "Der Ursprung der Helenalegende im Pilgerbetrieb Jerusalems." *JbAC* 32 (1989): 41–71.

Heine, R., trans. *Gregory of Nyssa's Treatise on the Inscriptions of the Psalms*. Oxford, 1995.

Hill, R. C., trans. *Theodoret of Cyrus: Commentary on the Psalms*. 2 vols. Washington, DC, 2000–2001.

Horbury, W. *Jews and Christians in Contact and Controversy*. Edinburgh, 1998.

Horowitz, E. "'The Vengeance of the Jews Was Stronger Than Their Avarice': Modern Historians and the Persian Conquest of Jerusalem in 614." *Jewish Social Studies* 4.2 (1988): 1–39.

Ioniță, A. "Byzantine Liturgical Hymnography: A Stumbling Stone for the Jewish–Orthodox Christian Dialogue?" *Review of Ecumenical Studies* 11.2 (2009): 253–67.

Janeras, S. *Le Vendredi-saint dans la tradition liturgique byzantine: Structure et histoire de ses offices*. Analecta liturgica 13. Rome, 1988.

Jeffery, P. "The Earliest Octōēchoi: The Role of Jerusalem and Palestine in the Beginnings of Modal Ordering." In *The Study of Medieval Chant: Paths and Bridges, East and West; In Honor of Kenneth Levy*, edited by P. Jeffery, 147–209. Woodbridge, 2001.

Jeffreys, E. "Old Testament 'History' and the Byzantine Chronicle." In *The Old Testament in Byzantium*, edited by P. Magdalino and R. Nelson, 155–74. Washington, DC, 2010.

Jeffries, E. "Kontakion." *ODB* 2:1148.

———. "Troparion." *ODB* 3:2124.

Jensen, R. *The Cross: History, Art, and Controversy*. Cambridge, MA, 2017.

Kaegi, W. "Arianism and the Byzantine Army in Africa 533–46." *Traditio* 21 (1965): 23–53.

———. *Army, Society, and Religion in Byzantium*. London, 1982.

———. "The Byzantine Armies and Iconoclasm." *BSl* 27.1 (1966): 48–70.

———. *Heraclius, Emperor of Byzantium*. Cambridge, 2003.

———. "Patterns of Political Activity of the Armies of the Byzantine Empire." In *On Military Intervention*, edited by M. Janowitz and J. van Doorn, 4–35. Rotterdam, 1971.

Kalavrezou, I., N. Trahoulia, and S. Sabar. "Critique of the Emperor in the Vatican Psalter gr. 752." *DOP* 47 (1993): 195–219.

Kaldellis, A. *Ethnography after Antiquity: Foreign Lands and Peoples in Byzantine Literature*. Philadelphia, 2013.

Kazhdan, A., and N. Ševčenko. "Kosmas the Hymnographer." *ODB* 2:1152.

Klein, H. *Byzanz, der Westen und das "wahre" Kreuz: Die Geschichte einer Reliquie und ihrer künstlerischen Fassung in Byzanz und im Abendland*. Wiesbaden, 2004.

Koder, J. "Imperial Propaganda in the Kontakia of Romanos the Melode." *DOP* 62 (2008): 275–91.

Kolbaba, T. "Fighting for Christianity: Holy War in the Byzantine Empire." *Byzantion* 68 (1998): 194–221.

Koopman, C. *Genealogy as Critique: Foucault and the Problems of Modernity*. Bloomington, IN, 2013.

Koroma, E. S. "Imprecatory Psalms as Prophecy: How John Chrysostom's Commentary on the Psalms Address the Moral Problem of Anger." *JEChrSt* 31 (2023): 33–56.

Kraft, A. "The Last Roman Emperor 'Topos' in the Byzantine Apocalyptic Tradition." *Byzantion* 82 (2012): 213–57.

Krueger, D. *Liturgical Subjects: Christian Ritual, Biblical Narrative, and the Formation of the Self in Byzantium*. Philadelphia, 2014.

Kyrou, A., and E. Prodromou. "Debates on Just War, Holy War, and Peace: Orthodox Christian Thought and Byzantine Imperial Attitudes toward War." In *Orthodox Christian Perspectives on War*, edited by P. T. Hamalis and V. A. Karras, 215–48. Notre Dame, IN, 2018.

Laiou, A. "On Just War in Byzantium." In *To Hellenikon: Studies in Honor of Speros Vryonis, Jr.*, edited by J. S. Allen, C. Ioannides, J. Langdon, and S. Reinert, 153–74. New Rochelle, NY, 1993.

Lash, E., trans. *On the Life of Christ: Kontakia*. San Francisco, 1995.

Lieber, L. "Portraits of Righteousness: Noah in Early Christian and Jewish Hymnography." *Zeitschrift für Religions- und Geistesgeschichte* 61.4 (2009): 332–55.

———. "The Rhetoric of Participation: Experiential Elements of Early Hebrew Liturgical Poetry." *JR* 90.2 (2010): 119–47.

———. "Setting the Stage: The Theatricality of Jewish Aramaic Poetry from Late Antiquity." *JQR* 104.4 (2014): 537–72.

———. "'You Have Skirted This Hill Long Enough': The Tension between Rhetoric and History in a Byzantine Piyyut." *Hebrew Union College Annual* 80 (2009): 63–114.

Lingas, A. "The Liturgical Place of the *Kontakion* in Constantinople." In *Liturgy, Architecture and Art of the Byzantine World: Papers of the XVIII International Byzantine Congress (Moscow, 8–15 August, 1991) and Other Essays Dedicated to the Memory Fr. John Meyendorff*, edited by C. C. Akentiev, 50–57. St. Petersburg, 1995.

Lombard, A. *Études d'histoire byzantine: Constantine V, empereur de Romains*. Paris, 1902.

Longenecker, B. *The Cross before Constantine: The Early Life of a Christian Symbol*. Minneapolis, 2015.

Louth, A. F. C. Review of A. F. C. Webster and D. Cole, *The Virtue of War: Reclaiming the Classic Christian Traditions East and West*. In *Communion* 33 (Spring 2004). https://incommunion.org/2011/07/22/review-of-the-virtue-of-war/.

Maas, P., and C. A. Trypanis, eds. *Sancti Romani Melodi Cantica*. Vol. 1, *Cantica Genuina*. Oxford, 1963.

———, eds. *Sancti Romani Melodi Cantica*. Vol. 2, *Cantica Dubia*. Berlin, 1970.

Magdalino, P., and R. Nelson, eds. *The Old Testament and Byzantium*. Washington, DC, 2010.

Maguire, H. *Art and Eloquence in Byzantium*. Princeton, 1981.

Mango, C. "Greek Culture in Palestine after the Arab Conquest." In *Scritture libri e testi nelle aree provinciali di Bisanzio: Atti del seminario di Erice (18–25 settembre 1988)*, edited by G. Cavallo, G. De Gregorio and M. Maniaci, 149–60. Spoleto, 1991.

Mango, C., and R. Scott, trans. *The Chronicle of Theophanes Confessor: Byzantine and Near Eastern History, AD 284–813*. Oxford, 1997.

Mango, M. M. "Imperial Art in the Seventh Century." In *New Constantines: The Rhythm of Imperial Renewal in Byzantium, 4th–13th Centuries*, edited by P. Magdalino, 109–38. Aldershot, 1994.

Maraval, P., ed. *Égérie: Journal de voyage (Itinéraire)*. SC 296. Paris, 1997.

Martin, D. "Jesus in Jerusalem: Armed and Not Dangerous." *Journal for the Study of the New Testament* 37.1 (2014): 3–24.

Mateos, J., ed. *Le Typicon de la Grande Église*. 2 vols. Rome, 1962–1963.

McGuckin, J. A. "A Conflicted Heritage: The Byzantine Religious Establishment of a War Ethic." *DOP* 65/66 (2011–2012): 29–44.

Mellas, A. "Liturgical Emotions in Byzantine Hymns: Reimagining Romanos the Melodist's *On the Victory of the Cross*." *Phronema* 32 (2017): 49–75.

———. *Liturgy and Emotions in Byzantium: Compunction and Hymnody*. Cambridge, 2020.

———. "Romanos the Melodist." In *Liturgy and the Emotions in Byzantium: Compunction and Hymnody*, 71–112. Cambridge, 2020.

Metreveli, E., C. Čankievi, and L. Xevsuriani. *Uzvelesi iadgari* [The oldest chantbook]. Żveli kʻartʻuli mcerlobis żeglebi 2. Tbilisi, 1980.

Métrévéli, H. "Les manuscrits liturgiques géorgiens des IXe–Xe siècles et leur importance pour l'étude de l'hymnographie byzantine." *BK* 36 (1978): 43–48.

Métrévéli, H., and B. Outtier. "Contribution à l'histoire de l'Hirmologion: Anciens hirmologia géorgiens." *Le Muséon* 88 (1975): 331–59.

Milliner, M. "Woman of Peace, Temple of War." *Public Orthodoxy*, 25 March 2022. https://publicorthodoxy.org/2022/03/25/woman-of-peace-temple-of-war/.

Mitchell, M. *The Heavenly Trumpet: John Chrysostom and the Art of Pauline Interpretation*. Tübingen, 2000.

Moffatt, A., and M. Tall, trans. *Constantine Porphyrogennetos: The Book of Ceremonies*. Leiden, 2017.

Mother Mary, and K. Ware, trans. *The Service Books of the Orthodox Church*. Vol. 2, *The Lenten Triodion*. South Canaan, PA, 1994.

Münz-Manor, O., and T. Arentzen. "Soundscapes of Salvation: Resounding Refrains in Jewish and Christian Liturgical Poems." *Studies in Late Antiquity* 3.1 (2019): 36–55.

Nietzsche, F. *On the Genealogy of Morals and Ecce Homo*. Translated by W. Kaufmann and R. J. Hollingdale. New York, 1967.

Noth, A. *Heiliger Krieg und heiliger Kampf in Islam und Christentum*. Bonn, 1966.

Olster, D. "Byzantine Apocalypses." In *The Encyclopedia of Apocalypticism*. Vol. 2, edited by J. J. Collins, B. McGinn, and S. J. Stein, 48–73. New York, 1998.

———. *Roman Defeat, Christian Response, and the Literary Construction of the Jew*. Philadelphia, 1994.

Papanikolaou, A. "The Ascetics of War: The Undoing and Redoing of Virtue." In *Orthodox Christian Perspectives on War*, edited by P. Hamalis and V. A. Karras, 13–35. Notre Dame, IN, 2018.

Parpulov, G. R. "Psalters and Personal Piety in Byzantium." In *The Old Testament in Byzantium*, edited by P. Magdalino and R. Nelson, 77–105. Washington, DC, 2010.

Pentcheva, B. "The Glittering Sound of Hagia Sophia and the Feast of the Exaltation of the Cross in Constantinople." In *Icons of Sound: Voice, Architecture, and Imagination in Medieval Art*, edited by Bissera Pentcheva, 52–100. London, 2020.

Peradzè, G. "Les monuments liturgiques prébyzantins en langue géorgienne." *Le Muséon* 45 (1932): 255–72.

Pertusi, A., ed. "Una akolouthia militaria inedita del x secolo." *Aevum* 22 (1948): 145–68.

Prelipcean, A. "Γένος μέν ἐξ ἑβραίων or the Jewish Origin of Romanos the Melodist: From *Overestimations* to *Underestimations* and Finding Bridges between the West and the East." *Review of Ecumenical Studies* 11.2 (2019): 199–208.

Rapp, C. "Old Testament Models for Emperors in Early Byzantium." In *The Old Testament in Byzantium*, edited by P. Magdalino and R. Nelson, 175–98. Washington, DC, 2010.

Regan, G. *First Crusader: Byzantium's Holy Wars*. New York, 2003.

Renoux, A., ed. *Le Codex arménien Jérusalem 121*. 2 vols. *PO* 35, fasc. 1, no. 163; *PO* 36, fasc. 2, no. 167. Turnhout, 1969–1971.

Renoux, C., trans. *Les hymnes de la Résurrection*. Vol. 1, *Hymnographie liturgique géorgienne: Textes du Sinaï 18*. Sources liturgiques 3. Paris, 2000.

———. *Les hymnes de la Résurrection*. Vol. 3, *Hymnographie liturgique géorgienne: Introduction, traduction, annotation des manuscrits Sinaï 26 et 20 et index analytique des trois volumes*. *PO* 52, fasc. 2, no. 232. Turnhout, 2010.

———. *L'hymnaire de Saint-Sabas (V^e–VIIe siècle): Le manuscrit géorgien H 2123*. Vol. 2, *De la Nativité de Jean-Baptiste à la Liturgie des défunts*. *PO* 53, fasc. 3, no. 237. Turnhout, 2015.

———. "Hymnographie géorgienne ancienne et hymnaire de Saint-Sabas (V^e–VIIIe siècle)." *Irénikon* 80 (2007): 36–69.

Riedel, M. *Leo VI and the Transformation of Byzantine Christian Identity: Writings of an Unexpected Emperor*. Cambridge, 2018.

———. "Nikephoros II Phokas and Orthodox Military Martyrs." *Journal of Medieval Religious Cultures* 41.2 (2015): 121–47.

Romanos the Melodist. *Hymnes*. Vol. 1, edited and translated by J. Grosdidier de Matons. SC 99. Paris, 1964.

Schwartz, E., and T. Mommsen, eds. *Eusebius Werke*. Vol. 2.2, *Die Kirchengeschichte*. GCS n.s. 6.2. Berlin, 1999.

Shahid, I. "The Iranian Factor in Byzantium during the Reign of Heraclius." *DOP* 26 (1972): 293–320.

Sharf, A. "Byzantine Jewry in the Seventh Century." *BZ* 48.1 (1955): 103–15.

Shaw, B. D. *Sacred Violence: African Christians and Sectarian Hatred in the Age of Augustine*. Cambridge, 2011.

Shoemaker, S. *Apocalypse of Empire: Imperial Eschatology in Late Antiquity and Early Islam*. Philadelphia, 2018.

---. *The First Christian Hymnal: The Songs of the Ancient Jerusalem Church; Parallel Georgian-English Texts*. Middle Eastern Texts Initiative 10. Provo, UT, 2018.

---. "'Let Us Go and Burn Her Body': The Image of the Jews in the Early Dormition Traditions." *ChHist* 68 (1999): 775–823.

---. "Passion Piety and Anti-Judaism in Late Ancient Jerusalem: Hymns from Holy Week from the *Jerusalem Georgian Chantbook*." In *The Byzantine Liturgy and the Jews*, edited by H. Buchinger and A. Ioniță. Münster, forthcoming.

Shurgaia, G. "L'esaltazione della croce nello Iadgari antico." In *L'Onagro Maestro: Miscellanea di fuochi accesi per Gianroberto Scarcia in occasione del suo LXX sadè*, edited by R. Favaro, S. Cristoforetti, and M. Compareti, 137–88. Venice, 2004.

Simocatta, Theophylact. *Theophylact Simocatta: Historiae*. Edited by C. de Boor. Leipzig, 1887.

Simon, M. *Verus Israel: A Study of the Relations between Christians and Jews in the Roman Empire, AD 135–425*. Translated by H. McKeating. Liverpool, 1996.

Sizgorich, T. *Violence and Belief in Late Antiquity: Militant Devotion in Christianity and Islam*. Philadelphia, 2009.

Starr, J. "Byzantine Jewry on the Eve of the Arab Conquest (565–638)." *JPOS* 15 (1935): 280–93.

Stein, E. *Histoire du Bas-Empire*. Vol. 2, *De la disparition de l'Empire d'occident à la mort de Justinien (476–565)*. Paris, 1949.

Stephenson, P. "About the Emperor Nikephoros and How He Leaves His Bones in Bulgaria: A Context for the Controversial Chronicle of 811." *DOP* 60 (2006): 87–109.

Stouraitis, I. "'Just War' and 'Holy War' in the Middle Ages: Rethinking Theory through the Byzantine Case-Study." *JÖB* 62 (2012): 227–64.

---. "State War Ethic and Popular Views on Warfare." In *A Companion to the Byzantine Culture of War, ca. 300–1204*, edited by I. Stouraitis, 59–91. Leiden, 2018.

Stroumsa, G. "Religious Contacts in Byzantine Palestine." *Numen* 38 (1989): 16–42.

Sweeney, C. "Grief and the Cross: Popular Devotion and Passion Piety from Late Antiquity to the Early Middle Ages." PhD diss., Fordham University, 2019.

---. "'The Wailing of the People': The Lay Invention of Passion Piety in Late Antique Jerusalem." *Journal of Orthodox Christian Studies* 2.2 (2019): 129–48.

Sykes, A. S. "Melito's Anti-Judaism." *JEChrSt* 5.2 (1997): 271–83.

Synkellos, Theodore. *On the Avar Siege of Constantinople*. In *Analecta Avarica*, edited by L. Sternbach. Krakow, 1900. Reprinted in F. Makk, ed. and trans. *Traduction et commentaire de l'homélie écrite probablement par Théodore le Syncelle sur le siege de Constantinople en 626*. Opuscula Byzantina 3, Acta Universitatis de Attila József Nominatae: Acta Antiqua et Archaeologica 19, 73–118. Szeged, 1975.

Taft, R. "Cathedral vs. Monastic Liturgy in the Christian East: Vindicating a Distinction." *Bollettino della Badia Greca di Grottaferrata*, 3rd ser., 2 (2005): 173–219.

Tieszen, C. *Cross Veneration in the Medieval Islamic World: Christian Identity and Practice under Muslim Rule*. London, 2017.

Treadgold, W. *Byzantium and Its Army, 284–1081*. Stanford, 1998.

———. *History of the Byzantine State and Society*. Stanford, 1997.

Treitinger, O. *Die oströmische Kaiser- und Reichsidee nach ihrer Gestaltung im höfischen Zeremoniell*. Jena, 1938.

Turtledove, H., trans. *The Chronicle of Theophanes*. Philadelphia, 1982.

van Tongeren, L. *Exaltation of the Cross: Toward the Origins of the Feast of the Cross and the Meaning of the Cross in Early Medieval Liturgy*. Leuven, 2000.

Viscuso, P. "Christian Participation in Warfare: A Byzantine View." In *Peace and War in Byzantium: Essays in Honor of George Dennis*, ed. T. S. Miller and J. Nesbitt, 33–40. Washington, DC, 1995.

Wade, A. "The Oldest *Iadgari*: The Jerusalem Tropologion, 4th to 8th Centuries, 30 Years after the Publication." In *Synaxis katholikē: Beiträge zu Gottesdienst und Geschichte der fünf altkirchlichen Patriarchate für Heinzgerd Brakmann zum 70. Geburtstag*. Vol. 2, edited by D. Atanassova and T. Chronz, 717–50. Vienna, 2014.

———. "The Oldest Iadgari: The Jerusalem Tropologion, V–VIII c." *OCP* 50 (1984): 451–56.

Webster, A. F. C. *The Pacifist Option: The Moral Argument against War in Eastern Orthodox Theology*. San Francisco, 1998.

Webster, A. F. C., and D. Cole. *The Virtue of War: Reclaiming the Classic Christian Traditions East and West*. Salisbury, MA, 2004.

Wellington, J. "Let God Arise: The Divine Warrior Motif in Theodoret of Cyrrhus' Commentary on Ps. 67." *StP* 96 (2017): 265–71.

Whitby, M., and M. Whitby, trans. *Chronicon Paschale 284–628 AD*. Liverpool, 1989.

Wilson, A. "The Blood of Christ and Christian Blood: A Model for Interpreting the Concept of Blood in Second- and Third-Century Christian Theology." PhD diss., Fordham University, 2022.

Yoder, J. H. *The Politics of Jesus: Vicit Agnus Noster*. 2nd ed. Grand Rapids, MI, 1994.

GENERAL INDEX

Subject Index

Scriptural citation index follows the subject index.

Abu Ubaidah, 111
Adam (biblical), 77–78, 80, 82–83, 125n59
Agamben, Giorgio: *Homo Sacer*, 86–87
Akathist Hymn, 71, 71n18, 137
Akolouthia before Battle, 26, 135–45, 158
    Christ's mercy and, 139–40
    compared to Akolouthia for Fallen Soldiers, 145–47, 151
    compared to Feast of the Exaltation of the Holy Cross hymns, 136, 141, 144
    compared to pre-Feast hymns, 141
    conditionality of worship based on victory against enemy, 140–41
    emperor's army as God's army, 26
    martyrs petitioned in, 138, 141n31
    petition for destruction of enemies of Rome, 136–37
    petition for protection vs. for destruction, 26, 138–39
    plunder and, 137–38
    repentance on part of army, 139
    sacralization of emperor and, 26, 141–45, 158
    sacralization of violence and, 138–41, 144, 151–52
    translation of text, 199–206
    troparion, 139
Akolouthia for Fallen Soldiers, 26, 135, 145–51, 158
    acrostic of stanzas' first letters, 135n13
    Christians vs. barbarians, 146–47
    Christ's mercy and, 145, 148
    Christ's Passion and, 145, 145nn43–44
    compared to Akolouthia before Battle, 145–47, 151
    Constantinopolitan origin and use, 26, 152
    deaths in line of duty or in captivity, 145
    focus on violence recalled, 145
    martyrdom of soldiers killed fighting Muslims and, 149–50, 150n57
    reflecting familiarity with Kosmas and other Palestinian hymnographers, 135n13
    sacralization of military service and, 151–52, 158
    sacralization of violence and, 135, 151–52
    salvation, expectations of, 148–49
    Saturday of the Souls and, 26
    service to Christ offered by soldiers as religious act, 26, 146–47
    sin, expiation of, 8, 26, 147, 152, 158
    translation of text, 207–13
Alexandrian School, 20
Ambrose (saint), 91–92n10
Amphilochius, 9n22
Anastasis. *See* church of the Anastasis (Holy Sepulcher)
ancient Egypt, 41–42, 149
ancient Israel, 19–21, 23n63

Anderson, Gary, 18n42
Andrew of Crete, 123n53
Annunciation, 71
Anthony (saint), 150
Antiochian School, 20
Apamea (Syrian town), 93n16
apocalyptic thinking, 23
apolytikion ("dismissal" hymn), 113
Arab conquest of Palestine (seventh century), 13, 108–11
    Christians vs. Muslims, 141, 144–45, 150–51
    decline in Greek learning and culture during, 122
    Feast of the Exaltation of the Holy Cross and, 129, 160
    Kosmas's kanon composed during, 131
    See also Islam and Muslims
Arentzen, Thomas, 68–69, 69n10, 71, 71n17, 76, 79
Armenian Lectionary, 29n9, 114
army. See Roman army
asceticism, 6, 50n6, 149–50, 150n57, 160
Athanasius, 10, 18n41
Athenian drama, 70, 82, 86n64
Avars, 21, 112n11
Avi-Yonah, Michael, 60n35, 61

Babylonian captivity, 43
Barabbas, 63n46
barbarians, 117–18, 118n37, 130–31, 134n4, 140, 146–47
    See also Arab conquest of Palestine
Barkhuizen, J. H., 73n23
Basil I (Byzantine emperor, r. 867–886), 22
Basil II (Byzantine emperor, r. 976–1025), Menologion of, 67n2
basileus as term for "emperor," 115–16, 115n28, 116n29, 128n68, 141–45, 160
    See also emperors
Basil of Caesarea, 9, 139, 150, 150n57
    Basil's Canon 13, 9n22, 9n25, 10

Basil of Seleucia, 75n29
Battle of Ninevah (627), 113n16
Battle of the Milvian bridge (312), 90
Bethlehem, massacre of innocent children in. See massacre of holy innocents by Herod
blood sacrifice, 150, 150n58
Book of Ceremonies, 119
Byzantine literature, genres of, 22
Byzantine military manuals, 10, 133n3, 134–35, 150n57
Byzantine Triodion tradition, 151, 153
Byzantine violence, 5–11
    hymns as evidence of Byzantine attitudes toward, 11–13
    See also enemies; Feast of the Exaltation of the Holy Cross; Passion, Crucifixion, and Resurrection; sacralization of violence

Caesarea, assault of Christians by Jews and Samaritans, 62
canonical tradition, 9–10, 70, 150n57
cathedral vs. monastic liturgy dichotomy, 50n4
Chalcedonian monks, 50, 62, 62n45
Chaldean children, 24n64, 43–47, 64n52, 125
chantbook. See *Jerusalem Georgian Chantbook*
Christ. See Jesus Christ; Passion, Crucifixion, and Resurrection; suffering of Christ
Christians/Christianity
    earliest Christians, cross not used as symbol by, 89, 89n1
    imitating violence suffered by Christ, 82, 159
    intertwining of Christian and Roman identity, 15–16, 118, 155, 158
    Jerusalem community of, in line of divine privilege, 42
    legalization of religion by Constantine, 58, 60, 160

Muslims vs., 141, 144–47, 150–51
righteous infliction of violence on their enemies, 159
spread of Christianity as consequence of Constantine's reign, 127–28
sunset as start of day for early Christians, 28n5
See also Jesus Christ; Passion, Crucifixion, and Resurrection; sacralization *headings*; salvation; *specific festal days and compilations of hymns*

Chronicon Paschale, 23n59, 112–13, 134n4

church of the Anastasis (Holy Sepulcher)
Constantine's commissioning of, 30, 105, 158
Egeria (pilgrim) on, 91n7, 92, 109, 109n2
feast of 13 September to commemorate consecration of, 92, 94–97, 94n21, 114, 125, 158, 168–81, 168n8
Idiomela and, 49–50
interaction with ascetic communities in city and desert, 50n6
location of, 91n7
Octoechos hymns performed at, 24
Persian destruction of, 109
relics of true cross in, 109, 109n2
two-day commemoration of, 91–93, 92nn11–12, 158–59
See also Octoechos hymns

communal singing, 3, 125, 152

confession by soldier prior to battle, 134

Constantine (emperor, r. 306–337)
army chaplains, Christian clergy as, 133–34
church of the Anastasis (Holy Sepulcher) commissioned by, 30, 105, 158
conversion to Christianity of, 94, 158–59
cross as Christian symbol and military standard for, 89–90, 103–5, 110, 112, 131, 159
divine favor shown to, 102–3
Feast of the Exaltation and, 94, 102–4, 159, 161
first hymns celebrating reign of, 94, 98
as instrument of God, 98

Jews and, 58n25, 59n31, 60
Kosmas's linking to veneration of cross, 127–28, 128n67
labarum adopted as standard by, 90, 90n4
legalization of Christianity by, 58, 60, 160
spread of Christianity and, 127–28
See also Eusebius of Caesarea

Constantinople
Akolouthia for Fallen Soldiers and, 26, 152
ancient Israel's relics brought to, 21n54
cessation of cathedral rite, 70n12
Feast of the Exaltation of the Holy Cross in, 15–16, 107–8, 112
influence in structure of liturgy, 12, 156
kontakion form unique to, 69
remembrance of the Passion, changes by sixth century in, 56, 58, 63–65
Romanos's life in, 68
"Save, O Lord" composed in, 114
Virgin Mary as protector of, 134n4, 137–38
See also Hagia Sophia

Constantinopolitan hymns. *See* Akolouthia before Battle; Akolouthia for Fallen Soldiers; Feast of the Exaltation of the Holy Cross; Romanos the Melodist

conversion of Jews, 59, 61, 61n39, 68

Council of Chalcedon (451), 22, 60, 60n32, 60n35

cross
authority conferred on Roman emperors via, 101–2, 109, 120, 129–30
as both symbol and physical relic, 101
call for devotion to, 126, 131
Christian rulers' appropriation of symbol of, 89–90, 89n1, 103, 107, 125
compared to triumphant armor, 101
cult of, origins of, 111–12, 126, 131
destroying gate barring entrance to Eden, 82
Feast of the Dedication hymns and, 95, 98–99, 101, 104
four-day period of adoration of, 114n20
Hell and, 83–84

Kosmas's canon linking to Constantine and spread of Christianity, 127–28
lifting of, 92, 119, 119n39, 125, 129, 158
Moses parting Red Sea by making sign of, 41–42
as most powerful symbol of Christian faith, 109
Octoechos hymns and, 38–42
popularity in centuries following Constantine, 90
prefigurations in Hebrew Bible, 41–42, 125–27
as promise of God's love and commitment, 39, 102
as throne of Christ, 84
as weapon against death, 47
as weapon against enemies, 41–42, 47, 83, 101–4, 107, 112, 112n10, 118, 118n36, 120, 126–31, 143
as weapon of peace, 120
as weapon of the faithful, 39, 47, 107
wood's role in salvation of humanity, 125n59
See also Feast of the Exaltation of the Holy Cross
Crucifixion. *See* Golgotha; Passion, Crucifixion, and Resurrection; suffering of Christ
Crusaders, 70n12, 151
Cyril of Alexandria, 23
Cyril of Jerusalem, 34n21, 59n29, 91, 91n9, 109n2
Cyrus of Panapolis, 68n4

Daniel. *See* scriptural citations *following the subject index*
David (biblical king), 18n42, 19, 21–23, 116n28, 117, 130, 136, 142, 142nn33–34, 160
David Plates, 21–22, 130, 142n33, 160
death
Christ's death conquering, 35–38, 46, 75, 77, 84–85, 97–99, 122, 156
cross as weapon against, 41, 83, 118
as enemy, 37–38, 40–41, 46
love defeating, 38
metaphorical violence of, 45, 100

See also Akolouthia for Fallen Soldiers; Passion, Crucifixion, and Resurrection
Dennis, George, 134
Détorakis, Theocharis, 26, 135, 207n1
double translations, 14, 31, 35n24, 100

Eastern Orthodox. *See* Orthodox Church
Eden, 82
tree of, 84, 85n60
Egeria (pilgrim), 50n7, 91n7, 92, 109, 109n3
emotional violence, 3, 53–55, 81, 87, 156–57
emperors
co-opting Christian message of salvation for imperial authority, 163
cross as insignia of, 89
divine power and, 85
dynasty of, 143
enemies of, as God's enemies, 16, 85, 139–40, 143, 160
establishing legitimacy of rule, 142n33, 143
as God's selected instrument, 16, 90, 98, 103, 131, 143–44, 147, 152, 160
Hagia Sophia typikon and, 121–22
Kosmas's kanon and, 128–29
post-seventh century hymns assigning Christian identity to imperial ideology, 161
relics and, 112, 112n10, 113, 131, 134
tied to liturgical feasts, 163
See also basileus as term for "emperor"; sacralization of emperors; *specific emperors by name*
encomia (short hymns or lamentation), 153–54
See also Triodion's encomia
enemies
Akolouthia before Battle on, 139–41, 152
condemnation by the church, 163
death as, 37–38, 40–41, 46
deniers of God as, 140
divinely authorized violence against, 163
emperor's enemies as enemies of God, 16, 85, 139–40, 143, 160
as faithless and lawless, 140

General Index

Feast of the Exaltation hymns seeking destruction of, 25
God's protection against, 100, 161
God's vengeance upon evildoers, 117
in *Jerusalem Georgian Chantbook*, 40
power of God to defeat foreign enemies, 42, 47, 117, 158
Satan as, 37–38, 40–41, 46, 100
vanquished by means of crucifixion, 37
violence against, 139–41, 156
"You Who Were Lifted upon the Cross" authorizing and compelling violence against, 120
See also Arab conquest of Palestine; barbarians; Islam and Muslims

Ephraim the Syrian, 11, 23, 81

Ericksen, Uffe, 69

eternal life. *See* salvation

ethopoiia. *See* speech-in-character

Eucharist
church of the Anastasis site and, 96
following matins service, 28n5
Octoechos hymns and, 28
soldier to receive prior to battle, 134
soldier who kills another in war abstaining from, 9

Euripides, 86n64

Eusebius of Caesarea
on Constantine's conversion, 89–90, 158
on Constantine's cross-shaped battle standard, 17, 105, 110
Life of Constantine, 63, 90
on Roman/Byzantine Empire as last stage before eternal kingdom, 23
on Roman emperor as *basileus*, 115, 115n28
on Roman soldiers ordered to attend Sunday's Divine Liturgy, 133

Evagrius Scholasticus, 93n16

exegetical tradition, 10–11, 18, 22, 70, 81, 124

Feast of the Apparition of the Cross in Jerusalem, 182n21

Feast of the Exaltation of the Holy Cross, 17, 25–26, 89–105, 107–32, 157–58
13 September hymns as commemoration of church of the Anastasis, 91–97,
92nn11–12, 94n21, 114, 125, 158–59, 168–81, 168n8
14 September hymns as veneration of the cross, 25, 95, 98–104, 114, 116, 116n32, 119, 121, 125, 158, 181–97
as annual and popular religious festival, 24, 129
combining multiple commemorations, 91–93
compared to Akolouthia before Battle, 136, 141–42, 144
compared to Akolouthia for Fallen Soldiers, 147
compared to Octoechos, 93, 97, 100–101
compared to Triodion's encomia, 155
Constantine and, 94, 102–4, 130, 159, 161
Constantinople's commemoration of, 107–8, 112–13, 119, 130
dating of hymns for, 93
development and import to Constantinople, 13, 15–16, 92–93, 129–30, 158
Egeria (pilgrim) on, 91n7, 92, 109, 109n3
"the enemy" in, 100–101
Herakleios and, 11n27, 15–16, 93, 107–8, 110–13, 120, 130, 142, 160
intertwining of Christian and Roman identity, 158
Justinian's reign as start of, 16, 93, 98, 131
Kosmas's kanon for, 108, 123–29, 131
military imagery in hymns, 101
oldest surviving hymns of Constantinopolitan origin, 98, 113–19, 156
relic of cross and, 113, 129, 159, 160
Roman identity of hymn singers and listeners and, 103
"royal sign," meaning of, 102
sacralization of violence, development of, 11n27, 13, 16, 38, 90, 95–96, 103, 118–20, 130, 140, 142, 157–60
"Save, O Lord" (*Soson Kyrie*) and, 113–19
split into two distinct feasts of 13 September and 14 September, 159
spread throughout empire, 16, 93n16, 110, 111, 127–28, 158–60
suffering of Christ and, 95–97, 136
troparia associated with, 116
Typikon of the Great Church and, 119–22

festal cycle of *Jerusalem Georgian Chantbook*, 14, 28, 28n6, 94, 128, 166

flight to Egypt by holy family, 72–73, 75
forgiveness of sins of soldiers who die in defense of Christianity, 8, 26, 136, 147, 152, 158
Forty Martyrs of Sebaste, 86n66
Foucault, Michel, 15, 15n37
Frøyshov, S. S. R., 28–29nn7–8

Gabriel's encounter with Mary, 71
Galadza, Daniel, 166
Garden of Eden. *See* Eden
genealogical approach to study of hymnography, 14–15, 15n37
Gentiles, 54–57, 55n18, 65
Georgian language. *See* Old Georgian (language)
Germanos of Constantinople, 123n53
God
  emperor's enemies as enemies of, 16, 85, 139–40, 143, 160
  Roman army as army of, 16, 26, 127, 160
  Roman emperor as chosen instrument of, 8, 16, 90, 98, 103, 107, 131, 143–44, 147, 152, 160
  Roman people as God's chosen, 23n63, 24, 104, 107, 118, 130, 136
  Yahweh as divine warrior in psalms, 19–20
  See also forgiveness of sins of soldiers who die in defense of Christianity
Golgotha, 81, 82, 91, 91n7, 109
  See also church of the Anastasis (Holy Sepulcher)
Goliath, 136
Good Friday, 24, 34n21, 37, 51, 51n8, 56, 81
  See also Idiomela of Good Friday
Gospels
  Christ's Passion, account of, 57, 65, 86
  hymnography telling events of, 12
  site of Crucifixion and, 81
  See also Passion, Crucifixion, and Resurrection; scriptural citations *following the subject index*

Greek Christians, factions warring against each other in alliances with Western and Turkish forces, 141
Greek drama. *See* Athenian drama
Greek hymns, 14, 24, 27, 29–30, 38, 51, 69, 93, 93n18. *See also* Octoechos hymns; Old Georgian (language) *for translation*
Greek mythology, 81n49
Greek Orthodox Church, Holy Saturday service in US, 153n1
Gregory Nazianzen, 10
Gregory of Nyssa, 10, 18–19, 18nn41–42

Hagia Sophia
  choral singing at, 18
  Feast of the Exaltation of the Holy Cross and, 112
  patriarch lifting of cross in, 119, 119n39
  "Save, O Lord" from, 114
  See also Typikon of the Great Church
Harakas, Stanley, 8, 151
Harvey, Susan Ashbrook, 11, 12
Hebrew Bible
  animal slaughter and, 3
  comparison of contemporary wars to, 10
  prefigurations of cross in, 41–42, 125–27
  prophecies of triumph of the cross in, 81–82
  prophetic language from, 64
  Septuagint (Greek translation), 115, 142
heirmos (music-setting melody and rhythm), 124
Helena (mother of Constantine), 59, 91, 91–92n10, 103, 158–59
Hell personified in Romanos's *On the Victory of the Cross*, 81–86
Herakleian-era hymnology, 85, 142, 159
Herakleios (emperor, r. 610–641), 25, 111–16
  basileus as title of, 115, 160
  David linked to, 21–22, 116n28, 130, 142, 142nn33–34, 160
  Feast of the Exaltation of the Holy Cross and reconceptualization of violence under, 11n27, 13, 15–16, 93, 107–8, 110, 111–13, 120, 130, 142, 157–60

forced conversion of Jews and, 61n39
"holy war" and, 110, 110n7
New Israel and, 21n54
overthrow of Phokas by, 112n12
Persian war and, 110, 122
relic of cross carried into battle by, 112–13, 131
Synkellos's panegyric and, 21–22
"You Who Were Lifted upon the Cross" and, 120

heresy under Justinian, 61

Hermogenes, 73n23

Herod, 25, 71–76, 86–87, 149, 157

Hesychius, 34n21

historical-critical methodology, 14

Holy Saturday, 153, 155

Holy Sepulcher. *See* church of the Anastasis

holy war, 6–8, 110, 110n7

Holy Week hymns, 28, 65, 156
See also Idiomela of Good Friday; Triodion's encomia

Homer, 70

hymnography
biblical literacy provided by, 11
celebrating postbiblical saints' lives, 3, 47
genealogical approach to study of, 14–15, 115n25, 116, 118, 143, 159
intended for public audience, 11, 14
organic, evolving nature of, 12–13
study parameters, 16–17
universal Christian knowledge of, 12
See also Akolouthia before Battle; Akolouthia for Fallen Soldiers; Feast of the Exaltation of the Holy Cross; Idiomela of Good Friday; *Jerusalem Georgian Chantbook*; Kosmas the Hymnographer; Octoechos hymns; Romanos the Melodist; Triodion's encomia

Iadgari, 165–66

Idiomela of Good Friday, 24–25, 49–65, 156
compared to fifth matins troparion, 122
compared to Octoechos hymns, 51, 53, 55, 58, 64–65, 156
compared to Sunday Resurrection hymns, 51, 53, 55
compared to Triodion's encomia, 154–55
composed in Greek and translated into Georgian, 49
dating of, 49, 49–50n3, 62
emotional violence and, 53–55, 156–57
in *Jerusalem Georgian Chantbook*, 49
Jews as responsible for Christ's death, 55–65, 154–55, 157
Jews depicted as lawless, 141
Mar Saba monks (Palestine) as possible composers, 49–50, 50n3
meaning of "idiomela," 49n2
oldest surviving hymns exclusively devoted to Christ's crucifixion during Holy Week, 24, 156
sequence differing by language, 51
speech-in-character mode of, 53
surviving in Greek manuscripts, 51
Sweeney redating of, 62

idolatry
Chaldean children refusing to engage in, 43–46
Christ child in Egypt and, 75
metaphorical violence of, 45

imperial power. *See* emperors

Islam and Muslims
Byzantine soldiers fighting against, 141, 150–51
comparison of sacralization of violence with Christianity, 6–7
martyrdom for soldiers who died fighting, 9, 149–50, 150n57
See also Arab conquest of Palestine

Jacob (biblical), 125

Jacob of Sarug, 11

Jerusalem
Arab conquest of, 13, 108, 111–13
feast of 14 September spreading from, 93n16, 159–60
including both urban and desert monastics, 50n4
influence in structure of liturgy, 12

Persian conquest and sack of, 13, 42, 62, 62n43, 101n47, 108–10, 113
as pilgrimage destination, 27, 103
relic of the cross returned to, 91, 93, 113, 130, 160
See also church of the Anastasis (Holy Sepulcher); *Jerusalem Georgian Chantbook*; Palestine

Jerusalem Georgian Chantbook, 24, 27–47, 156, 165
Chaldean children's story in, 43–47
compared to fifth matins troparion, 122
compared to Kosmas's kanon, 127n63, 128
compared to Romanos's kontakia, 71–72, 87
compared to "Save, O Lord," 117, 118n35
compared to Triodion, 154
cross in, 38–42, 47
Feast of the Exaltation of the Cross and, 93
festal section of hymns composed for specific days, 94
hymns for 13 September, 94–97, 114, 168–81
hymns for 14 September, 25, 98–104, 114, 116, 116n32, 119, 121, 125, 158, 181–97
Idiomela of Good Friday in, 49
metaphor of military campaign in, 36–37, 47
no contemporary threat to people of God in, 42
number of hymns, 98
Octoechos as oldest surviving collection of hymns in, 27, 46, 49n1
older recension's hymns no longer in use at time of Greek manuscripts, 27, 27n2, 165
originated in Jerusalem, 27
purpose of hymns in, 28
salvation tied to Christ's suffering, 33–34, 46
sequence of "regular" Sunday services, 28
Sinai Georgian 18 as source of translations, 166–67
structure of, 28
translated by Shoemaker, 24, 27
two recensions in, 27n2

versions as Old Iadgari and New Iadgari, 165
violence of Crucifixion and its soteriological consequences, 24, 31–34
See also Idiomela of Good Friday; Octoechos hymns

Jesus Christ
as advocate for humans against Satan, 84
Akolouthia before Battle and, 137
Chaldean children's suffering as anticipatory of, 24n64, 43, 64n52
conditionality of worship based on victory against enemy, 140
in conversation with Mary in Romanos's *On the Lament of the Mother of God*, 76–81, 157
David and psalms as anticipatory of, 19–20
feet washing and, 70
first-person speech in idiomela, 53, 56, 156
mercy sought in akolouthia, 139–40, 145, 148
mercy sought in Octoechos, 41
miracles performed by, 53, 56, 77
as pacifist vs. leader of armed resistance movement, 4
preaching to the dead, 37
sense of betrayal experienced by, 53–55
See also Passion, Crucifixion, and Resurrection; Resurrection

Jewish apocalypses, 23

Jews
absolved for Christ's death, 85n62
anti-Christian violence in Palestine by, 61–62
armed resistance to Romans, 60
Constantine and, 58n25
conversion to Christianity, 59, 59n31, 61n39, 68
failure to recognize Christ as God, 57
implications of anti-Jewish invective, 63–65, 157
included in Christ's salvific work, 85n62
Justinian's anti-Jewish legislation, 60, 61, 157
Orthodox Church's revision of hymns due to anti-Jewish sentiments, 65

General Index

proselytizing by, 59, 59n28
relationship with Christians in Palestine, 14, 25, 58–62, 65, 157
relationship with Christians in Syria, 68
as responsible for Christ's death, 25, 55–65, 79–80, 85, 154–57
sunset as start of day, 28n5
as threat to Roman Christians in mid-sixth century, 101n47

John Chrysostom, 10, 19, 19n44, 23
John of Damascus, 123–24, 182n22
Jonah (biblical), 125
Joseph (biblical patriarch), 84, 125
 Egyptian queen and, 84, 84n59
Judas (biblical), 76, 155n10
Judas Cyriacus, 92n10
Justinian (emperor, r. 527–565)
 anti-Jewish laws of, 60–61, 157
 change in hymnography and, 16, 125, 158
 Feast of the Exaltation of the Holy Cross and, 93, 98, 158
 Jewish-Christian relations in Palestine and, 14, 61–62
 Romanos the Melodist's reference to, 116n29
Justin of St. Catherine's monastery in Sinai, 166
just war, 6–8, 10

Kaegi, Walter, 5
kanons
 Akolouthia before Battle and, 135
 Akolouthia for Fallen Soldiers and, 135, 148
 compared to kontakia, 124, 124n54
 defined, 123
 development of form, 123, 131
 heirmos (music-setting melody and rhythm) of, 124
 intended for monastic settings, 123–24, 124n54, 131
 Kosmas's Feast of the Exaltation kanon, 108
 odes of, 124
 troparion and, 116
Kirill, Patriarch of Moscow, 1–2, 4, 163

Klein, Holger, 112–13
Klentos, John, as translator of Akolouthia before Battle, 26, 135, 199
kontakia, 51, 54, 67–71, 74, 76
 compared to kanons, 124, 124n54
 compared to other Greek-language hymns, 69
 complex metrical structure of, 69, 69n10
 disappearance from Byzantine liturgical cycle, 67n1, 70n12
 exegetical nature of, 70, 124
 heirmos (first stanza) of, 69
 length of, 69
 prooemion (prelude) of, 67n1, 82
 Romanos and, 16, 24–25, 67–71, 81–82, 157
 troparion and, 116
 "You Who Were Lifted upon the Cross" as, 120
 See also speech-in-character
Koroma, Elizabeth Sunshine, 19
Kosmas the Hymnographer (saint), 108, 114, 122–29
 Akolouthia for Fallen Soldiers' author familiar with, 135n13
 background of, 124
 Constantine linked to veneration of cross, 127–28, 128n67
 Feast of the Exaltation kanon by, 108, 124–25, 131
 Hebrew Bible's prefiguration of cross and, 125–27
 Jerusalem Georgian Chantbook and, 127n63, 128, 131
 at Mar Saba, 123–24
 Roman empire as nostalgic memory for, 132
 sacralization of violence and, 126–27, 131
Krueger, Derek, 12
Kubinka cathedral (near Moscow), 1–2
"Kyrie eleison," 119, 119n39

labarum (Constantine's battle standard), 90, 90n4
lamb metaphor, 51, 76
last emperor motif, 23

Lent, 28, 81n48, 123n52
　Akathistos performed during, 71, 71n18
　Triodion (Lenten service book), 151, 153
Leo VI (emperor, r. 886–912), *Taktika* (military manual) of, 6n12, 133n3, 134
Leontius, 56n21
Licinius (emperor, r. 308–324), 90
Lingas, Alexander, 69n11, 70n12
liturgical tradition, 10
　cycles of, 24, 94, 98, 98n36
　Eastern Christian liturgy's order, 28n5
　festal days and, 28n6, 39
　kontakia's disappearance from, 67n1
　monastic vs. cathedral liturgy, 50n4
　Octoechos and, 28–29
　services explicitly for imperial soldiers, 15, 20
　Typikon of the Great Church and, 114
liturgical violence, changing language of, 14
lived religion, 12–13
Lord's Prayer, 29
love
　Christ's offering of, 52, 54
　cross as sign of God's love, 39
　defeating death, 38
　God's equal love of all humanity, 162

Maas, Paul, 71, 86n66
Magi, 70, 72
Maguire, Henry, 74–75n29
Malalas, John, 23n59
Mar Saba monastery (Sabaites), 50, 50n3, 50n5, 62, 123–24
Martyrium basilica (Golgotha). *See* church of the Anastasis (Holy Sepulcher)
martyrs
　asceticism akin to, 150
　assisting soldiers going into battle, 138, 141n31
　dispute between Polyeuktos and Nikephoros II Phokas over martyrdom for soldiers who died fighting Muslims, 9, 149–50, 150n57
　Forty Martyrs of Sebaste, 86n66
　saints as equal to, 149

Mary. *See* Virgin Mary
massacre of holy innocents by Herod, 25, 71–76, 80, 84, 86–87, 149, 157
matins
　13 September commemoration of the Anastasis, 94–97, 94n21
　14 September celebration of Feast of the Exaltation, 98, 98n36, 100–101, 104
　Akathistos during Lent, 71n18
　encomia for Holy Saturday morning, 153
　Hagia Sophia typikon adding four hymns for 14 September, 121–22
　Idiomela of Good Friday and, 52n12
　kontakia and, 67n1, 69n11
　Kosmas's kanons for, 114, 123, 125
　Octoechos hymns and, 28–29, 31–32, 35–37, 40–41, 43, 43n35, 45–46
　"Save, O Lord" sung with hymns on 14 September, 114, 119
　at sunrise, 28n5
Mauricius (emperor, r. 582–602), 112, 112n11, 134
McGuckin, John, 10–11, 142n34
Melito of Sardis, 63
Menologion of Basil II, 67n2
Miaphysite monks of Gaza, 50, 50n3, 62
military, sacralization of. *See* Akolouthia before Battle; Akolouthia for Fallen Soldiers; sacralization of military service
military imagery, 36–37, 47, 84–85
　cross as military insignia, 89, 105
　in Feast of the Exaltation of the Holy Cross hymns, 101
military manuals (Byzantine), 10, 133n3, 134–35, 150n57
military plunder, 137–38
miracles, 53, 56, 77
monastic hymnographers during Muslim occupation, 131
monastic vs. cathedral liturgy, 50n4
Moses (biblical), 41–42, 80, 125, 127
Mossay, Justin, 26, 135, 207n1
Muslims. *See* Arab conquest of Palestine; Islam and Muslims

nationalism, Christianity tied to, 1, 1n3
natural law approach to war, 7
Nebuchadnezzar (king of Babylonia), 43, 46
New Israel, envisioning of, 17, 21, 21n54, 90, 104, 130
New Testament. *See* scriptural citations *following the subject index*
New Testament studies, 4
Nicodemus, Gospel of, 81n49
Nietzsche, Friedrich, 15, 15n37
Nikephoros II Phokas (emperor, r. 963–969), 9, 10n25, 135, 150–51, 150n57

Octoechos hymns, 28–47, 156
  assignment of culpability for Crucifixion, 55, 64, 154
  authorial or editorial consistency throughout, 41
  codification of original Greek hymns of, 30
  compared to hymns of Feast of the Exaltation of the Holy Cross, 93, 97, 100–101
  compared to Idiomela of Good Friday, 51, 53, 55, 58, 64–65, 156
  compared to Kosmas's kanon, 131
  compared to today's Orthodox Church, 163
  cross as weapon against enemies, 41–42
  cross as weapon of faithful, 39
  dating of Georgian translation of the Greek, 30
  dating of original Greek hymns of, 29, 29n11, 49n1, 61
  Eastern Christian festal days and, 28n6
  eight musical tones used in, 28–29
  eight-week cycle and, 28–29, 94, 154
  enemy presumed to be Satan or death, 41
  God's love and protection in, 39
  Jews mentioned in, 55
  as oldest surviving collection of hymns, 27, 46, 49n1
  performed at church of the Anastasis (Holy Sepulcher), 24
  rebounding of violence and, 35–39, 45–46

translation of text, 167
violence in description of Crucifixion and Christ's suffering, 24, 31–34, 40, 46–47, 87
oikonomia (lessening of reprimand to achieve pastoral good), 9
Old Georgian (language), 14n35, 25, 27, 31, 165–66
  Idiomela of Good Friday composed in Greek and translated into, 49
Old Testament, 22–23, 23n59
  See also Hebrew Bible; scriptural citations *following the subject index*
Orthodox Church
  Akolouthia for Fallen Soldiers not retained by, 152
  compared to Western Christian tradition of sacralized violence, 151
  drifting from Octoechos's emphasis on violence Christ suffered to benefit humanity, 163
  eight-part tonal register, 29n8
  Holy Saturday, 153n1
  hymns originated by Palestinian Christians used in, 111
  Idiomela used in, 51
  revision of hymns due to anti-Jewish sentiments, 65
  Romanos's hymns and, 67
  "Save, O Lord" (*Soson Kyrie*) and, 113, 119n42
  "Today Was Hung upon the Cross" hymn and, 51n8, 52
  "You Who Were Lifted upon the Cross" and, 119n42
O Ypsotheis en to stavro. *See* "You Who Were Lifted upon the Cross"

Pachomius (saint), 150
Palestine
  Christian majority in early fifth century in, 58
  Christian pilgrimages to, 60
  end of Roman rule of, 111
  Feast of the Exaltation celebrated in eighth century in, 158
  kanon form flourishing in, 123

monastic vigilantism against Jews in, 60, 60n32
relationship between Christians and Jews in, 14, 25, 58–60, 65, 157
Roman beneficence to, 59
Romans' expulsion as goal of Jesus and his followers, 4
See also Arab conquest of Palestine; Jerusalem
Palestinian Christians
under Arab rule, 111, 125–26
Good Friday Idiomela composed by monks of, 24, 49–50, 50n3
hymnographers composing works used in today's Orthodox Church, 111
interactions between patriarchal churches and ascetic communities, 50n6
Mar Saba monastery (Sabaites), 50, 50n3, 50n5, 62, 123–24
as Romans, 57–58, 101
separation in prayers from Jews, 56
settlements of, 60
See also church of the Anastasis (Holy Sepulcher); Feast of the Exaltation of the Holy Cross; Idiomela of Good Friday
Passion, Crucifixion, and Resurrection, 13
Akolouthia before Battle and, 152
Akolouthia for Fallen Soldiers and, 145, 145nn43–44, 152
assignment of culpability for, 55–64, 154, 157
as Christ's plan and willful sacrifice, 36, 76–78, 84, 120–21
Christ's victory over death through, 35–38, 46, 75, 77, 84–85, 97–99, 122, 156
Constantinopolitan hymns moving beyond tradition of, 131
Feast of the Exaltation of the Holy Cross hymns and, 95–96, 136
Gentiles and, 54–57, 55n18
Gospels' account of, 57
Herod and, 86
hymnography on, 11–13, 16
Idiomela of Good Friday and, 49–65
Idiomela of Good Friday devoted exclusively to Christ's crucifixion, 24, 156

Jews as responsible for Crucifixion, 25, 55–65, 79–80, 85, 154–57
Octoechos hymns and, 24, 28, 31–34, 40, 46–47, 87
Pilate as culpable for death of Jesus, 85
rebounding of violence in, 35–39, 45–46, 97
Resurrection's emphasis over Crucifixion, 31–34, 154
retribution for violence against Christ, 38
Romanos's conversation between Jesus and Mary at time of, 72, 76–81
Romans' role in, 57–58, 85
soldier's lance and, 84
sponge at Crucifixion as relic, 112
suffering of children of Bethlehem as typology for, 87
suffering of saints and, 16, 47
Triodion's focus on, 154
See also salvation; suffering of Christ
patronage, 105, 132
Pauline writings, 40
Pentcheva, Bissera, 115, 119–20, 120n45
persecution, history of, 4, 6
Persian War (602–628), 160
barbarians, Persians as, 118n37
conquest of Palestine and sack of Jerusalem, 13, 15, 42, 62, 62n43, 101n47, 108–10, 113
Herakleios's securing peace, 113, 113n16, 130
relic of the cross returned to Jerusalem from Persians, 91, 93, 113, 130, 160
turn in favor to Byzantines, 21
Pertusi, Agostino, 26, 135
Peter (saint)
compared to Christ, 75–76
first-person speech in idiomela, 53, 156
Romanos's character development of, 70, 75–77
Phokas (emperor, r. 602–610), 112, 112n12
Pilate, 57, 63n46, 85–87
Pitra, Jean-Baptiste-François, 69n11
Polyeuktos, Patriarch of Constantinople, 9, 150, 150n57
psalms, 17–20, 94n20

Byzantine Christians' use of, 17–18
engagement with violence in, 154
history of, 17
as prophecy, 19–20
recitation as part of liturgical services, 29
See also scriptural citations *following the subject index*

psalters, 18, 18nn41–42

Rapp, Claudia, 21–23, 23n59

Rashidun caliphate, 111

relics of cross
battlefield empowerment of Christian rulers, 112–13, 112n10, 131, 134
in church of the Anastasis (Holy Sepulcher), 109, 109n2
Cyril of Jerusalem offering earliest evidence of, 91
discovery of "true" cross and Helena's involvement, 91, 91–92n10, 102, 158–59
Feast of the Exaltation of the Holy Cross and, 91–93, 113, 129
local communities with, 93n16
looting by Persians, 109, 113
protective powers of, 107
return to Jerusalem, 91, 93, 113, 130, 160
wood of the cross, 101–2

Renoux, Athanase, 29n9, 29n11

repentance, 19, 139, 157

Resurrection
anticipated in psalms, 20, 20n49
Christ's suffering tied to, 31, 33
described in militarized language, 37
on Easter, 37
hymns emphasizing over Crucifixion, 31–34, 154
transforming existence of death, 35
weekly Sunday liturgy devoted to, 28
See also Passion, Crucifixion, and Resurrection

Riedel, Meredith, 10n25, 150, 150nn57–58

Roman army
Christian clergy as chaplains, 133–34
divine intervention responsible for battlefield events, 134
Divine Liturgy on Sunday, mandatory attendance, 133
as God's army, 16, 26, 127, 160
prayers of non-Christian soldiers, 133
religious rites prior to Christianity, 133
Trisagion recited by soldiers, 134
victory dependent on moral purity of soldiers, 133
See also Akolouthia before Battle; Akolouthia for Fallen Soldiers

Roman Empire and Romans
Akolouthia before Battle's mention of "Romans," 144–45
as Christian empire, 25, 105, 133, 155, 160
Crucifixion, role of Romans in, 57–58, 85
David Plates linked to, 22
as God's chosen people replacing the Jews, 23n63, 24, 104, 107, 118, 130, 136
Jews and, 60, 60n33
military losses, 15, 110–11
as New Israel, 90, 104, 130
Romanos's *On the Victory of the Cross* and, 85
sense of political and religious superiority, 118
See also Roman army; *specific emperors and wars*

Romanos the Melodist, 16, 25, 67–87, 157
Agamben at odds with, 87
Akathist Hymn, 71
celebrating defeat of Hell and Satan, 86
compared to chantbook and idiomela collections, 25, 71–72, 87
compared to encomia of Triodon, 154
compared to Feast of the Exaltation hymns, 93
Herod and his soldiers as wicked perpetrators of violence in, 73, 75
hymns of (kontakia), 16, 24–25, 67–71, 81–82, 157
on Justinian as *basileus*, 116n29
life of, 67–68, 67n2
On Judas, 76
On the Lament of the Mother of God, 25, 76–81, 84, 157
On the Massacre of the Holy Innocents, 25, 71–76, 80, 84, 86–87, 157
On Peter's Denial, 75–76
On the Victory of the Cross, 81–86
popularity of, 67–68

speech-in-character and, 25, 54, 70–71, 74, 82, 157
on suffering of the righteous, 25, 71, 76
Royal Hours, service of (Good Friday morning), 51, 51n8

Sabaites. *See* Mar Saba monastery
sacralization of emperors
  Akolouthia before Battle and, 141–45, 158
  Akolouthia for Fallen Soldiers and, 151
  as chosen by God, 8, 16, 90, 98, 103, 107, 131, 143–44, 147, 152, 160
  cross conferring authority on, 101–2, 109, 120, 129–30
  incompatibility with universality of Christianity, 162
  intertwined with sacralization of violence, 144, 152
  as sacralization of empire as a whole, 144
sacralization of military service, 1, 8, 16, 26, 98, 149, 151–52, 158, 163
sacralization of violence
  Akolouthia before Battle and, 138–41, 144, 151–52
  Akolouthia for Fallen Soldiers and, 135, 151–52
  consequences of, 161–63
  as contradiction to eternal life, 162
  Feast of the Exaltation of the Holy Cross and development of, 11n27, 13, 15–16, 25, 38, 90, 93, 95–96, 107–8, 110–13, 118–20, 130, 142, 157–60
  holy war and, 7
  incompatibility with Christianity's universality when limiting to imperial causes, 162
  intertwined with sacralization of emperor, 144, 152, 162
  in Justinian's reign, 16, 125, 158
  Kosmas's kanon and, 126, 131
  missing from Octoechos and Idiomela, 64–65
  Orthodox East compared to Western Christian tradition of, 151
  as precedent for political opportunists of today, 163
  prior studies of, 6–8

similarities between early Christianity and early Islam, 6
of sixth- and seventh-century Byzantine hymnology, 156, 162
war and, 7, 112n10
saints
  Chaldean children's references as antecedents to hymns celebrating, 47
  cults of, 10
  plunder enabled by, 138
  suffering of, 16, 25, 47
  Synaxarion of Constantinople's biographies of, 67n2
salvation
  Akolouthia for Fallen Soldiers and, 148–49, 152
  massacre of holy innocents and, 75
  military metaphor of plan for, 84
  as purpose of Christ's suffering, 33–35, 46, 77, 82, 118, 122, 154, 156
  sacralization of violence as contradiction to, 162
  suffering of virtuous and, 81
  universality of, 155n10, 162
  See also Passion, Crucifixion, and Resurrection
Samaritans, 58, 60, 60n35, 62
Sasanians, 108–9
  See also Persian War
Satan
  conversing with Hell, 81–86
  cross as weapon against, 41
  as enemy, 25, 37–38, 40–41, 46, 100
  metaphorical violence of, 40, 45, 100
  Romanos's *On the Victory of the Cross* and, 71, 81–86
Saturday of the Souls, 26, 135, 135n12, 151
Saul (biblical), 18n42, 19
"Save, O Lord" (*Soson Kyrie*)
  barbarians (those living outside the empire) as enemy in, 117–18
  basileus as term in, 115–16, 143
  brevity of, 116
  compared to *Jerusalem Georgian Chantbook*, 117, 118n35
  compared to Kosmas's kanon, 126, 131
  compared to Octoechos, 131
  compared to troparion #1 and #3, 121–22

General Index 241

compared to "You Who Were Lifted
  upon the Cross," 120–21
contrary to history of salvation, 162–63
origins of, 113–14
petition for military victory and, 117, 131
Psalm 28 (27) linked to, 116–18
as troparion, 116
in *Typikon of the Great Church*, 114, 119
scene recognition, 81–82
Second Council of Constantinople (553),
  62n45
Septuagint (Greek translation of Hebrew
  Bible), 115, 142, 150n58
Shahid, Irfan, 115, 115nn26–27
Shaw, Brent, 3
Shoemaker, Stephen
  on forced conversion of Jews, 61n39
  on Jews remaining in Palestine in 300s,
    58
  on lay composers of hymns, 30
  on Old Testament connection of
    Roman people, 23, 23n63
  translations by, 24–25, 27, 165, 167
singing and singers
  Chaldean children's singing and
    escaping violence, 45
  communal singing linked to acts of
    violence, 3, 125, 152
  ecclesial singing to build political
    legitimacy and military loyalty, 143
  female participation in public singing,
    11
  Hagia Sophia, choral singing at, 18
  idiomela distinguishing community of
    singers from Jews, 141
  Romans as singers, 107
sins, remission of. *See* forgiveness of
sins of soldiers who die in defense of
  Christianity
sixth-century hymns. *See* Idiomela of
  Good Friday; Romanos the Melodist
Sizgorich, Thomas, 6–7
Skylites, John, 150
Socrates, 22
Solomon (biblical king), 22
Sophronios of Jerusalem, 111

Soson Kyrie. *See* "Save, O Lord"
Sozomen, 22
speech-in-character, 3, 53–54, 53n14, 56,
  124, 156
  Romanos's kontakia and, 25, 54, 70–71,
    74, 82, 157
speech as violence, 3
sticheron/stichera
  Akolouthia before Battle and, 135, 138
  Akolouthia for Fallen Soldiers and, 135
  idiomela and, 135
  troparion and, 116
Stouraitis, Ioannis, 7–8
Strategikon (military manual) of Emperor
  Mauricius, 134
suffering of Christ
  acknowledgment allowing infliction of
    violence on enemies of Christians,
    121
  on behalf of all humanity, 45, 52, 64, 78,
    122, 126, 132, 156, 162
  emotional distress of Christ, 53–55,
    156–57
  imagery of encomia of Triodon and, 154
  linked to call for devotion to cross, 126
  salvation as purpose of, 33–35, 46, 77,
    82, 118, 122, 154, 156
  as told in hymns of Feast of the
    Exaltation of the Holy Cross, 96–97
  as told in Idiomela of Good Friday, 24,
    51–52, 156
  See also Passion, Crucifixion, and
    Resurrection
suffering of saints, 16, 25, 47
Sunday
  Divine Liturgy, Roman soldiers
    attending, 133
  as "eighth" day, 29n7
  hymn cycle compared to Idiomela, 51,
    53
  See also Octoechos hymns *for eight-
    week cycle*
sunset as start of day, 28n5
Sweeney, Christopher, 33–34, 34n21, 50n3,
  51n9, 62
Synaxarion of Constantinople, 67n2
Synkellos, Theodore, 21–22

Synod of Constantinople, 9n25
Syria, Jews' relationship with Christians in, 68

Taktika (military manual) of Leo VI, 133n3, 134–35
tenth-century rites before battle and after death, 26, 133–52
   See also Akolouthia before Battle; Akolouthia for Fallen Soldiers
Theodoret of Cyrrhus, 20
Theodosian Code, 60n33
Theodosius (archdeacon), 92n14
Theodosius I (emperor, r. 379–395), 91n10
Theodosius II (emperor, r. 402–450), 109
theological interpretation of violence, 10–11, 15–16
Theopaschite controversy, 50n3, 62
Theophanes Confessor, 109n4, 110n7
Theophylact Simocatta, 112n11
Ti Ipermachon (added to Akathist Hymn), 137–38
"Today Was Hung upon the Cross" hymn, 51n8, 52
tonal register, 29, 29n8
   See also Octoechos hymns
Treadgold, Warren, 5
tree in Garden of Eden vs. tree of the cross, 125n59
Trinity, 43, 57
Triodion's encomia (for Lent and Holy Week), 151, 153–54
   compared to Feast of the Exaltation of the Holy Cross, 155
   compared to Idiomela for Good Friday, 154–55
   compared to Octoechos cycle, 154
   Jews as responsible for Christ's death and, 154–56
   no imperialized violence in, 155
Trisagion, 134
troparia, 51, 51n10
   Akolouthia before Battle troparion, 139–40

Hagia Sophia typikon's matins on 14 September, 121–22
Kosmas's references to Constantine, 127
"Save, O Lord" as, 116
"You Who Were Lifted upon the Cross" as, 120
Tropologion, 165
Trypanis, Constantine, 71
typika of local churches, 12
   definition of typikon, 114n19
   of Evergetis monastery, 120n45
Typikon of the Great Church (Hagia Sophia), 67n2, 114–15, 114n19, 115n23, 119–22
   hymns for matins on 14 September, 121–22
Tyrpannis, 86n66

Ukraine invasion (2022), 2, 2n4, 4
Umar (Rashidun caliph), 111

vespers
   for 13 September commemoration of Anastasis, 94
   for 14 September Feast of the Exaltation, 98, 98n36, 116n32
   all-night vigil service with kontakia and, 69n11
   Octoechos hymns and, 24, 28–29, 32–33, 36, 39
   "Save, O Lord" singing in, 114, 114n20
   at sundown, 28n5
violence
   Byzantine, 5–11
   Byzantine Christian attitudes toward, 2, 11–13, 15, 86n66, 149
   emotional, 3, 53–55, 81, 87, 156–57
   forms of, 2–3
   hymns as evidence of Byzantine attitudes toward, 11–13
   See also enemies; Passion, Crucifixion, and Resurrection; sacralization of violence; *specific battles, wars, and events*

General Index

Virgin Mary
　Akolouthia before Battle and, 136–38, 140–41
　burning bush and, 190n26
　conditionality of worship based on victory against enemy, 140–41
　conversing with Jesus in Romanos's *On the Lament of the Mother of God*, 25, 70–71, 76–81, 157
　enemy deserving violence and, 140–41
　grief of, 77, 154, 157
　as protector of Constantinople against Avars, 134n4, 137–38
　voiced by singers of encomia of Triodon, 154
　as voice of the people expressing sorrowful joy, 79

Webster, Alexander, 8
Wellington, James, 20

women
　Mary's maternal grief and, 77
　Mary's military persona and, 137–38
　participation in public singing, 11
"The Wood of Your Cross," 119n42

Xanthopoulos, Kallistos, 68n4

Yahweh. *See* God
"You Who Were Lifted upon the Cross" (*O Ypsotheis en to stavro*), 115
　compared to Kosmas's kanon, 126
　compared to "Save, O Lord," 120–21
　compared to troparion #1 and #3, 121–22
　contrary to history of salvation, 162–63
　Herakleios and, 120
　Roman Christians and, 130

Scriptural Citation Index

1 Kingdoms 2:1–10, 171, 185

1 Peter 2:24, 187
1 Peter 3:19, 37

1 Samuel, 18n42, 19

2 Chronicles 7:5, 169

3 Kingdoms 8:63, 169

Colossians 2:14, 188, 190

Daniel, 23, 43
Daniel 3:1, 169
Daniel 3:26–56, 175, 190
Daniel 3:57–88, 176, 191

Deuteronomy 28:66, 196
Deuteronomy 32:1–43, 171, 183

Ephesians 6:10–17, 40n31

Exodus 3:2, 190
Exodus 14, 41
Exodus 15:1–19, 170, 182
Exodus 17:11–13, 184
Exodus 19, 190

Habakkuk 3:2–19, 172, 186

Isaiah 26:9–20, 173, 187
Isaiah 60:14, 180

Jonah 2:3–10, 174, 189

Luke 1:46–55, 177, 192

Matthew 2, 74
Matthew 16:18, 168

Proverbs 6:23, 188

Psalm 27:8, 196
Psalm 27:9, 196
Psalm 28 (27), 116–17, 116–17n32, 118
Psalm 28:2, 182
Psalm 28:10, 182
Psalm 45:11, 196
Psalm 64:5, 180
Psalm 65:1, 170

Psalm 65:4–5, 170
Psalm 73:12, 197
Psalm 85:5, 180
Psalm 85:9, 180
Psalm 106:19–20, 174
Psalm 118 (119), 153
Psalm 140, 168, 181
Psalm 148, 178, 193

Psalms 57/58, 18
Psalms 67/68, 19–20
Psalms 68/69, 18
Psalms 108/109, 18
Psalms 136/137, 18